Long Road to Love

Long Road to Love

Darlene Bogle

Published by
chosen books

FLEMING H. REVELL COMPANY
OLD TAPPAN, NEW JERSEY

Certain Scripture quotations are from *The Living Bible,* copyright © 1971 by Tyndale House Publishers, Wheaton, Illinois. Used by permission.

Library of Congress Cataloging in Publication Data

Bogle, Darlene.
 Long road to love.

 "Chosen books."

  1. Bogle, Darlene. 2. Converts—United States—Biography. 3. Homosexuals—United States—Biography.

I. Title.
BV4935.B63A35 1985   280'.4 [B]
85-22465
ISBN 0-8007-9129-0

A Chosen Book
Copyright © 1985 by Darlene Bogle
Chosen Books are Published by
Fleming H. Revell Company
Old Tappan, New Jersey
Printed in the United States of America

Contents

To Mom Hollowell,
who appears in this story
as Marie Fuller

Acknowledgments

My deepest appreciation to Karen Ann Wojahn, who patiently edited each draft of this manuscript. A gift of editing is a gift of love.

I also wish to acknowledge all the editors and authors I have met through Mount Hermon Writers Conferences, who have encouraged and loved me as I worked on this book—especially Bonnie Wheeler and Jan Rodger.

A special thank-you to Jane Campbell for her encouragement as my editor; for her challenges to grow; and her participation in friendship as God has developed a spiritual bond between us.

To all who have prayed and believed in God's timing for this book, thank you.

1.
Getting Involved

Anticipation merged with resentment as I watched the cars pulling into the circular drive to deposit loads of students in front of the college administration building. I had worked on campus all summer trying to earn enough money to continue another year at this Christian school. From my vantage point at the second-story dormitory window, I scanned the crowd, looking for familiar faces.

I wonder if Joy will be back this year, I pondered reviewing the few friendships I had developed during my freshman year. Resentment gnawed at me with the realization that most of these students had parents who cared, who supported them emotionally and financially as they studied for careers.

Financially I qualified for a federal grant for the underprivileged, and emotionally my family had long ago granted me independence. I was eighteen and determined to make something of my life. Although I thought God was calling me to be a missionary, inside I struggled with doubts and resentments, and my feelings of inadequacy were beginning to surface.

I had spent many hours alone this past summer walking along the canal smoking cigarettes and feeding the ducks. They were my only frequent companions. Smoking was against the rules, but it was summer and no one would know.

Another reason I had enjoyed the summer was that I could wear jeans, which during the school year were forbidden. I glanced down at the faded, short-sleeved sweatshirt and pale blue jeans that had been my summer uniform. *Guess these go back into the closet.*

I turned from the window and the happy activity.

"I'll never be like them," I muttered.

I started packing my belongings into cardboard boxes for the move up the hill to my new home for the semester. An elderly woman had rented a room to me for half of what dorm costs would be. I would still have meals in the cafeteria, but my grant and the money I had earned during the summer would put me half-a-year closer to a degree.

A voice startled me as I carried the first of my boxes into the hall. "Hi! Are you coming or going?"

I spun around and faced a tall, good-looking girl with coal-black hair, which hung several inches below her shoulders. Her arms were loaded with coats and sacks.

"I'm just moving out. I've been in this room all summer." I hesitated. "My name's Darlene. Can I help you with those?" I moved to help without waiting for her response.

"I'm Barbara," she smiled. "Thanks for the help. Where are you moving?"

"I'm off-campus this semester. I'm renting a room in a private house up the hill."

"Oh, an upperclassman, huh? I'm a freshman." She avoided eye contact, as she started hanging coats in the closet I had just emptied.

"It's only my second year," I murmured. I didn't feel like explaining that I lacked the money to live on campus this year. To change the subject, I asked Barbara where she was from while I packed the last of my boxes.

She shared about her family. Barbara was the youngest of four and the only girl. Her brothers were a doctor, a lawyer, and an engineer. Although she was only sixteen, she had graduated with honors from high school. She had been voted outstanding youth leader in her church group and was talented in drama. Overall, I decided she fit the model of the perfect Christian student who attended this college.

Still, something seemed different. She rattled off personal information on a surface level. Despite her apparent successes, her expression appeared troubled, not what I would expect from an excited freshman anticipating the adventure of college. An invisible magnet drew me to know her better.

I lifted the largest box and headed out the doorway. "I'll move my things. Then we can go to dinner together. O.K.?"

She nodded with a vague smile. Then her attention returned to the suitcase in front of her.

As cute as she is, she'll be popular with the boys, I reflected, carrying boxes downstairs. *I wonder why she looks so pensive?*

My weeks flew by with a full schedule of classes and twenty-five hours of janitorial work each week. Barbara became one of my closest friends, and we spent time together nearly every night. We studied together and talked frequently about religion. We agreed that although Christianity seemed to work for other people, it never quite met our own needs.

During our talks Barbara often had a faraway look in her eyes, as though she were not paying full attention to what I said. But she always responded in a thoughtful manner, so I shared about my loneliness and not feeling accepted because of my non-Christian background. I also confessed my growing anger and hurt because I did not have the emotional support of my family.

Barbara confided that she too felt lonely and insecure. She dated several boys on campus but found them immature. Being from a Christian home, she told me, didn't always mean you felt loved and accepted. And she sometimes seemed on the verge of telling something more.

I felt our bond strengthened one afternoon when we went for a walk down by the canal. She pulled a cigarette from her jacket pocket and lit it.

"I didn't know you smoked," I exclaimed, drawing a cigarette from my own pocket.

"You can't exactly tell the world, Dar." She giggled, twisting a strand of her hair around her index finger. "I had to be sure you wouldn't tell."

"Why would I tell? I'm fighting that battle myself and losing, more than anything."

"Well, maybe it wouldn't make much difference if you did tell." She paused. "And maybe someday I'll tell you more of my secrets." She started walking faster, as if to avoid further conversation.

What did she mean? Then I decided she would tell me what was on her mind when she was ready. Besides, I couldn't begin to tell her some of my own secrets.

I hurried after her. "Hey, wait up!"

The Christmas recess between semesters approached almost without warning. I walked into Barbara's room one December afternoon and dumped my books on the bed. She was due back any time from taking a final, so I busied myself looking at the Christmas cards on her dresser.

Emotion overwhelmed me as memories of Christmases past paraded through my mind and I blinked back the tears. It hardly seemed fair that everyone else, including Barbara, got to spend Christmas with families. Except for the janitorial crew, the campus would be silent for two weeks while everyone enjoyed presents, family times, and shared love. Everyone, that is, except me.

It was not as though anyone was making me stay on campus during the holidays or that Barbara had not invited me—out of pity, I thought—to go home with her. But my self-pity stemmed not from homesickness but from knowing that going home would only mean more pain.

Childhood Christmases of Goodwill donations and drunken celebrations by alcoholic parents had caused me to choose to stay on campus and work rather than go home to emptiness. I renewed my vow not to spend this holiday with a family who not only did not know the meaning of Christmas but also would be too drunk to care. Despite attending a Christian college, I struggled with my fledgling Christian faith when it came to unmet emotional needs. And the previous seventeen years of painful memories did not help my inner battle.

The sound of footsteps invaded my thoughts as Barbara walked through the doorway. "Hi, Dar. You finished with classes?"

"Uh-huh. Just finished my last final." In an attempt to push away the unhappy thoughts and regain my composure, I busied myself straightening her dresser. I tried to hide the lump of emotion still lodged in my throat.

"You all packed for vacation?" I asked.

"Almost. My folks won't be here until tomorrow morning." Barbara stared intently. "Are you sure you don't want to come home with me for the holidays?"

"No," I murmured, still fiddling with the Christmas cards. "I can earn more money toward next semester by working through the break."

Besides, I thought, *it wouldn't be the same. I wouldn't really be part of her family. And I don't want people feeling sorry for me.*

"I hope you have a good Christmas. You *are* returning next semester, aren't you?" I glanced at the nakedness of the room then back at Barbara. "You know, sometimes I feel I don't even know you, although we've shared so much this past three months."

Barbara flopped on the bed, propped her head against a pillow, and stared at me. "To tell you the truth, I haven't really decided about next semester. Darlene, do you remember I told you once that I had a secret I would tell you someday? Well, I'm going to tell you now."

She motioned for me to come sit on the bed beside her. "This will probably blow you away." Her forehead tightened into furrows.

"I really like you, Dar, and know how out-of-place we both feel sometimes. I haven't been able to share this with anyone here, but I hope you'll understand Darlene, I'm a homosexual."

The words sank like a brick to the pit of my stomach. There was a light pause, an embarrassed silence. Then I blurted, "A lesbian? You can't be! You're a Christian."

I wanted to run away and hide, yet I sat rigidly on the edge of the bed.

"Yes, I love Jesus," Barbara replied softly, "but I also love women. I've tried to change, but there's no way out, so I live with my secret."

I rushed to the window, which was open a crack. My face felt hot and my eyes burned. Looking out into the cold, wet December world, I saw cars moving like snails, hesitating only to pick up students for the trip home—home to warm fireplaces and caring families. I suddenly felt isolated from my friend, while intense feelings of abandonment surged through my confused emotions. Loneliness seeped in around me like the damp Portland fog hugging the ground. My mind whirled with objections and questions I didn't know how to verbalize.

For a minute I watched the greetings and departures and resented the embraces that didn't include me. Anger began to surface. Once again I was separated emotionally from someone I cared for and I felt betrayed by Barbara's confession. It seemed an inappropriate backdrop for the scenes of love I was witnessing out the window.

I don't know how long I stood staring, but finally I took a few gulps of fresh air and turned to face my friend.

Waiting for my reaction, Barbara looked more vulnerable than I had ever seen. My feelings alternated between fear and bewilderment.

"Help me understand," I pleaded. "How can you be that way and still be a Christian? You're my best friend. I've grown to care about you so much this semester. How am I supposed to respond?"

The tension in Barbara's face relaxed. She looked less vulnerable and more relieved as she sat up and fluffed her pillow. "It's a long story, Darlene. Why don't you spend the night and after supper I'll tell you the whole thing? My roommate left for the holiday, so you can have her bed."

"All right," I said, ignoring a stab of nervousness. "I'll go get clothes for tomorrow and pick you up for supper."

I sprinted up the hill, my heart pounding with excitement and a strange attraction toward Barbara. The fondness that had been growing over the past semester seemed greatly intensified. I had fought feelings of curiosity about her before. And maybe now Barbara in turn could help me understand myself.

A few minutes later as I headed back down the hill with a change of clothes and a nightgown, I suppressed the strongly-worded biblical admonitions against homosexuality that echoed in my mind. Although I had once before encountered a woman who was a homosexual and had had a frightening sexual experience myself with a girl friend several years earlier, Barbara was the first person I had ever cared about who admitted she was a lesbian.

Suddenly homosexuality was more than a word, more than a source of off-color jokes, and more than one of the sins listed in the Bible. Now homosexuality had a face, which belonged to one of the few people I had been able to love and trust and be myself with. I understood now that Barbara must suffer from guilt, loneliness, and pain and that homosexuality must play a major role in this pain.

But I was hurting too. I wanted not only to help Barbara but to understand myself. I slowed down as I approached her room. Heart pounding, I tapped on the door. "I'm back!"

"I wondered if I'd scared you off." Barbara laughed self-consciously.

"I don't scare that easily," I lied, putting my things on the bed across the room.

After supper that night, I leaned a pillow against the wall and propped myself against it. "Well, let's hear the story."

Barbara, propped against the wall on her own bed, gazed thoughtfully into space. "I guess it all started a couple years ago. I was housecleaning for a woman. One day while we were having a conversation, she made some advances toward me. I liked her and felt flattered that she was complimenting me and stroking my hair. Before I knew it, we were embracing. It seemed so right, and I felt she cared for me.

"I've talked to a counselor, and he feels I was susceptible to her advances because of my great need for love and affirmation. My father is heavy on achievement but not on showing affection. I've never known real closeness. . . .

"Well anyhow, I saw this woman many times, and she introduced me to other lesbians. I felt guilty at first, so I tried to change my feelings and really care about men. But it's just not there."

I had a strange impression that Barbara was repeating a well-rehearsed monologue, a defense of her feelings rather than a true expression of them.

"How can you feel it's right, Barb," I countered, "when the Bible says it's a sin? Just because it seems good. . . . Don't you feel bad or dirty?"

I remembered how uncomfortable I had felt when I had met the homosexual woman and how guilty I had felt after the sexual encounter with my girl friend.

"Not anymore. God loves me, and He understands my feelings. I don't love Him any less just because I choose to care for women."

Intrigue was being spun like a web around me. Barbara and I continued to talk late into the night. Around midnight we got ready for bed and turned out the light. In the darkness, I shared more of my confusion about my childhood experiences, lack of love, and feelings of abandonment. I told Barbara I had always been searching for someone to care.

Barbara's voice wove the smooth web of seduction tighter. "I care, Darlene. I want you to know that. I'll always be your friend."

"I care about you too, Barbara." I gulped hard. "I'll really miss you over the holidays."

"You could still change your mind and come visit my family. We could have a good time."

"But I do need to earn money toward next term. Maybe I can visit over New Year's weekend. I'll see." I lay with my hands cupped behind my head, staring into the darkness. "Barb?" My throat was tight; my voice barely a whisper. My heart was pounding so violently that I wondered if she could hear it too.

"Yes?"

"Do you think I could be a lesbian too?" I held my breath, fearing the answer.

"I know one way to find out."

The covers moved on her bed, and instantly she stood beside me in the darkness.

"Darlene, don't be scared. You'll know for sure one way or the other. Move over."

I complied almost mechanically.

We didn't talk any more that night, and I received my first explicit lesson in lesbian love. Barbara was back in her own bed when I woke up the next morning, and we did not discuss what had happened. She left with her parents a few hours later. I gave her a quick hug through the open window of the car.

"I'll call you in a few days," I promised.

"Have a good Christmas, Darlene. Remember, I'll be thinking of you." She squeezed my arm.

My mind was a jumble of conflicts and guilt as I walked across campus. What had I done? Was I really a lesbian? Holding Barbara seemed so right, but I felt dirty, and now part of me inside seemed dead.

The campus was quiet except for a few faculty members. Mrs. Fuller, the dean of women with whom I had spent many hours talking and praying during the past year and a half, came down the steps of the administration building.

"Are you staying over for the holidays?" She smiled.

"Yeah. I'm working in janitorial. I need to keep earning

money so I can come back next term." I scuffed my shoe against the sidewalk and avoided eye contact. Do you have any time to talk?"

"Matter of fact I do, dear. I'm not leaving campus until tomorrow. Would you like to come up for tea?"

She slipped a maternal arm through mine and steered me up the path toward her apartment, not waiting for my reply.

Moments later we were settled in front of her fireplace, warming our hands and drinking cups of steaming Russian tea. Marie sat in her favorite high-backed maple rocking chair. I snuggled against a pile of throw pillows on the floor.

"This quarter has been too busy for both of us, Darlene. I've missed our talks. Tell me what's happening in your life." She rocked slowly, her shoulders a little hunched, revealing the weariness of her fifty-plus years with the added responsibility of over six hundred women on campus.

I glanced up quickly, then took a sip of tea. "It's been a frustrating quarter for me," I began slowly, my mind whirling with cautions.

If I tell her everything, she'll hate me. She certainly won't understand. What if she has me kicked out of school? I don't even know if I really am a homosexual! I love Barbara and want everything to be O.K., but nothing seems sane.

I weighed my words. "Marie, do you remember last summer when I came back from my work with Teen Challenge? I told you something had happened that I wanted to share with you. Oh, this sounds dumb. I don't even know where to begin."

"Honey, we have all day. Why don't you start where you want? We'll make sense of things." She sipped her tea.

I love her so much. If she rejects me. . . .

"Well, there was a girl at the center. I felt attracted to her in a wrong way. She told us she was a lesbian. And I was— well, afraid of my own curiosity. Nothing happened though," I added quickly.

Marie's expression remained friendly. "What does that have to do with how you're feeling now, Darlene?" Her words sounded warm, accepting.

"Well, I spent last night in my friend Barbara's room. We talked most of the night. She—she told me she is a lesbian." I sighed deeply, waiting for a response.

Marie encouraged me with a nod. "Go on."

"Mrs. Fuller, I'm so confused. She's a Christian, but what she does is a sin."

I hesitated, then blurted out, "I slept with Barbara last night and I think I'm a lesbian too!"

I stared at my teacup, ashamed to look at her.

"Honey, what you're telling me about Barbara isn't a secret. I've been aware of her problem for some time. But I'm sorry you got involved over your head. You know the Bible says homosexuality is a sin, and we need to pray and ask forgiveness for that sin."

"I know," I mumbled, moving closer and burying my face in Mrs. Fuller's lap. I still couldn't look at her. "Will you pray with me?"

She set her cup on the table and laid her hands gently on my head and shoulders.

"Jesus, please bring healing to Darlene. Clear the confusion in her heart and help her not only to confess her sin to You but also to walk freely away from the fractured emotions that bind her to making wrong choices. Help her to know You are committed to making her whole and that You have promised never to abandon her."

I trembled with emotion as I prayed silently along with her. While I tried to control unshed tears, another prayer echoed in my mind.

But God, I really love Barb! I want to help her. I don't want to abandon her like Daddy abandoned me.

Marie prayed for a long time; then I asked forgiveness for my sin. But inside another voice taunted me.

You'll never be free! You can't change your family, your childhood, or the pain.

Still kneeling, I hugged Marie. I was afraid to look up and afraid to let go for fear this momentary feeling of warmth and acceptance would disappear when I opened my eyes. Why had I been born into a family like mine?

2.
Shattered
Beginnings

With few exceptions, what I can remember from my early years are legends derived from tongues loosened by alcohol or puzzle pieces snatched from photo albums and faded "Remember when?" conversations.

My father had not wanted any children, although he was pleased that his first child would carry on the family name. Mom's second pregnancy angered him, and he went immediately for a vasectomy without consulting her. Anger changed to shock when Daddy was presented with twin daughters.

Marlene and I were the first twins born in 1944 in that coastal Oregon town. We brought Mom and Daddy lots of attention. I looked a lot like my brother Bobby, who had father's blue eyes and, according to Mom, the blackest mess of curls the nurses had ever seen on a newborn.

Because of the wartime economy, Daddy was forced to hold a variety of jobs to support us. Working in the lumber mill, driving a bus and bartending on weekends kept him away from home much of the time. Daddy also liked to party, and on the nights he wasn't working, he went out on the town with the boys. He usually brought a crowd home after the bar closed and drank till he passed out, leaving Mom to make conversation with these strangers. Perhaps in anger, perhaps from frustration, Mom eventually began drinking too.

Except for the money that went for alcohol, she tried to save expenses whenever possible. She began taking in ironing and kept Marlene and me in the same crib until we were more than a year old. She received hand-me-downs gratefully and dressed us identically as often as possible.

When Daddy was home, he was too tired to help raise the kids he never wanted in the first place. When I tried to crawl into his lap to be held, he would set me back on the floor with a swat, remarking that when we were old enough to tell him what we wanted, then he would spend time with us. So Mom was left with dirty dishes, piles of dirty laundry, and three youngsters under the age of two.

Marlene and I were different from the start. Although we dressed in frilly dresses and ruffles, Marlene was the only one who took to that attire naturally. I chose to play with anything but a doll. I was slightly larger and more assertive than Marlene, and my natural inclination was to protect her as we grew older. I wrestled with Bubba my brother and climbed trees, woodpiles, and hills with the boys, tumbling back to Mom with cut lips or broken bones.

Marlene hung close to Mom while I explored my world. She mothered her dolls and brushed dirt smudges from her dresses. When buttons fell off or tears appeared in seams, Marlene would not settle for safety-pin repairs. She insisted on permanent repairs or she wouldn't wear the dress.

I started kindergarten with more than the usual trauma. We had dragged a cat home and apparently I was allergic to cat hair. Sores had erupted all over my head. The doctor shaved my head, painted it with purple medicine and gave me ultraviolet treatments for several months before the sores went away. I couldn't wear a hat or scarf during that time and had only a fringe of hair around the base of my neck.

When the kids made fun of me, I withdrew, venting my hurt through occasional displays of belligerence. The teacher often pinned a note to my coat telling Mom I had disrupted the class by talking out of turn or beating up a child who called me names.

Marlene learned quickly that she could get her own way by telling our classmates I would beat them up if they didn't give her a certain toy. They believed her, and I acquired few close friends in grade school.

One day at recess I was playing with a basketball. A new kid walked up and grabbed it from me. I threw myself at him and knocked him on the ground, beating him with my fists. "It's my ball!" I screamed.

Suddenly I was lifted, kicking and yelling, into the air by the yard-duty teacher.

"I swear, Darlene," she said, her head wagging, "you're going to grow up to be a lady wrestler!"

I took another note home.

Along with my growing awareness of the outside world was the awareness that things were not right between Daddy and Mom. They spent a lot of time arguing and fighting, though we never knew what it was about. I had just turned five when they brought us into the front room and sat us on the couch. Mom knelt in front of us.

"We have something to tell you," she began. "Daddy is going to go away for awhile and live in another house." She watched our faces, then continued. "He'll come visit sometimes, but he won't be living with us anymore."

"How come, Mommy?" Bubba's lower lip trembled as he looked at both of them. "Don't you love us anymore, Daddy?"

"Sure I do, son." Daddy walked over and picked Bubba up. "I have to move closer to my work, that's all. Everything's going to be all right."

He hugged Bubba, then Marlene and me. Then he walked out the front door without looking back.

I threw myself against the overstuffed purple cushions of the couch and cried, "Daddy, don't go! Daddy, don't go!"

"Raymond, you'd better come back here and talk to your daughter!" Mom yelled after him with a look of despair on her face.

My racking sobs were interspersed with panicked pleadings: "Daddy, please don't go."

Suddenly he appeared in the doorway again, towering over Mom's five-foot frame. He said something angrily to her, then walked over and picked me up. I buried my head against his chest and wrapped my tiny arms around his neck. He removed my arms, held me at arm's length, and looked into my eyes.

"Come on, Darlene," he said. "Be Daddy's big girl. Big girls don't cry. See, Bubba and Marlene aren't crying."

He wiped my tears with a rough, calloused thumb, then set me on the floor. "I'll be back, honey. Just don't cry anymore, O.K.?"

I nodded and gulped back the growing lump in my throat. He walked out the door once again without looking back.

But this time I wouldn't cry. Though my lower lip trembled with emotion, I was determined to be Daddy's big girl. No matter what happened, I would try to please Daddy.

Birthdays and Christmases for the next three years brought a card from Daddy with a dollar for each of us, but it wasn't like having him be part of our life.

Bubba had an asthma condition that grew worse, and Mom had to buy special air filters for the vaporizer that ran constantly in his room. Sudden attacks would monopolize her attention for hours. The doctor said that the attacks were brought on by emotional stress. Mom would call Daddy and after Bubba spoke to him, he seemed to get better.

Then when I was eight, Daddy reappeared with a large truck and two friends. As Mom packed suitcases and the men moved furniture, we kids raced around the house throwing our toys into boxes and making sure our own possessions were secure on the big truck. "Hurray! We're going to live with Daddy!"

I ran next door to say good-by to my friend Lois, two years older. "We're moving! Maybe I can come visit you sometime. Will you write to me?"

"Sure." Tears spilled down her cheeks. "I'll miss you, Darlene."

"Me, too." I threw my arms around her. "I gotta go now. My daddy is taking us to live with him. Bye!"

I ran back home and took one last look around the empty house. Any sadness was overshadowed because the five of us would be together again.

Mom and Dad did not tell us it was only a trial time to see if they could piece their marriage back together. They did not tell us they were not going to remarry. They told us only that we were moving a long way away.

We moved into an old stucco house about five miles outside the town of Crescent City, California. We were surrounded by towering redwoods and a half-dozen neighbors who lived between us and town. We children played in makeshift treehouses and on a mountain of sawdust scraps from the lumber mill down the road.

I was happy we were living with Daddy again and so afraid he would leave us that I looked for things to do to please him. One night Mom was ironing some of his dress shirts. He liked to have them perfect for his bartending and was a fanatic for a clean, starched white shirt every shift. I asked Mom if I could iron his shirts as a special surprise. I was very careful and took several hours to iron about a dozen shirts for him.

"Let's not tell Daddy I did it," I said excitedly, "and see if he notices."

The next night as Dad was dressing for work, I grinned from ear to ear. As he splashed on Old Spice cologne and headed for the door, I could wait no longer.

"Do you like the way your shirt is ironed, Daddy?"

He glanced down. "Sure, honey. Your mom always does a great job." He reached for his suit coat.

"Mom didn't do it this time" I announced. "I did!" I was proud that he saw no difference and waited for words of praise and approval.

"You didn't iron this shirt," he snapped. "Little girls can't iron this well." He walked toward the door.

"Yes, I did, Daddy. I really did."

"Darlene, quit your lying or I'll backhand you!" He slammed the door without looking back.

Stabbed with hurt, I ran outside and found Mom.

"He didn't believe me that I did the ironing, Mama. Will you tell him I really did? Please?" I fought to keep the tears from spilling down my cheeks.

"I'll tell him, Darlene." She patted my head. "You did a fine job."

Mom did tell him, but Dad never acknowledged that he knew. Nor did I ever iron for him again, although my desire to please him flourished.

Shortly after that, Mom introduced Marlene, Bubba, and me to Daddy's bar life. She said she was tired of sitting home night after night while he went to work at the bar and came home drunk. So she took us with her and put us in a small room behind the bar to watch television while she visited with Dad. After Dad closed at 2 A.M., he carried us to the car for the five-mile trip home.

But it wasn't practical to pack up three children night after night, so we began to spend the nights alone at home, dialing the tavern number when we got scared.

Since we didn't have the money for a television, we invented fun games like running through the woods pretending we were pioneers. The Evans girls next door, five of them ranging in age from five to twelve, were our near-constant companions. Their parents spent a lot of time in the bar with Mom and Dad.

The only other kid in the area was a seventeen-year-old named Curt. His family owned the property directly behind ours next to the edge of the forest. One day when the Evans girls, Marlene, and I were trying to figure out how to build a secret fort for a clubhouse, Curt walked up.

"I know where there's a good place for a fort," he said smugly.

"Tell us, tell us," we begged.

"Nope! It's my secret." Picking up a pole for a staff, he headed toward the forest.

"Come on, Curt, tell us," pleaded the twelve-year-old

Evans girl. She ran up and grabbed his arm and whispered something in his ear. They both laughed.

"All right, girls! Let's have a race. If you can keep up with me, I'll show you a secret place where no one will find you." He turned and sprinted toward the trees.

We all gave chase.

"What did you whisper to him?" Marjorie yelled to her sister as we ran.

"I told him he could teach us the facts of life," she laughed. "We can teach *him* a few things, I'll bet!"

Marlene and I looked at each other as we raced to keep up. What were the facts of life? We were eight years old.

We were well out of sight of the houses when we finally caught up with Curt. We grabbed his coat and hung on.

"Show us your secret place," we yelled in unison. "We caught you."

"All right," he chuckled. "Look over there!" He pointed to a cluster of trees. The branches twisted together, forming the perfect foundation for the floor of a treehouse. Slits had been hacked into the trunk of the largest tree for stairs.

"All you need is a few boards and some nails. I'll help you, girls." He braced himself against a tree. "Now, who wants to be first to learn the 'facts of life'?"

"I do, I do!" The five-year-old Evans girl was jumping up and down, waving her hand in the air.

"No, you're too little to be first." He scanned the group. "Darlene, you be first." Reaching out and grabbing my hand, he pulled me away from the clearing.

A disappointed wail rose from the group as Curt and I disappeared into the brush. My heart was pounding wildly.

"What are we doing?" I asked, trying to free my arm.

He tightened his grip. "I'm going to show you what big people do. It's a secret."

He was breathing harder as he pulled me into a small circle of trees that formed a natural wall. Removing his jacket, he spread it on the ground. "Just lie still," he whispered hoarsely, as he forced me to the ground.

I looked up at the treetops. They seemed miles high. "I don't want to be first!" I tried to get up.

"It won't hurt," he said between clenched teeth. Pulling me back down, he pinned me against the ground with his body. With one free hand he tugged at my dress.

I closed my eyes tight and began to struggle. He cupped one hand over my mouth to stifle my screams and pulled off my panties with the other. Forcing my legs apart with his, he thrust his body against me. Red lights and clanging bells exploded in my head as I bit my lip. His hand pressed tighter against my mouth to silence any sounds. The stabbing pain continued for what seemed like ages. Then he lifted his body away and fell aside, leaving warm, sticky white stuff across my legs.

I lay in terror, afraid to move.

"Get these on." He threw my panties at me and zipped his pants.

Slowly I became aware of a loud commotion heading in our direction. Then Daddy burst into the small area. Although he was slender and of average height, he now resembled a raging giant. He stood still for a moment, blue eyes blazing behind his wire-rimmed glasses. Then he lunged at Curt.

"You son of a bitch!" he yelled, pinning him against a tree. "I ought to kill you!"

His fist was doubled to punch Curt when Mr. Evans burst into the clearing. "Don't kill him, Ray! We'll take him back to the house and call the cops. We'll throw him in jail."

He grabbed Curt and shoved him toward the house.

Then Daddy reached down to where I was lying terrified on the ground and scooped me into his arms. "It'll be O.K., baby. It'll be O.K."

Mom was calling a doctor to come and check me as Daddy carried me into the house. The other girls stood watching Curt, who was pinned to a chair by Mr. Evans. The youngest girl had run home to tell on him because he had chosen me to be first instead of her.

Mama held me close, trying to soothe my tears. Daddy paced the floor yelling and calling Curt bad names. Mr. Evans was yelling at the girls who pressed against the doorway to watch what would happen. The uproar at the house was almost as frightening as the actual event, adding to my fear and confusion.

When the doctor arrived, Mom and Dad watched over his shoulder as he examined me in the bedroom. I felt embarrassed. "There was penetration and an obvious presence of semen. You can clean her up now." The doctor wrote a report, and Curt was taken away by the policemen who had arrived while we were in the bedroom.

Daddy had told me it would be O.K., but it never was O.K. again. I felt dirty inside and afraid to play in the woods. Almost nightly I dreamed of Curt or some older man chasing me through the woods and throwing himself on top of me. I would wake up screaming, drenched in perspiration, though I never told anyone what the nightmares were about. I overheard Dad tell Mr. Evans that Curt would be in jail a long time, but that didn't help me forget or stop the dreams.

3.
Replacement Father

Mom and Dad continued to fight almost nightly. Just before my ninth birthday we returned to Oregon, leaving Dad in California. It was fun seeing my good friend Lois again. We moved back to the same neighborhood into a small two-story place with four bedrooms upstairs, although we had no furniture to go in them.

Mom bought a wooden dinette and an iron double bed frame. We children slept on mattresses in a corner of the front room because it was too expensive to heat the entire house. Somehow Mom scraped together enough money for food and clothes. We didn't have new things, but at least we could start school with warm clothing. Within a few weeks, Mom brought a red-haired man home from the bar. Frank, she told us, was her new husband and our new daddy.

Life with Frank was hell from the beginning. He had just undergone a divorce, after his wife left him for another man and resented Daddy for refusing to meet his responsibility to support us. The court had decreed $75 per month for each of us, but the hundreds of miles between Oregon and California prevented enforcement of the order. We were a daily reminder to Frank that he had married not only a wife but also a built-in family with needs for food and clothing.

Every trip to the grocery store started a fight. "Why should I put food on the table for your brats?" he would demand of Mom.

"You knew I had three children when you married me," she replied. "They came as part of the package."

"So why doesn't their father support them?" he would

shout. "They're not my responsibility. I didn't bring them into the world."

"Ray has a mind of his own. When you married me, you married my kids. They have to eat too."

"Well, I hope they appreciate my spending all my hard-earned money so they can grow up fat. When I was their age, I spent my time in an institution eating leftovers and scraps that the state provided. I had to work sixteen hours a day for every single thing I got."

"All right Frank, that's enough. I'm not going to fight you for every dime to put food on the table." The discouragement in Mom's voice signaled the end of the conversation.

"Oh, sure, go ahead and spend. I work my fingers to the bone so they can fill their guts!" Frank would stomp off, get a beer from the refrigerator, then slam the back door as he went to the woodshed to chop logs for the heating stove.

"Mom, why do we even have to eat his food?" I would pout. "I'd rather starve."

"Yeah, me too!" Marlene and Bubba would chime in.

"Knock it off, kids. I can't handle you and Frank too. None of us is going to starve." She would pick up her purse with determination. "I'm going to the store. Who wants to come?"

"I do! I do!" We would all yell at once and race for the door.

In spite of the fights, there was always food in the house. We tried to avoid being alone with Frank so he wouldn't have the opportunity to make sneering remarks about our father. But inwardly I began to wonder. Daddy didn't come to see us and hardly ever sent a letter. What if he didn't really love me?

Feeling rejected, I would climb a tree in the backyard and let the rough juncture of the limbs form a secure hiding place. I pressed the length of my body against a horizontal limb and snuggled under the huge leaves for shelter. This was my favorite place. I could watch the children in the next yard playing and having fun while I created a make-believe world that accepted me. Strong and brave, I saved lives and conquered new frontiers.

Another favorite place was the wooded hills behind the stadium about three blocks from our house. Marlene, Bubba, and I went there often to pick berries and swing at the park. One day we were joined by an elderly man. He helped us pick berries and asked if we'd like him to play in the park with us. Someone to push us high! We ran toward the swings.

"Here, little girl. I'll carry you." He picked me up and sat me on his shoulders before I could object.

As we moved toward the swings, his hands moved up my legs. "Don't want you to fall." He chuckled.

I panicked. "Let me down!" I tried to wiggle off his shoulders.

"We'll be at the swings in a minute." His fingers probed between my legs.

"Bubba!" I yelled.

The old man swung me to the ground and went the opposite direction.

"Let's go get Mom!" I screamed.

We rushed home and told Mom the story. She called the police with a general description. The man was picked up a few hours later. He was a known child-molester.

A policeman took us to identify the man. Once again I felt embarrassment as I told a roomful of adults how he had put his hand where he shouldn't have.

Mom looked over at me with a scowl. "Don't you ever let any man you don't know give you a ride!"

Even after Mom told me the man was in jail, I was afraid someone would attack me, and my nightmares intensified. I dreamed of old men chasing me down the street, and just when they were about to grab me, I woke up screaming.

Marlene, Bubba, and I had separate upstairs bedrooms now, and they never came to check on me. I would lay awake in my darkened room listening to the sounds of the night. Mom and Frank wouldn't check on me either because they spent every night at the tavern.

Afraid even of the dark, I made a secret cubbyhole in the

back of my closet. Every night I stuffed pillows under the blankets on my bed to make it look like a person, then crept into the closet so no one could attack me during the night. Bundled in my blanket, I would wait for the sound of a car door slam around 2:30 A.M..

Why doesn't Daddy ever come back? Doesn't he know I need him? And how come Mom has to go out every night? Doesn't she love me? When will she get home? What if she doesn't come home?

A hundred questions bombarded me. When I heard the car door slam and footsteps on the front porch, at least I knew Mom was safe. Then I would creep back into bed and fall asleep.

Many nights I was awakened with the sound of voices and a sudden brightness as the overhead light was switched on.

"This is one of my twins." My mother's words, though slurred, were filled with pride.

"Oh, she's cute!" Some strange woman would reach down to pat my cheek.

"The other one is in here." Mom turned off the light and led her guests down the hall toward Marlene's room.

Often the sound of voices downstairs told us Mom and Frank were throwing a party. "You kids can come down if you stay out of the way," she would say as she went to act as hostess.

The three of us would tumble downstairs. We learned to dance at those weekend parties. The men would stand us on their shoetops, and we would hold on to their belt loops while they moved to the music. We were allowed to drink the foam off a glass of beer and soon learned to shake the glasses so there would always be foam. It was exciting to be part of the world of stale beer smells and stuffy smoke-filled rooms.

But the fighting between Mom and Frank worsened during the next two years. Every time Mom tried to defend us against his abuse, Frank started shouting at her, too. He was convinced that when Mom wasn't with him she was sleeping with other men. The names he called her had no meaning to my nine-year-old ears, but I understood the anger all too well. We began to plot how we would run away and take Mom with us.

My immediate escape was to start attending Sunday school with my friend Lois. Her dad was the minister. I enjoyed the peaceful atmosphere of the church. The stories fascinated me, and the testimony services described a loving, caring God. One older man stood up each week with a speech committed to memory.

"God is so good," he would say with tears. "I wasted my youth in the pursuit of pleasure and fell into sin. Oh, I learned at my mother's knee of the saving power of Jesus Christ, but I spurned it. God took me back, but now I have nothing to offer. The best years of my life were spent for the devil"

That's dumb! I would think. *If God is such a good God, why would anyone ever turn away and waste life on the devil? Why wait until you're old with nothing left to give God?*

The old man wiped the tears from his eyes. "The few years I have left, I plan to give to the gospel. Young people, don't ever turn your back on Him. It's not worth the price you pay!"

Several people would respond, "Amen, brother."

I still could not understand.

When I was ten the church got a new pastor, and Lois moved several hundred miles away. I stopped going to Sunday school shortly after she left.

At home things worsened. Frank set strict rules for us to be home and in our rooms by seven each night. If we failed to get home on time, the door would be locked. Many times if Mom were at the tavern, it would be hours before Frank let us in. We would walk the streets, visit friends, and sometimes break into the church bus until we heard Mom come home.

As we entered the house, Frank would be huddled by the woodstove drinking beer. He would fly into a drunken rampage, shouting obscenities and accusations. He would recall in vivid detail every wrong he had experienced including his bad childhood and remind us constantly of every mistake we had made.

At other times when we forgot to put away books, toys or clothes, he threw them into the stove. He was more generous with coats and shoes: these he scooped up and threw out the back door onto the woodpile. We were not allowed to get them until the next day. Many times Mom went out and rescued them from the rain.

With the years, our hate for Frank increased. We asked Mom constantly why she stayed with him.

"It isn't easy to find a man who wants a woman with three kids," she explained.

But she had many men friends who wanted a woman and finally decided that if she were being accused, she might as well justify the accusations.

Frank vented his anger at us in nearly every conversation. "You kids are just like your father, no good! Every one of you will end up in jail and have bastard kids."

I bit my tongue, clenched my teeth, and glared defiantly at him.

"I know you earn your quarters on the street corner letting the boys cop a feel," he said to me. "Won't you be lucky when you're older and can sell your ass all over town like your mother?"

"Shut up!" I screamed as I fled the room.

Night after night the scenario was repeated, drilling hatred and resentment into us. I could feel myself hardening inside. We children had few friends and seldom asked schoolmates to come to the house. I felt strongly protective toward Marlene, although I also felt inferior. She was pretty and never seemed to gain weight; I was several inches taller and twenty pounds heavier.

Meanwhile our older brother was wearing under Frank's constant baiting. Some arguments ended with Bubba's loud, wheezing gasps as he ran from the room with another asthma attack. Frank accused him of faking them to get Mom's attention, but it was obvious Bubba could not continue to live under such pressure. So Dad agreed to let him live with him in California.

Dad also agreed to let Marlene and me visit for the summer but said we couldn't live with him permanently until we were twelve. That was a year away.

Dad had moved into town, and our summer in Crescent City passed all too quickly. We earned money cleaning up the bar where Dad worked and spent it at movies and the skating rink. He left us alone as much as Mom did but didn't yell at us as Frank did.

Nothing had changed when Marlene and I returned to Oregon at the beginning of the new school year. We still lived in the old two-story house, and Mom still spent every night at the tavern with people who would listen to her tales of Frank's insane jealousy.

One night Frank got off work early and went to the bar to drink with Mom until closing. It was slightly after two when his 1949 Chevrolet pulled up. I was wide awake, and the stillness of the street seemed to amplify their voices.

"Why don't you just go shack up with your lover?" he shouted.

From my dark bedroom, I heard the car door slam and the heavy thud of footsteps on the porch. The front door opened and slammed shut; the chain latch slid into place.

Another car door slammed shut, and a second later, lighter footsteps sounded across the porch.

The front door opened and pushed against the chain. "Frank, if you don't open this door, I'll break the window."

"Go right ahead. I'm not letting you in."

Several loud thumps and the shattering of glass brought me to the top of the stairs. I grabbed a baseball bat and crept down the stairs until I could see what was happening. Mom was reaching through the broken window and unlocking the chain. Frank swung at her as she pushed the door open and entered the hall. Marlene joined me on the stairs just as Mom spotted us on the landing.

"You girls go back to bed. Everything is all right."

"But Mom—"

"Get!" Her tone was firm.

I returned to my room, wide awake in the darkness. *It will never be all right as long as we live with him!*

Every creak in the long hallway, every sound in the night, I imagined to be Frank, and I clutched the baseball bat under the covers. Sleep did not come easily. The voices downstairs were muffled, but I knew the fighting would last all night. Confusion and anger clamored in my mind. Why didn't she leave him? Why?

Within weeks we had the reason. Mom was going to have a baby.

Up until the day Emily Ann entered our lives, Frank said he wouldn't claim her unless she had red hair and looked like him. The newborn's features were the source of many fights, but she did have red hair. And Frank reluctantly acknowledged he had a daughter.

Within two weeks Mom returned to her nightly bar routine to escape spending time with Frank. I cared for Emily as though she were my own child. When I took her for walks in the stroller, people thought I was her mother. I was twelve years old going on thirty.

Mom did not seem to notice the change of roles. For my part, I resented her long absences and the growing responsibility of caring for Emily. I rejected Dad and Mom's rejection and vowed never to let my children hate me as I hated Frank. Why couldn't she make him leave? And why were neither she nor Dad there to protect me from his relentless verbal abuse?

4.
Looking for Love

When school was over, Mom announced that Marlene and I were going to live with Dad. We were almost thirteen.

But the warm, loving family atmosphere I hoped for was another illusion. Dad worked days at his own cabinet-making business and had a part-time job as a bartender. We went to the bar with him occasionally but were left alone most of the time with no supervision. We managed to find just enough trouble to keep life interesting.

Dad had moved to Oakland, and the junior high schools were nothing like the small ones we had known. Our campus included at least two city blocks and was fenced with six-foot wire mesh. Eighth-grade students were not allowed to leave the grounds during school hours, and the iron bars across the windows earned our school the nickname of "the prison."

The student body was mixed. Almost fifty percent of the students were black, fifteen percent were Hispanic, and the rest of us were white. We learned quickly how to survive— form a gang.

Marlene and I joined the "Black Daggers." There were twelve of us, all in the eighth grade. Since I was the biggest, I was elected president and chose Marlene as my vice-president.

My best friend in the gang was Kathy. She had been supporting herself on the streets for two years, mostly by stealing and sleeping in abandoned houses and cars. I admired her because she was so smart that she had never gotten caught, and I listened to her advice.

We were standing outside a department store one Saturday afternoon as she delivered one of many lectures.

"Look, kid. You don't need money to get by on the streets. You have to be a good thief." She puffed hard on her cigarette, her eyes hard and intense.

"What if I get caught?" I reached out to share her smoke.

"That's your first mistake!" Her words drove deep. "You can't even *think* you'll get caught. Act like you have every right to what you're taking. It's yours."

She leaned closer. "And never look around to see if someone is watching. Always buy one thing from the store and never have more than two people with you at one time."

"Did you ever get caught?"

"Once they tried to hold me, but I knew they hadn't seen me, so I just held to my story. Look them straight in the eye and lie!"

She grinned. "You can do it, Darlene. You look so straight no one will catch you if you do as I say."

Kathy was right. Under her tutelage I learned quickly and became adept at stealing.

My only involvement with the law came when the leader of a rival gang, a Mexican-American girl, challenged me to a fight. Margaret didn't back down with threats. I had to either fight or lose face with my gang. Besides, I wanted to be tough and learn to protect myself. So I stole a switchblade from a hock shop in case Margaret had more than a fair fight in mind, and we agreed to meet one block south of the school at four on Friday.

A large group of kids followed us there. My throat was dry, and my hands were sweaty. It was my first real fight. But I was not going to let her get the better of me.

"Come on, chicken," I taunted, gripping the knife handle in my pocket.

Margaret was positioned in front of her gang. "Man, I'm going to kick your face."

"Well, come on out here and do it, if you've got the guts

without your little gang behind you." My brave words belied the sickening fear in the pit of my stomach.

"You're nothing but a lily-white lizard," she responded, "and I'm going to turn you into a bloody one!"

The jeers of my gang encouraged me. I lunged at her, and we tumbled to the ground.

"I'll kill you," she sneered through clenched teeth.

We rolled several times, scratching, pounding, and kicking as we smashed into bushes and flowers. Margaret pinned me to the ground and began choking me. I brought my fist up under her rib cage and threw her off balance.

Then something snapped inside my brain and pounding explosions blurred my vision. I rolled on top of her and tightened my fingers around her throat. A torrent of pent-up violence surged through my body. I began to pound her head against the ground as I choked her.

"I'll kill you! I'll kill you!" I gasped between breaths, gripped by a blinding rage. I was unaware of the sea of faces around us and oblivious to the cheers.

Suddenly a fist hit my back. "Darlene, let her go! The cops are coming!"

The sound of approaching sirens snapped me to my senses. A woman had grown alarmed at the sight of so many kids on her street and called the police. I gave Margaret one last push against the ground and jumped up. "You ever cross my path again, and I'll kill you!" Then I took off running with everyone else.

Had I actually come that close to killing her?

With the exception of a half-dozen girls, the street cleared in seconds. One of the girls who stayed behind was Marlene, who had not been fighting and saw no reason to run. I was a block away when the police cars screeched to a stop. The officers jumped from their cars and confronted the small group. One knelt beside Margaret, who still lay on the ground. Suddenly I saw a cop push Marlene toward the patrol car and shove her into the back seat. I ran back.

"Where do you think you're taking her?" I demanded.

"Who are you?" replied the officer, standing between me and the police car.

"I'm her sister. She didn't do anything."

"Oh? Good. Then you can keep her company."

Another cop came up behind me and snapped cuffs onto my hands before I could resist.

They shoved me in beside Marlene. But I started to laugh as they shut the car door. "Well, at least you aren't going alone. Why didn't you run, Marlene?"

"I wasn't fighting," she pouted. "Margaret told them I was your sister, so they stuck me in the car."

Suddenly I remembered the switchblade in my pocket. "Marlene, they're going to search us at the station. Reach into my pocket and get that knife out. Push it between the seats."

Our tones grew hushed as we tried to dispose of my illegal weapon. I pushed aside a new fear: What if they locked us up for the night?

Suddenly the area was alive. Four boys from a male gang decided to rescue us. With sticks and chains flying, they jumped on the hoods of the patrol cars, smashing windows and attacking the cops. Shortly another half-dozen cars were on the scene and a paddy wagon at the rear. Marlene and I were hysterical as we watched from the safety of the back seat.

A single gunshot into the air stopped the assault, and the four boys were placed under arrest. I remembered from a television show that all we had to tell the police was our name and address, so that was all I planned to give.

We were transferred into the paddy wagon and taken to the downtown police station. After being searched, Marlene and I were placed in a small cell. She paced the floor.

"I told them where Dad usually hangs out," she whimpered. "What is he going to say?"

"What can he say? He doesn't care what happens to us.

Besides since this is our first offense, they can't keep us very long."

"Dad does too care, Darlene."

But I was no longer sure.

As the minutes ticked into hours, I lay on a wooden bench with my coat wadded up as a pillow and wondered what was keeping Dad. Did he really love us as Marlene thought? How come he was never around when I needed him? Hands cupped behind my head, I stared at the waterstained ceiling and the graffiti on the walls. My hurt turned to anger against Marlene.

I'll never get caught for anything again! If I hadn't gone back for her, I wouldn't be here now.

Metal clicked against metal as a key was inserted into the lock behind us. A policewoman swung open the iron door and told us to follow her. We were led into an office where Dad had just finished signing our release.

We walked in silence to the car. As I climbed into the back seat, Dad's eyes caught mine in the rear-view mirror. "Did you win?"

"Yes. I didn't start it either, Dad. She did. You told me once that if someone else started it, I could finish it."

He didn't say another word about the fight, but all the way home he mumbled about the police finding him in a bar.

When I returned to school the following Monday, I was called into the principal's office and given a week's suspension. Dad went to school on Tuesday and insisted they reinstate me because he didn't want any kid of his running the streets of that town.

For example, Bubba had taken a paper route to earn spending money. The Sunday morning issue had to be started at 2 A.M., and Dad thought it was good for me to keep Bubba company. We would leave the house about midnight and walk the streets for two hours, breaking into cars and stealing anything of value. We made more money that way than what Bubba's route paid.

Sometimes we slit convertible tops just for the fun of it or we would set fire to a car if it had nothing worth stealing. My conscience became so hardened that I neither cared about personal safety nor regarded other people's property. People didn't care about us; why should we care about them? Besides, doing pranks at night and not getting caught ignited my excitement and boldness.

My own neighborhood also offered ample opportunity for daytime experiments. Several boys who were high school dropouts invited me different times to cut school and spend the day drinking and smoking pot in their apartment. I talked a couple of girls from my gang into joining me. I was an expert at forging Dad's signature and could write excuses for everyone.

I had a great time until the third booze party.

"More wine?" Tony held up a half-empty bottle of Tokay. His wavy black hair and tanned muscular body had the girls chasing after him.

"Sure," I giggled. I held up my glass, my head already spinning.

Tony glanced around the room. "There's six of us today. Let's play strip poker!" He winked at me.

The alcohol and the excitement of acting grown-up overshadowed the fear that had haunted me for years.

"Yeah! Good idea." I struggled to keep my balance, as I staggered to the table. "You guys chicken?"

The other two couples joined Tony and me at the dining room table. The boys grinned. Several hands later we were all down to our underwear. While the girls traded passionate kisses for not having to remove anything else, Tony produced more wine.

The room was beginning to spin, and suddenly I felt uneasy. "I think you're dealing from the bottom of the deck!" I said to Tony.

"I wouldn't do that." He chuckled and gestured to the others who were kissing and stroking each other. "Looks like they have better things to do than play cards. Come on."

He rose to his full six feet, grasped my arm, and propelled me toward his bedroom. I pulled away, trying to clear my mind enough to object. "Let me get my clothes."

"You don't need them," he whispered hoarsely.

He kicked the door shut with his foot and shoved me onto the bed. Struggle was useless as he pressed his mouth against mine and removed what little clothing remained. As he thrust his body hard against mine, I could hardly breathe beneath his weight. My ears were ringing, and I squeezed my eyes shut, fireworks flashing in my mind.

Never again, I thought. *I will never again let a man get me drunk or trick me.*

I wanted to kill him, but I shut off my mind and waited until he was finished.

I continued to lie trembling, wrapped in the sheet after Tony went back to join the others. Why did it always happen to me? What if I got pregnant? Why couldn't someone really love me? At thirteen, I seemed always to be on the receiving end of anything but love.

I staggered from the bed to the bathroom and threw up. I couldn't look at myself in the mirror. Still wrapped in the sheet, I opened the door to the dining room, grabbed my clothes, and dressed while I make another resolve. *I'll never drink again.*

That resolve lasted less than a week, but my attendance at school was regular for the rest of the year. I relaxed a little when I started my period after two months, but my stomach knotted whenever I thought of that day with Tony, and I decided never again to go through the fear of being pregnant.

When summer started, I told Dad I was returning to Oregon to live with Mom.

Marlene was dumbfounded. "How can you even think of living with Frank again?"

"Yeah," Dad said. "After the way he treated you kids, why do you want to go back to him?"

I wasn't sure why. Living with Frank had been tough, but living in Oakland had been tough too. Since I had not found the love I was looking for from Dad, winning his approval seemed less important than it had been.

"I can handle Frank," I muttered. "I just want to be with Mom."

"Well, I'm not going!" declared Marlene defiantly.

"You girls are old enough to make your own choices," Dad said. "If Darlene wants to leave, she can. You can stay with Bubba and me." He gave Marlene a reassuring hug.

I motioned for Marlene to follow me into the bedroom. "You write me and keep me informed about the gang, O.K.? Since I'm going, you can be president!" I smiled to cover up a growing feeling of lostness and punched her on the shoulder. "Just don't get caught, sis, whatever you do!"

"I won't." Her voice lowered. "I'll miss you, Dar. We've never been apart."

"I guess we need to grow up sometime," I said, trying to sound tough and composed. "I'll write, O.K.?"

"Sure." Her face brightened. "And you can come back next summer."

"Right!" I picked up the phone to call Mom.

And within the week, I was on a bus headed north. The year had dulled my hatred for Frank, and after all my new experiences, I was not afraid of anything. At least, I wouldn't admit it.

5.
A Fresh
Start

Although being back in a rural community forced me to curtail my gang activities, I remained cocky, while hungering inside for acceptance and love. I didn't know what I expected from Mom; however, she was drinking and fighting with Frank as much as ever.

Nor was my search fulfilled through my classmates in high school. I had no close friends, and the few dates I accepted with boys ended up as backseat wrestling matches. So to avoid dating, I used the excuse of having to take care of Emily. I withdrew into a private world of fantasy and seldom went anywhere except to school.

When the pastor of a local church invited me to a youth retreat over Thanksgiving and even offered to pay my way, Mom agreed to let me go. I welcomed the chance to get away from Frank and see my old friend Lois. We had written a few times during the past year. Her family was living in Portland, and she was anxious to see me.

The camp was several miles east of Portland, situated on property bordering the Columbia River. Many of the buildings were under construction, so we sat on rough wooden benches and knelt on sawdust floors.

I had heard sermons before, but didn't ever recall being confronted personally to accept Jesus Christ as my Savior. The camp evangelist changed that.

The Reverend Henry Steele was from Michigan. He was a tall, barrel-chested, athletic type with a prematurely receding hairline. Although he was in his early thirties, his sermons were filled with illustrations from his teenage years.

I felt, sitting next to Lois in the chapel, that he was not preaching at me but talking to me. And when he shared several tragic moments in his life, the most recent being the loss of his seven-year-old son to leukemia, a lump of emotion filled my throat.

"I spent months asking God why," he said, "and pouring out my agony. One night God spoke to my heart. *My Son died in pain and agony too. Isn't it enough to know that I understand even if you never know why?*

"I fell asleep for the first time in weeks," concluded Henry Steele, "completely at peace. God understands what you and I are going through and wants us to commit our entire lives to Him."

During the altar call Lois reached over and took my hand. "Darlene, wouldn't you like to ask Jesus to come into your heart and forgive your sins?"

I looked down at my feet, kicking the sawdust into small piles. "I don't think even Jesus could straighten out my life after all I've done," I whispered back.

"Sure He could. The Bible says He came into the world to save sinners if you'll just believe on Him."

"But you don't know what I've done." My mind raced back over the last few years. "I might only be fifteen, but I've committed every sin in the book except kill someone!"

"It doesn't matter what you've done, Darlene. Jesus will forgive all your sins." She paused for a moment. "Do you think you can change yourself?"

"No." I fidgeted nervously on the bench. "But don't pressure me, Lois. I know I'm at rock bottom and I need help to get out, but I can't do it right now. O.K.?"

"Sure, Darlene." She leaned closer and whispered in my ear. "But I want you to know that I'll be praying for you!"

I didn't look up.

The service seemed to drag that night, and I was glad when they finally dismissed us so I could take a walk. Apparently I had a new question to answer.

Since I liked the Reverend Steele, I found an opportunity

to talk with him the very next day. He talked in a strong, fatherly way, as my own father seldom had. And when he took time to pray for God's leading in my life, I felt he really cared.

That night he spoke again. "In high school I was on the track team. I was scheduled to run in the late afternoon for the last qualifying heat. During a lunch break, several of us went to a soda fountain where I ordered the largest hamburger and milkshake they made. The other boys ate very little. They were scheduled to run soon after lunch. So I teased them and tempted them with my food, which I thought would have time to settle before I ran my race.

"But when we arrived back at the field, the schedule had been changed. I was to run immediately. It was a hot day, and on a full stomach I made it *almost* to the finish line. Then I passed out!"

He smiled, while everyone laughed.

"The next day my name wasn't even listed as a runner," he continued, "because I hadn't finished. Life is like that race, kids. We get the program all figured out, then someone changes the schedule. When you're an athlete you can't afford to partake of the goodies at the soda shop and when you're a Christian you can't afford to partake of the sins of this world, no matter how good they look to you."

He paused for a moment and looked at the faces, not smiling now. "The most important thing in the world is to have everything right between you and Jesus. We don't know when our time to run might be changed. We don't know when we are going to die."

His voice tightened and then cracked with emotion. "You know, I always thought I had forever. But my doctors tell me it could be anytime. You see, I have cancer. I know I'm in that last race heading for the finish line, and Jesus will be there to meet me. I'd like to meet you there. Are you ready to meet Him? Don't leave this room tonight until you're sure that Jesus is your Savior."

Tears were rising from deep within me. I shut my eyes

tight while a painful lump filled my throat. A feeling of desperation swept over me.

You can't die, my thoughts screamed. *Why did you bother to care about me if you were going to die?*

Soothing music from the piano interrupted my thoughts. We stood to sing "Almost Persuaded" as I wrestled with grief and conviction. I wasn't ready to meet Jesus but I knew I needed Him. I wasn't ready to lose my new friend either and I knew I wanted to see him in heaven.

I laid the hymn book down and stepped into the aisle. I didn't look around while I walked to the makeshift altar. My heart pounded wildly as I knelt in the sawdust.

"Dear Jesus," I began, "You know I'm not ready to meet You. I've done some pretty bad things. Please forgive me for my sins and come into my heart and be my Savior. And Jesus, if it isn't too much to ask, please don't let Reverend Steele die. Amen."

I rose and found a seat near the front. When an opportunity came to tell everyone what God had done, I stood with legs trembling.

"I don't know exactly what happened inside me," I said, "but I felt a load lift and I feel clean. I asked Jesus to save me and I want to serve Him forever."

I smiled at Lois, sitting farther back in the chapel.

In the months after camp weekend, I attended church regularly, taking Emily as often as possible. It was time away from Mom and Frank's fighting.

But although being a Christian meant my sins had been forgiven, my awful ache to be loved had not gone away. Scenes of Tony and even of Curt often flashed across my mind and tormented my dreams. I had never felt more alone.

As my sophomore year drew to a close, Lois's father called and asked if I wanted to spend the summer with Lois on a fire lookout near Mount Hood. I was elated. He promised to pay me a dollar a day so she wouldn't have to spend the summer alone.

Lois and I anticipated a time of Bible sharing and Christian fellowship for an entire summer. It took the better part of a day to backpack in our supplies and personal effects for the three months. Our new home was a two-story cabin perched on a peak some five thousand feet up the mountain. Lois's father was to come up once a week with a fresh supply of food. Our water supply was from an underground spring about a half-mile down the back side of the peak. My job was to pack it up to the cabin because one person had to be in the lookout at all times. We both learned to use the instruments to spot smoke after a lightning storm.

The first month met our expectations. We had special times to read the Bible and share what we were learning. Every night we sang hymns from the church hymnal Lois had brought. I memorized most of them so I could sing as I carried water each day.

One morning we were awakened by an electrical storm outside the window. The peak was covered with dense grey fog. There wasn't any way to watch for fires. So we sat on the single bench bed and began to talk about my year in California.

For the first time I shared the rape experience with Tony. I told her about my fear of being close to boys. I told her about Frank's prediction I would end up pregnant and my resolve not to let that happen. I told her about my nightmares and fear of dirty old men.

Never having verbalized these thoughts to anyone, I felt embarrassed as I finished my monologue.

Lois wrapped her arms around the pillow, leaned forward, and watched me with interest.

"I think about sex a lot," she confided. "I was molested once. I never told anyone." She had a faraway look in her eyes.

"You never forget it," I whispered.

The cold dampness of the fog pressing against the windows and door of the cabin sent a chill through me. Or perhaps it was a sudden feeling of isolation rather than the fog.

"I don't think anyone will ever love me" I said suddenly.

"I love you, Darlene." Lois moved closer and put her arms around me.

"Yeah, but that's different. We're girls." I didn't move away.

"I spent the night with a girl friend once. She taught me how to masturbate. It feels good and it's not like sex with a boy."

Almost as if we had identical inner cue cards, my next thought and her next words matched.

"I do love you, Darlene. We could—"

"Are you serious? How?"

With thick fog clouds covering the mountaintop like a shroud, we slipped beneath the covers for warmth and exploration. Girl kisses weren't the same as boy's; they were not violent or threatening. We both knew we shouldn't be touching each other, but we didn't stop. For several hours we lay together and talked, letting our mutual curiosity become a sexual encounter.

Later that night I asked Lois guiltily, "Do you think we'll go to hell for what we did?"

"No. We just wanted to see what it was like. We should pray for forgiveness and promise never to do it again though."

"O.K.—and never to tell anyone either. Promise?"

"I promise." She gave me a hug.

We read the Bible and prayed about our activities that day. But her promise not to tell lasted only until her father came up for his weekly visit.

Lois told the entire story while I was getting water. So that night before we went to bed, her father read from the Bible about all sexual activity outside marriage being wrong in the sight of God. He explained that what we had done was normal childhood curiosity, but that we should not do it again.

The next day, overwhelmed by a sense of betrayal, I confronted Lois.

"You promised not to tell," I exploded.

"But I still felt guilty," she said. "I had to confess to Daddy." Tears began to run down her cheeks.

"But you lied to me," I said, shaking my head. "I'll never trust you again. And I'll never tell you anything I do again either."

The next morning things between Lois and me were better. We agreed never to talk about the experience again. But my sense of betrayal turned to deep, seething anger. I no longer wanted to share personal feelings with her, and because we never talked, she thought all the effects from our experience were over.

But the feelings awakened in me that day on the mountaintop did not end. I had felt safe being intimate with Lois and knew I could not get pregnant.

Now my awakened sexuality grappled with new desires, and I had no idea what to do about them. Although I went to church each Sunday, I struggled with what it meant to be a Christian. Isolated from my classmates at school, I began to pour my feelings into poetry. I discovered I had a knack for taking sermon themes and composing verse. Mom liked to listen to my poetry, and I used it to communicate to her what I knew about Jesus.

During my senior year I was asked to write the poem for the school yearbook and looked forward to reciting it on graduation night before receiving my diploma. To my crushing disappointment, however, Mom bowed out of attending at the last minute, explaining she couldn't stand to be closed in with so many people and she knew I understood.

I understood only that she went to the tavern every night with a crowd and it didn't bother her there. After the ceremony I did not go to the senior ball but walked the streets and smoked cigarettes, too hurt to cry and too mad to go home.

I was only seventeen and had not found the love I was looking for in either my own family or in the life I had known thus far. It continued to hover just out of reach.

6.
The
Outsider

Within a week after graduation I received my acceptance from a Christian college in Portland and notification of a federal loan. I was even offered a job for the summer if I wanted to start earning money toward tuition.

So I packed for school, moved to Portland, and spent the summer with Lois and her family. We were still friends, although I had kept my vow never to trust her with my feelings again. When school opened in the fall, Lois's older sister let us both stay in her apartment near the campus.

From the beginning of the semester, I realized I was different. Almost everyone I met came from a Christian home and had been raised by both parents. They talked about a warm, loving family life that I thought existed only on "Father Knows Best."

Classwork proved easy for me. I read the material, attended classes, and never had to study further. When I wasn't working in the janitorial department, I made new friends in the dorm and listened to their family stories. And as I caught a glimpse of a life that was more than bars, fighting, and raising unwanted children, I became determined to avoid marriage and make more of my life than either of my parents had.

Resentment and bitterness motivated me: I would succeed! I would not bear children to hate me the way I hated Dad and Mom for the years of neglect. I remembered Frank's taunts: *You'll never be any good! You're not worth anything!*

Then I met Lance. He was the son of a minister and was

studying for the ministry. He seemed to embody the gentleness of a butterfly in the frame of a football tackle! I was attracted by his outward strength and his inward commitment to Jesus Christ.

Lance was on a ministry team that went out every Sunday evening to surrounding churches. I sat in the front row each place he preached. He would catch my eye from time to time as he delivered messages about living a sanctified and holy life. As the weeks passed, we began spending more and more time together. I started to dream of love. Perhaps I was being too hasty about avoiding marriage.

Then my dreams were shattered.

We were walking along a secluded path near the campus one afternoon when Lance stopped and pulled me close to him.

"I really care for you, Darlene," he said and kissed me gently on the lips.

My head spun. How I had longed to hear those words!

"I'm fond of you too, Lance," I murmured, melting against his strong build as his arms encircled me.

"If you love me, Darlene, go to bed with me," he whispered urgently into my ear.

"What?" I pushed him away and stared in disbelief.

"I love you and you love me. I need you to show me by making love with me." He tried to pull me close again.

"I don't believe I'm hearing this! You preach purity from the pulpit and then you want me to have sex with you? I thought Christians were different!"

I pulled away and ran back up the path, choking back angry tears. Just when I had thought I was finding real love! Despair surged through me. All men were alike!

As I raced across the campus I almost ran over Joy, one of the girls I had met from the new girls' dorm and a member of Lance's gospel team.

"Where are you going in such a hurry?" she laughed, then stopped. "Hey, what's the matter?"

"Nothing." I pressed my lips tight together and fought back the tears. Joy of all people, privy to Lance's talks on holiness, would not understand.

"Come on, Darlene. I can tell something is wrong."

"All right!" I spun around and faced her. "I'll tell you what's wrong. I come to a Christian school because everyone here loves each other, and you can learn about God's loving you. I meet a Christian boy who preaches that the Bible is true and who says he loves me. Then we go for a walk and he says if I love him I'll have sex with him."

My face was flushed with hurt and anger. "Well, I've got news for you. In the world men tell you right away what they want and they don't disguise it in Christian love. I can't take it anymore. Christians aren't any better than anybody else. God doesn't care. No one cares. I wish I were dead!"

Joy looked stunned. "You mean Lance?"

I bit my lower lip until I tasted blood. "I don't belong here," I said dully, my anger beginning to turn to depression. "I don't belong anywhere."

Joy reached out and touched my arm. "Darlene, I hardly know what to say. But why don't you talk with Marie Fuller, the dean of women? She's understanding. Maybe she can help."

"I don't think anyone can help, Joy. God is supposed to make such a difference. Everyone says He does. But people everywhere act the same." I gritted my teeth. "And I hate · men!"

"You can't hate men because of Lance, Darlene. Besides, you care too much about people."

"Oh, really?" I pulled a leaf from a bush along the path. "Then why don't people really care about me?"

"I care about you. And Darlene, God didn't work miracles to get you here just to have you toss it all away. College is your opportunity to break the mold, to learn a whole new lifestyle. Why don't we pray together?"

"I don't think it'll do any good, Joy. But you're right about one thing. Lance isn't worth it!" I forced a smile as we walked slowly back toward her dorm. "You know, sometimes I hurt so much I don't think I want to keep living. Why can't anyone love me for me?"

"Jesus does," she replied quietly. After a moment of silence she added, "And I do too."

In Joy's room we talked and prayed for several hours with her roommate Sharon. I felt better after sharing my struggles with them and discovered both Sharon and Joy had conflicts too.

It was after midnight when I slipped into my apartment and got ready for bed. Lois and her sister were sound asleep. I lay in the dark thinking about the events of the evening. If everyone else had struggles too, then maybe Dean Fuller would be able to understand. But why did I continue to feel so alone?

The next day I stopped by Marie Fuller's office. She had an open-door policy for her apartment as well as her office. She had been widowed as a young woman and chose not to remarry. Now in her early fifties and with her children married, she had a heart for college-age women.

During my first session with her, I found a haven from the pressures of my inner struggles and a sounding board for my endless questions. Week after week she took time for me and did not seem to mind my frequent visits.

Because she made me feel loved and accepted, I could be truthful with her. I did not tell her about the occasional cigarettes I still smoked contrary to college policy. But I shared my disappointment about Lance, with whom I now refused to talk. And I related accounts of my childhood and the circumstances that led me to a Christian college. She listened sympathetically, sometimes for hours with nothing more than a nod and always suggested we pray and commit my feelings and my past to God.

Not everyone at the school possessed Mrs. Fuller's unique

ability to love me unconditionally, so I tried to camouflage my growing emotional and spiritual struggles from everyone but her.

One Sunday night at church I heard about a Christian drug rehabilitation center in San Francisco. After my own teenage experiences in Oakland, I wondered if God might want me to take a semester off and volunteer at the center. It would certainly be better to leave school voluntarily rather than get caught smoking, I reasoned. So I went to talk with Marie Fuller, whom I now considered my best friend and called by first name.

Marie was dubious. "Darlene, I can't make a decision for you. I think you need to consider that it would put you right back into the environment of street gangs and drugs. How do you think you would handle that?"

"Well, since I used to be in a gang and I've seen the drug scene firsthand, I'd really like to help people and tell them how Jesus can change their lives. It would be exciting."

Inwardly I hesitated. Had I really changed so much that I *could* tell others? On the other hand, maybe I would find where I really belonged.

"But do you think you're strong enough to handle that pressure?" persisted Marie.

I decided to ignore my feelings of failure, like my guilt over smoking and my continuing sense of isolation.

"I've had some shaky times this year," I replied confidently, "but I think I've got it together now. I guess I won't know until I'm there. Besides, I don't have enough money to stay in school without another loan, and this will give me the opportunity to do something for God."

The words sounded phony even to me, but I had already made my decision.

"Oh, Darlene, I'm not so concerned with your doing something for God as I am with your getting to know Him and letting Him heal your life. Whatever you decide, I'll back you in prayer, but honey, please pray about it. You could find yourself in a real problem if it isn't His place for you."

"Yeah, I know that. I will pray about it. But I really want to go." I sat on the floor by her rocking chair. "Will you still love me if I go?"

She smiled and patted my head. "Of course I'll still love you, Darlene. Why wouldn't I? Let's just pray and ask for God's wisdom. All right?"

Our time ended as it always did with prayer and a feeling of her complete acceptance. I never felt that unconditional love with anyone else, even with God.

Within the week I was packed and on my way to San Francisco, assured of the prayers of Joy and Marie. But almost immediately I was brought face-to-face with feelings I had thought were dead. I felt the old sense of excitement remembering when I was on the streets, although I kept to myself and shared my struggle with no one.

On my one day off each week, I could either explore the city or visit with my father, who lived just across the bay. As the months passed, I chose to explore the city.

One spring afternoon I was wandering down Market Street and passed a bookstore that opened onto the street. On the front rack I noticed a paperback with two women in an embrace. I bought the book, heedless of what the store clerk might think, and found a secluded place in a nearby park to read. A knot formed in the pit of my stomach, as I realized I was feeling the same feelings described in the book! I finished reading, then threw the book into a trashcan.

On my return to the center, I was greeted with a new candidate to help get settled into the dorm. Connie was a prostitute, dope addict, and lesbian who said she wanted help. I wanted to run away. I was both attracted and frightened by her sleeping in the same room.

That first night I sat watching her as she slept, while pictures from the book danced through my head. Perhaps I should never have left school. I certainly couldn't tell anyone about what I was thinking, least of all Marie; I would get thrown out of college.

One morning Connie was getting dressed and caught me watching her in the mirror. She smiled and winked. I turned away, embarrassed at having been caught.

I avoided being alone with her over the next few weeks, wrestling with guilt and confusion over my feelings of attraction. I had to get out! So I went to the director and informed him I would be returning to college. Summer was approaching, and he never questioned the decision, although I had enough questions for both of us.

My "ministry" had lasted three months. I felt once more like a failure and hoped Marie would not ask the real reason I had left the center. I wanted to please her but could not shake my feelings of sexual attraction toward Connie, while memories of the summer with Lois also crept into my thoughts.

Back at school, I got my janitorial job for the summer and another loan to finance the new semester. I could live rent free in the dorm until the fall quarter started. During those summer months, an invisible magnet drew me to more and more students who were struggling with Christian values. Most of my relationships lacked stability; most of my conversations left me with more questions than answers.

I was still smoking and struggled with a new impulse to get drunk and forget everything. At eighteen I hated the thought of using the same escape my parents used, yet alcohol seemed like a temporary solution. The problem was I was too young to stay drunk, and if I got kicked out of college, I had no place to go but home. I had run from the drug rehabilitation center but could not run from my own desires.

It was at this point that I met Barbara. By Christmas our friendship had grown solid, and she provided me with an acceptance I had never known. Because of our sexual encounter on the last night before Christmas vacation, I was forced to admit my own lesbian feelings, yet I needed the counsel and love that only Marie Fuller could offer.

So here I sat on the floor in front of Marie, my face buried in her lap. She had listened to my confession. I was too embarrassed to look in her eyes and too ashamed of being involved in a relationship I didn't understand.

But Marie's words were healing.

"Honey, I've never loved you for what you do. I love you just because Jesus does, and nothing you do will change that." She paused thoughtfully. "Barbara's problems are deeper than either of us has knowledge to heal. I have committed her to Jesus, as I have you. I will never stop loving either one of you." She cupped my face in her hands and looked into my eyes.

I gulped hard and straightened into a sitting position in front of her. Pulling my knees up to my chest, I wrapped my arms around them and rested my chin on one knee. "Promise?"

She smiled. "Cross my heart! I know you really care for Barbara. I know, too, that you've been going through a rough time emotionally. You're a loving person and you need to be loved. But the Bible calls homosexuality sin, dear, and we can do no less! I don't have any other help to advise than God Himself. We must trust Him with your life and Barbara's."

"I've tried to trust Him, Marie. I've prayed for her all semester. But people just don't know what she's going through."

"I'm aware of it, honey. I've spoken with her mother, and she won't be returning next semester. She's not strong enough emotionally to handle school."

The news stunned me. I stood up and paced the floor. "If she quits, I'll quit too! I want to take care of her."

"Maybe a semester away from her will help you gain perspective. I'm here anytime you need to talk. God loves you and He loves Barbara. She needs professional help, Darlene. Will you stay at least one more semester without her? I'd like you to."

I hesitated, then nodded. For her I would do it. "I'll give it a try, Marie. But maybe I'm the one who needs professional help instead of Barbara."

"Let's let Jesus be our Helper!" She stood up, wrapped her arms around me and whispered, "Don't ever forget I am praying for you, Darlene."

A giant lump filled my throat. "Thanks. I need it."

When I left Marie's apartment and returned to the almost empty dorm, I was overwhelmed by a sense of isolation.

I'll get my degree so I can really take care of Barbara, I vowed silently. *We can be just good friends, not lovers.*

All through the break I worked part-time in janitorial and tried to ignore the loneliness that the holidays always brought. But on Christmas Day when there was no work, I lost my battle with the guilt and tormenting thoughts. Although I cared for Barbara, nothing had been right since we had slept together.

Then a new idea crept into my mind. If I slept with a man, that would prove whether or not I was queer!

I took a bus to the center of downtown Portland, ignoring the protests of my conscience because this would resolve the question of my sexual identity. The only way I could do it was to act quickly.

It was early evening, and the theater marquees flashed titles of enticement to the winos and sailors seeking refuge from the chilly night air. Christmas was nothing special here either, and certainly no one from school would frequent this section of town. I wandered into one theater and sat near the back. Would someone pick me up?

Moments later a young sailor moved into my row. "Excuse me, do you have a match?" He sat down next to me.

"Sure." I reached into my purse.

"Are you alone?" he whispered, lighting a cigarette.

I gulped down my fear. "Yes."

"Want to go for a drink after the movie?"

"Sure." I lit a cigarette of my own and tried to act older than my eighteen years.

I resisted his advances during the movie with promises for later, while voices in my head argued.

I'm not a lesbian.

Yes, you are!

No, I'm not. I'm going to bed with this sailor.

That doesn't prove anything! Remember what Barbara said?

I didn't even see the movie.

When it was over, my companion's lopsided grin told me what he had in mind. Could I actually go through with it?

He led the way to the nearest bar. It was full of sailors, women, and loud music. We pushed our way to a rear booth. "Sit here, I'll get the drinks."

He disappeared into the crowd.

I spotted a red exit sign next to a sign for *Restroom.* Casting one glance toward the crowd, I made my way quickly to the door. I pushed it open and stepped into an alley. Though I was swallowed up into the night, my thoughts flashed like the neon signs.

You're queer! You're queer!

7.
Dykes and Queens Aren't Reservoirs and Royalty

As a second-semester sophomore, I grew increasingly depressed and isolated while I struggled to understand the new identity within me.

Then with no warning, Marie Fuller announced she had accepted a position with the American University in Beirut, Lebanon. She was the one person who loved me with all my conflicts. Fear seized me when I contemplated college life without Marie. Because she listened to me and loved me unconditionally, she had become the mother figure I had never known.

A few days later as I watched her airplane leave the runway, tears spilled down my cheeks. I felt as jumbled as a grocery-store shelf after an earthquake.

Marie's last words echoed in the silence. "Darlene, you can't depend on me. Only God can help you. Please seek professional counseling. Please do. And keep in touch with me. I don't want to lose track of you in this big world."

I remembered her words as I resolved anew to finish school and make Marie proud of me.

In January I called Barbara, who had been hospitalized for depression, to see how she was coming along.

"I'm doing all right," she said dully. "I've been out a week now."

I tried to ignore the haunting tone in Barbara's voice. "Did you hear Marie Fuller left school? I went to the airport and saw her off."

"She's a neat lady." Barbara was silent for a moment, then continued with new seriousness. "Darlene, I've been thinking about us."

I panicked. Didn't she love me anymore?

"Hey, we've got great plans for the future, Barb! Don't go thinking too hard!"

"Darlene, I really feel guilty about 'bringing you out.' If it weren't for me, you'd be straight."

"That's not true," I said. "If it hadn't been you, then it would have been someone else, somewhere else. Besides, it was my choice too. Don't blame yourself for my choices."

"No. . . ." Her voice trailed off. "If it weren't for me, you'd still be straight."

"Just forget about that kind of talk! Look, I'm coming down during Easter break. We'll discuss it then."

When we hung up a few minutes later, I knew I could set her mind at ease when we were together.

I wrote to her every day, alluding to an in-depth discussion in a few weeks. Her mother might read one of my letters, I reasoned, so I avoided details.

I finished my work schedule for the Easter holidays and made plans for a week-long trip to Barbara's hometown. As I walked into the dorm on Friday night to pack for my bus trip the next morning, the phone was ringing in the empty lobby. I picked it up.

"This is the operator. I have a person-to-person call for Darlene Bogle."

"Speaking."

What a coincidence!

"Go ahead please," said the operator.

"Darlene, this is Barbara's mom."

My heart beat faster, and my face was flushed. I envisioned her reading the last letter I had sent Barbara. Maybe she didn't want me to come.

"Oh, hi." I tried to sound casual.

Her next words hit like a brick. "Darlene, I have some bad news for you. Barbara is dead."

My knees buckled, and I grabbed the counter for support. "What do you mean? She can't be! I just talked with her on Tuesday."

Her voice was monotone. "She took an overdose of pills on Tuesday night and went into a coma on Wednesday. She never regained consciousness. She died this morning.

The room was spinning. "But I loved her! I told her it would be all right. She can't be dead. She just can't be." I was whispering the words, my voice tight with emotion.

"I know you cared for her, Darlene. The funeral is on Monday. You're welcome to come and stay with us if you want. I know she would have wanted me to let you know."

I felt sick. "Thanks. . . . I don't think I should come. But thanks for letting me know."

My brain spun, mixing up the silent screaming in my head. Barbara couldn't die! I hadn't explained to her yet that it wasn't her fault. She didn't have to feel guilty.

Tears spilled down my cheeks as I let the receiver fall back into the cradle. Then anger exploded and surged through my body. I slammed my fist against the wall.

"God, are You punishing me?" I shouted to the empty lobby. "Are You going to take away everyone I love? If that's the kind of God you are, the hell with it! Why? Why Barbara? But even if You take everyone away, I won't live for a God who kills what I love!"

I bolted through the doors and down the steps.

Joy was striding toward me. Apparently she had not yet left for Easter break.

"Barbara's dead!" I screamed. "God can't be a God of love and let this happen." I was shaking uncontrollably. "Barbara can't die. She just can't!"

I sat on the stairs, my face in my hands.

"Darlene, I was just coming to tell you." Joy sat next to me and put her hand on my shoulder. "Barbara's mother called the office first to see how she could reach you. I'm sorry. I know how deeply you cared for her."

"Do you? Do you really?" Desperation filled my voice. "I never told you the real story, Joy. I loved her. She was a lesbian and she killed herself because she introduced me to the homosexual world."

Tears streaming down my cheeks, I looked up at Joy through blurred vision.

Tears filled her eyes. "I had heard rumors. What will you do now?" Her tone was compassionate.

"I don't know. I just don't know." I threw my head back and cleared my throat. "I can't go there. I can't stay here! I think I'm going to find something to drink. It's the only thing I know that really helps."

"That won't help. Why don't you come to my room and let's talk?" Her voice was firm. "You don't need to be alone."

"Why? You think I'll kill myself or something?" I stood to my feet.

"I just think you need a friend, Darlene." She guided me to her room, where I collapsed on the bed. Although I fought to control them, hot tears continued to trickle down my cheeks. I spoke with great effort.

"I can't stay in school anymore," I mumbled. "Maybe I'll go to California with my dad or even join the Army."

Her eyes widened in surprise. "The Army? Are you serious? I don't think that's what you need!"

"I could support myself that way. I need space away from everyone." Fresh tears stung my eyes. "I don't even want to live without Barbara."

"The only One who can make life worth living is Jesus. I don't know how to help you, Darlene, other than to tell you He loves you and so do I."

I lay with eyes closed for several minutes.

"Thanks, Joy," I said at last. "I feel so alone. I need to know that someone cares. I don't know where I'll end up, but I've got to leave."

She sat cross-legged on the floor next to me. "Please don't run from God, Darlene. I'll pray that you talk things out with Him."

"I don't feel like talking with anyone right now. I think I'll withdraw from school tomorrow and just leave. Easter is a good time to make the break. I'll let you know where I go."

I rose wearily to my feet. "But thanks for caring."

It was almost dark outside, and only a few students remained on campus. What would happen next? Marie was gone. Now Barbara was dead. Why was I living? In less than an hour my whole life had changed.

By the end of the week I had withdrawn from school, taken my belongings back to Mom's, and packed for a month-long trip to visit Dad. I stayed drunk most of that time, trying to drown the memory of Barbara and erase the guilt that she had killed herself because of me. The agony of these recurring thoughts drove me into a deep depression.

Influenced by a whim I stopped by the Army recruitment office and signed induction papers. Starting a whole new life, I fantasized, would make the pain go away. I didn't want a replacement for Barbara, but maybe I could meet another lesbian and just be friends.

Two weeks later I stared at the nameless faces of people looking at our bus. We had just entered the military base and were being driven to the processing unit. Somehow I recognized the lesbians! Could they also recognize me?

Within hours an invisible magnet pulled small groups of women together. Everyone seemed to know who was gay and who was straight without saying a word. I was amazed to see officers who appeared to be gay and watched with growing interest the eye contact between women.

During our second week of training, a girl from my platoon accosted me in the ironing room. "Darlene, if I ask you a question will you give me a straight answer?"

"Depends on the question," I smiled.

She looked at me directly and whispered, "Are you a dyke?"

"Are you?" I whispered back.

"I think so," she said and moved to the ironing board next to me.

"Me, too."

The other girls from the platoon entered the room, and I

fell silent. Shelley's eyes told me we would talk later. And I was glad. Maybe caring for someone else would help me forget Barbara.

Over the next few weeks Shelley and I did talk. We also met in secluded areas around camp and found an unlocked room in the basement of the barracks where we met during unscheduled activity. A sexual relationship with Shelley wasn't the same as with Barbara, but day by day I felt less guilty. I created a shrine for my love for Barbara in my nineteen-year-old mind by deciding to commit myself fully to a lesbian lifestyle.

In the seventh week of training, I was called before the commanding officer and presented with documented evidence of homosexual activity. Shelley turned out to be a plant. Her job was to involve women, document it, and get them out of the military. I could choose to cooperate and incriminate others or receive a dishonorable discharge. I was scared and chose to cooperate.

Three weeks later I was on my way back to California, my discharge papers reading *Inability to adjust to military life.*

When I arrived at Dad's house in Oakland, he had just been arrested for drunk driving and was in jail. But Bubba insisted on some answers. We talked for several hours and I shared the experiences of the past year. Though he did not understand, he promised to listen anytime I needed to talk.

Within weeks I began to look the part of the lifestyle I now embraced. I had always been more comfortable in pants than a skirt; and now, less than three months after leaving college, I put on motorcycle boots, black Frisco jeans, and a black leather jacket. I carried a hunting knife inside one boot and sometimes a stolen .22 revolver in my jacket pocket. I cut my hair short, combed in a fifties style. I wore only men's shirts, and a man's wallet bulged in my right hip pocket.

Outwardly I appeared self-confident and strong; inside I still felt empty. My ability to love was buried in the grave with Barbara.

Then Bubba told me about a bar where only lesbians and queens were allowed.

"You're under the drinking age," he added, "so why don't you get some fake I.D.? Maybe you can find some new friends there. But you'd better make sure the I.D. says you're female. You're starting to look as much like a man as I do!"

"Very funny," I sulked. "I'm not trying to be a man. I just want to feel comfortable, that's all. Besides Bubba, I'm going crazy with no job. Maybe I'll change the dates of my discharge papers and birth certificate. That should get me past the door."

I altered the forms, then held them for Bubba to inspect. "Do they look real?"

"Pretty good, Sis. Want me to drop you off at the bar?"

"Would you? I'm kind of scared. I don't suppose you'd want to come in?"

Bubba scowled. "Not hardly! We both like women, Sis, but I like mine to like men!"

"I've never been in a bar all by myself. What do I do?"

"Just walk in as though you belong there. Order a draft beer and wait for someone to talk to you. Just be sure to leave early enough to catch a bus home."

When Bubba pulled up at the curb in front of Jean's Place, I thanked him and promised a full report when I got back. Then I lit a cigarette for courage, took a deep breath, and stepped through the door.

The bar was quiet. Candles on the small rectangular tables were the only light other than the jukebox. A middle-aged woman with silver white hair looked up from behind the bar.

"Evening," she said, scrutinizing me. "What can I do for you?"

I walked over to the bar and leaned against a black leather stool, trying to look confident. "Uh, I'll have a draft beer, please."

"Can I see some identification?"

"Sure." I took out my wallet and handed her the papers. "I

just got out of the service and don't have a driver's license yet."

She reached for a flashlight to examine my documents. "New in town, huh?" She handed back the papers. "You'd better get something with your picture on it. A lot of places require it."

"I will."

I puffed nervously on a cigarette while she reached for a glass, pushed forward a lever to fill it with beer, and placed it on the bar in front of me. Then she smiled, leaning against the back bar that supported a full-length mirror.

"My name's Jean. Darlene's yours. I read the papers."

I smiled back. "Hi Jean. When does this place come alive?"

"Not until after nine."

I sat on the stool, my knees knocking together so hard I thought Jean could hear them. When other customers entered the bar, she introduced me, saying with a smile, "Meet Dar. She's new blood in town and just barely old enough to be in here!"

After a few drinks, I began to relax and enjoy talking with other women who sat nearby. I answered questions and tried to appear experienced. Just before closing Jean walked over. "Hey kid, want to go out to breakfast with us? We meet some queens from downtown and take over a restaurant."

"Sure, but I don't have a car."

"You can ride with me." She winked, then went back to her job behind the bar.

Jean introduced me not only to the regulars at the bar, but also to the world of one-night stands and transitory relationships. I did not go home that night and returned to the bar every night. Jean bought my beer and taught me to shoot pool well enough to win almost every game.

Bar life became a part of me and I became community property, eventually spending the night with all the regulars. I wanted to fill the growing void in my life and was determined to experience all that gay life could offer in pursuit of that goal.

One of the regulars was Randi who was more interested in talking than in a sexual relationship. Over the blare of the jukebox, she leaned closer for a more intimate conversation. "Dar, you're just starting this life. Why don't you get out while it's still possible?"

I looked down at my beer, than back to her penetrating gaze. "Do you think it's ever possible to change, Randi?"

"If you get out while you're young, you could find a man who would care for you." She looked wistful.

I looked at her carefully. Her once-blazing red hair had telltale streaks of gray, and her face had lost its youthful smoothness. Her green eyes seemed cold.

"Did you ever try to change?" I asked, leaning forward to hear her response.

"Many long years ago I was married to a loving guy who said it didn't matter what I had been. He loved me for who I was right then. I cared deeply for him but I'd been gay too many years for it to work."

Randi paused for a long swill from her glass, then cleared her throat with a racking cough. "The more years you spend in this life, the tougher you become inside and out! We've grown used to the life, Dar. We won't change. But you've still got a chance. You're young and you're smart. These bars are filled with losers."

Her tone grew more intense. "You don't want to spend your life turning tricks with someone new every night. Why don't you go back to school and make something of yourself?"

"So who are you, my mother or something? I haven't had a lecture like that in months." *Not since Joy talked with me in her dorm room the night before I left college.*

"I just don't want to see you wreck your life, kid. If I could change, I'd be out of here in a minute. It's too late for me."

"It's too late for me too, Randi, because I don't want a straight life. Men have molested me, raped me, hurt and deserted me all my life. At least here I'm a little more in control of things."

She put her arm around my shoulder and leaned close to my face. "I wish there were some way I could make you see. . . . But you'll do your own thing." She tightened her hold on my shoulder, pulled me against her, and kissed me lightly on the cheek. "Don't mess up your life, kid. You deserve a lot better than this."

I moved away. "Thanks, Randi. Tomorrow can take care of itself. I've got tonight to handle!"

I sauntered to the pool table, refusing to get pensive about what I was doing with my life, and challenged the game in progress. If gay life were so bad, why were the bars full every night? And when had I found love or fulfillment any other way? No, I was on my own now and would live my own way. The last thing I wanted was a lecture!

I could tell one was coming the next morning, however, when I returned to Dad's apartment to change clothes. I had avoided time alone with him since his release from jail for drunk driving. Now he stopped me in the hall.

"Where have you been sleeping?" he demanded.

"With friends," I said flatly. "What difference does it make?"

"You smell like booze. You're not old enough to drink."

"That's a joke. If I'm old enough to pay for it, I'm old enough to drink it."

I pushed past him, but Dad reached out and grabbed my arm. "Someone told me you've been hanging out at that dykes' bar. If that's true, you can pack your bags."

"Fine! I'll let you know where to forward my mail." I pulled away and glared at him.

"What do they do for you?" he sneered.

"A hell of a lot more than you ever did!"

I slammed the bedroom door and began pulling clothes out of my closet, muttering, "Where were you when I needed to talk to someone or when I needed someone to protect me?"

The front door slammed, and Dad's footsteps clicked down

the sidewalk outside. I was overwhelmed with a feeling of abandonment. *You never cared about me anyway!*

I sat on the edge of the bed feeling once again like a five year old watching her daddy leave. *Don't cry, Darlene. Big girls don't cry.*

I bit my lip to keep it from trembling. I *was* Daddy's big girl now, and it was too late to change the program.

I finished packing my suitcase and scribbled a note to Bubba with the bar phone number if he needed to reach me.

All the way to the bar I was still muttering to myself about Dad. *I don't need him. I don't need anyone!*

8.
Treacherous Facades

I told myself I did not need Dad, but I did need a place to stay and a job to pay the rent. Jean solved the first problem for me with an offer to share her apartment until I got on my feet financially.

"You have a roof over your head as long as you need it, babe. We'll work out the payment!" She smiled and winked.

I winked back. "I'm sure we will. Say, who's that?" I nodded toward an older masculine woman sitting at the end of the bar. Even from this distance, her athletic build and dark tan reminded me of a physical education instructor.

"Oh, that's Billie. She just broke up with her lover. She's a teacher, babe, and way out of your class."

"Oh, really? Well, maybe I can get her to teach me some new tricks. No one's out of my class!" I grinned. "Send her a drink on me."

I watched in the mirror as Jean took Billie a drink. When she looked my way, I lifted my glass in a toast.

Jean came back over. "You're something else, babe. She wanted to know your name. Must be that youthful, clean-cut look."

"Let me go check it out."

I eased my way down the bar. "Hi. My name's Darlene."

"Thanks for the drink." Billie leaned back, crossed her legs, and stretched out. In navy blue cut-offs and a dark lavender velour sweatshirt, she looked as though she had just stepped off a tennis court. "Are you new around here?"

"I've been here a few months. Do you shoot pool?"

"I'd rather just talk." She fingered her glass, appearing deep in thought.

"Fine." I sat on the stool next to her, resting my right foot over my left knee, and locked her gaze with mine. "Do you go with anyone?"

Her brown eyes sparkled like a puppy's. "You don't waste time, do you? I don't go with anyone now. How about you?"

"I'm committed only to myself."

She looked amused. "You sound more educated than most of the women in here. Did you attend college?"

"I put in a couple of years at a Christian college up north."

"A Christian college? Then why are you in a lesbian bar?"

I rubbed the design on my cowboy boots. "God and I disagree about my sexuality. I decided to ignore Him instead of women."

"You can have both. God doesn't care who you sleep with. He created us to love one another." She leaned her elbows on the bar, an amused twinkle in her eyes. "The Bible does say that, doesn't it?"

"The Bible calls homosexuality a sin. The love He says to love with isn't sexual. Anyway, there are a lot of things the Bible says that I just can't do. I'm not sure anymore if I even want to live by what it says. I have a lot of questions about God's supposedly being a God of love. My first 'friend' died because she couldn't figure it out either.

"I'm sorry." Billie looked at me closely. "If you're mad at God, why do you even care if being gay is a sin?"

"I don't know. I guess because I still believe the Bible is true."

"Just what we need, another barstool preacher!" She shook her head and gulped the rest of her drink.

"Hey, I'm not preaching. I spend most of my time trying to forget about God. You're the one who asked the questions."

She nodded. "I forgot. Well, I can help you forget about all that Bible stuff. Want to go to a movie?"

"Sure."

I flashed a smile at Jean, watching from the other end of the bar. "God loses again," I said to Billie.

Then I remembered my suitcase behind the bar and excused myself for a minute. "Jean, can I leave things here for the night? We'll move them to your apartment tomorrow."

She reached across the bar and patted my arm. "Go ahead, babe, enjoy yourself. Maybe she's not out of your league after all."

The next afternoon I bounded through the door of the bar shouting, "Yippee! I'm in love!"

Jean glanced up from where she was stacking boxes behind the bar. "That's great, honey. Will you give me a hand?"

"Sure. But I expected a little more enthusiasm than that! Billie and I had a great time. I think I might be ready to settle down."

She set the box on a stool. "Darlene, did Billie tell you about her lover?"

"No. I didn't ask. The past doesn't matter."

"Maybe you should have, babe. She lives with a woman who was her lover; now they're just friends. She's known all over town for short-term affairs. She has financial investments tied up with her roommate, and she won't leave for a permanent relationship with anyone. I'll bet you went to a motel and not to her home."

I leaned against the padded railing. "I thought it was because I was special."

"You *are* special, kid. We all love you. I don't want to see you get hurt. Enjoy the excitement of a new lover, but don't think it's the one to last forever. That just doesn't happen."

"It will with me," I said emphatically. "How long have you known Billie?"

"Years. The last woman she went with? Name was Nancy. She's left town now, but her lover of three years killed herself when Billie took Nancy away. Most people are impressed with status and money in this life, babe, and they don't really see the person behind the money. You're different, kid. I knew it the day you walked in. That's why I've tried to protect you and give you a place. You're not like most of the regulars. You should be some man's wife!"

She picked up the box again. "Ever think of going straight?"

"What is this? All my lesbian friends keep trying to get me to go straight. Randi was on my case last week." I paused. "I've thought of it. But I don't like men the same way I like women. Besides, we were all straight once, remember."

"Yeah, I was married once myself. If I could ever find a loving man who would be all right for me, I'd probably try it again."

"Really? I figured you a confirmed lesbian."

She smiled. "You've got a lot to learn, babe. Just remember, you have a friend anytime the going gets rough."

"Thanks, Jean." I gave her a quick hug. "I still hope things will work out with Billie. I may be young but I could handle a place with someone and not go home with a different body every night!"

"Oh, speaking of a place. I decided to fix up a room for you right above the bar. You can watch the place for me and be paid fifteen dollars a week. You can make that much in tips, just helping here. Have you checked on any other jobs yet?"

"No, but a gas station across town is looking for an attendant. I'm on my way there this afternoon."

"Good. Also, Darlene, your brother brought some mail by this morning. It's over by the register."

"Thanks." I walked behind the bar and picked up a stack of letters. The top one was from Marie Fuller in Beirut. I tore it open, devouring the words of encouragement. Letters from Marie were a welcome invasion into my world, although they left me with a tight knot of emotion.

"Don't you think I'd change if I could?" I muttered aloud. "There's no way out!"

Jean emerged from the storeroom. "What'd you say?"

"Nothing. I was just talking to this letter from my friend. She's a missionary in Lebanon."

"A missionary! What does she think about your life?"

"She tells me it's a sin. She still loves me though. She is about the only real Christian I know who is going to heaven when Jesus Christ calls an end to this world." I folded the letter and put it in my wallet. "She also thinks I would benefit from professional counseling. You know, Jean, sometimes I wish alcohol were enough to make me forget everything!"

"It never is, babe." Jean busied herself, stocking the cooler. "I never understood all that Bible stuff. Someday you'll have to explain it to me." She stood and put her hand on my shoulder. "If it really bothers you, you could go straight."

"Yeah." I shrugged her hand away. "I could fly if I got high enough too! See you later."

My stomach churned. Although I had been out of school for just over a year, I hated even thinking about God, let alone having to explain the Bible to a lesbian. I wanted to forget what I was doing, to erase the painful knowledge of failure. Marie's letters were a constant reminder, but I loved her too much ever to break the connection.

I interviewed for the service station job and was hired on the spot. Later that evening I came back to the bar to celebrate. Billie was waiting for me and greeted me with a hug.

"Hi, Darlene. Want to go out for dinner and spend a quiet night in a motel?"

I stiffened. "Thanks for the offer. I want to celebrate my new job. I think I'd like to just stay here and shoot pool all evening."

Her smile faded. "That's more important?"

I decided to test what Jean had told me. "Well, we could move in together. Then we could spend a lot of quiet nights together."

"Let's not be too quick about setting up housekeeping." Her voice hardened.

"Why? I thought you didn't have any commitments."

"I don't, but I'm not looking for anything permanent right now." Her face reddened with anger.

"Well, I am."

So it was true. Everything Jean said was true.

I spun around and laid a quarter on the edge of the pool table. "I challenge," I said to the queen who seemed to be winning.

Then I looked back at Billie, the familiar knot of isolation forming in the pit of my stomach. "Maybe pool is a safer game."

"Darlene, let's talk."

She waved me over to a table, but I ignored her. Then the man who won the game joined me.

"I'm Ramon," he cooed, sticking out his hand for a limp handshake.

"I'm Darlene." I stooped to rack the balls. "You new in town? I don't think I've seen you before."

I watched Billie out of the corner of my eye.

"I usually don't hang out with the girls. But you know how we boys are. Sometimes we just feel like peace and quiet." His lisp fit the stereotype queen.

All night long I drank heavily and took verbal pot shots at Billie. Ramon and I shot pool for hours. About midnight he walked over and whispered, "Want to get a bite to eat?"

"Sure, why not?" I slurred. It would make Billie mad to see me leave with a queen. "Let's go."

I glanced in her direction. She had rejected me; I would reject her. And I ignored the angry look that crossed her face as I walked out with Ramon.

He opened the door and guided me to his car, a bashed-in green Chevrolet parked just outside.

"Where to?" he asked.

The night air felt good against my cheeks. I settled into the front seat. "There's a restaurant just down the street."

I leaned against the car door and lit a cigarette. "So tell me, do you have a lover?"

"No," he said quietly. The car picked up speed as we turned off the main street and headed for the skyline area in the hills.

"This isn't the way. Hey, where are we going?"

He reached over and grabbed my upper arm, pulling me toward him. "We're not going to a restaurant," he hissed, beginning to breathe harder. "And I'm not gay!"

The noted lisp was gone.

My stomach tightened, and my hand reached instinctively for the door handle.

He tightened his grasp on my arm and pulled me down toward the seat. "Don't try it. You'll be killed if you jump out of this car."

Anger swelled in me and all my hatred focused on Ramon. How had I been so deceived? Although stunned and panic-stricken, I started looking for identifying marks on the car and on this man intent upon raping me. He couldn't. He just couldn't!

The car came to a jolting stop. He had pulled into a secluded wooded area overlooking Oakland. As he turned off the ignition and lights, he released my arm with his right hand and flashed a hunting knife with his left. Chill bumps ran down my arms.

First he told me in specific detail what we were going to do as he brandished the knife dangerously close to my face. Paralyzed by fear, I heard the words as if from a distance. My throat was so dry I did not think I could even breathe, let alone speak.

Then I heard myself gasp, "But I'm gay."

"I know," he wheezed.

He lurched across the seat like a madman and tore away my clothing. Visions of Curt and Tony came to mind, and I struggled against his attack, trying to push his sweaty hands away from me. But his strength easily overpowered mine, and the next several hours were a nightmare.

Red lights flashed and burst inside my head as I sank into a deep, black pit. Ramon raped me repeatedly, all the while telling me how good he was and that I would never want sex with a woman again. My body grew numb from pain, and I knew despite the darkness that the seat was soaked with blood.

I'll kill you. If I live, I'll kill you. The words echoed and reechoed through my brain.

At the end of each session he picked up the knife and detailed the next event.

"I'll kill you if you scream," he warned, and even though I refrained from screaming, I was afraid that before the night was over he would slit my throat anyway. Ramon was a man possessed.

At one point I became physically sick, and tears filled my eyes. "Please stop. Please," I pleaded. But though I vomited on him in revulsion, he was far from finished with his conversion tactics.

Ramon stopped only when the blackness of night gave way to early morning gray. I huddled on the floor of the car with my clothing pressed against me. Would he kill me now?

But strangely enough, once he was finished he offered to drive me back to the bar. I got out of the car and stumbled over the curb to the sidewalk, clutching my torn clothing to my body. Somehow I made my way to the new apartment above the bar and collapsed on my bed.

I felt so dirty. Who could I tell? I couldn't even call the police because I was not yet twenty-one and could be arrested too.

So I stumbled into the bathroom and took a long, hot shower. Then I went to bed and lay awake the rest of the morning plotting how I could find Ramon and kill him. Despite my resolve not to let another man trick me, I had once again been deceived and violated. The hard knot of anger began to tighten deep inside me. Never again would I get into a situation where I was not in control.

That afternoon I told my brother. Bubba's anger erupted with volcanic force, and together we spent three days searching Oakland for a bashed-in green Chevrolet. We never found him.

Over the months that followed, I began to drink more heavily to chase away the nightmares that haunted me. Hatred boiled inside me against all men. I made a game of playing up to any straight men who came into the bar, then lifting their wallets.

"Any man who comes into a lesbian bar looking for women," I told Jean, "deserves what he gets."

"Just watch yourself, babe," she advised. "If you ever get caught in the act we'll have trouble on our hands."

"Trouble's my middle name!" I laughed.

Nor did I confine my stealing to men at the bar. I stole from the men I worked with too. That way I made enough money to pay the rent and drink every night.

After a year and a half at the service station, I was fired for being late and having a hangover. I returned to the bar, where Jean was sweeping up cigarette butts, which littered the black tile floor.

"What are you doing here in the middle of the day?" she asked.

"I just got canned. Give me a beer." I hopped up on the stool at the end of the bar.

"You what?" Jean leaned the broom against the jukebox and walked behind the bar.

"I just got fired. They said it was because I've been coming to work late with hangovers. They accused me of stealing money too."

She set the beer down in front of me. "Did you? I know the hangover part is true."

"Well, I always balanced each shift, but if I happened to see some spare bills that were unattended, could I help it if they jumped into my pocket?"

"Darlene! What am I going to do with you?"

"Just love me, I guess," I chuckled. "I can guarantee you one thing, Jean. I'll never steal from you. I don't steal from friends."

"If I thought there was any danger of that, I'd never let you behind the bar. I trust you, babe; I just worry about your getting caught somewhere else."

"It'll never happen," I assured her.

In fact, I had felt no fear about getting caught since my gang days in Oakland. And I had become so adept at stealing that it no longer bothered me. I was surprised, however, that I also felt nonchalant about being fired, although I was determined to prove to myself—and for some strange reason to Dad—that I could support myself.

I drank and shot pool all afternoon. And by closing I staggered upstairs to my room, crumpled in an intoxicated heap on the bed.

After a long shower the next morning, I recovered enough to buy a newspaper and check the classified section for jobs. I also pulled out a skirt and blouse left over from college days and dressed for job hunting. The second agency I visited thought they could place me in an electronics firm as a file clerk and part-time assembler and arranged an interview for the following morning.

So I returned to Jean's Place for another night of drinking and pool.

A woman I knew only casually seemed to monopolize my time that night. Carol was about thirty with a full, friendly smile. She kept me well-supplied with drinks because she lost every pool game and paid me with beer. We talked and joked all night as I gave her pointers about how to improve her game. Suddenly I realized she was asking a serious question.

"Darlene, would you move into my place and see if we could make a life together?" She ran nervous fingers through her thick, curly brown hair.

I was stunned. "I hardly know you."

"What do you want to know? I work in publicity, I like you, and I think you'd like my daughter. She's eight years old."

"I didn't know you had a daughter. What's her name?"

"Debbie. I was raped one night leaving a bar in Denver. I

thought about an abortion but decided to go ahead and have the baby. There's not much more to tell. I've watched you for a long time and think we could be good for each other. I think you need to get out of this bar."

"You do, huh? Well, why not?" I raised my glass. "Here's to a new start. I'll have a new job, a new home, and a new daughter all at once."

The next morning after my interview at the electronics firm, I was hired as a floater, someone who could fill in for all departments. I moved in with Carol that night.

The first few weeks were exciting as Carol and I worked at getting to know each other. The nights were spent in long conversations by the fireplace and drinking hot chocolate. Debbie and I became good friends from the day I moved into the house. She was small for her age with flowing blond curls framing a round, wide-eyed face. I showered Debbie with attention, and she clung to me when we were together. Every weekend we all went on family outings to the park or zoo.

But I still felt empty inside and increasingly dissatisfied with home life. I missed the booze and jukebox music at the bar and found that my relationship with Carol was confining.

One night about six months after moving in with her, I couldn't resist stopping by Jean's Place before catching the bus home. I bounced through the doors of the dimly lit bar and breathed deeply the stale beer and cigarette odors.

"Hi, Jean," I beamed. "How's it going?"

"Just great, stranger!" She kissed me affectionately. "I guess home life agrees with you?"

"I guess." I picked up a pool cue. "Got time for a game?"

"Sure." We walked over to a table, and I racked up the balls. "What do you mean, you guess? Aren't you guys getting along?"

"Yeah. Carol's good for me. But I miss bar life, and we don't drink much around home with the kid there."

"I see." She missed her shot. "Does Carol know you're here?"

"No. I just figured I'd drop in for one drink. Her schedule is different from mine. She never starts dinner until I'm home."

"Think you should call?"

"Hey, I don't check in with anyone! Living with Carol is just an experiment anyway. Maybe married life isn't for me. I always thought I wanted a permanent relationship, but after six months I'm wondering if Carol is the right one. Something seems to be missing."

"Well, babe, we sure miss you around here. Things aren't the same. Say, do you remember Roxie? She drove into a freeway divider last weekend after her love split."

"You're kidding! Sure I remember her. Good pool player. That's too bad."

As Jean and I finished our game, I dismissed the news about Roxie with a blasé lightness. But it reminded me of Barbara's suicide, and I shuddered to think of the unhappiness of most of the women who frequented the bar and the emptiness of my own life. Was anyone ever really happy?

"You'd better get on home, girl. It's almost six. Carol will be furious." Jean picked up the broom and pretended to sweep me outside.

"If she gets too mad, maybe I'll be back," I grinned.

Twenty minutes later I walked through the front door. Carol was waiting in the living room. "Where have you been?"

"I stopped by Jean's for a drink. I wanted to catch up on news."

"You care for her, don't you?"

I ignored her accusing tone and walked into the kitchen. "I only stopped for a drink. What's for dinner?"

"I want to go out for dinner." She barely glanced at Debbie, who now stood beside her in the kitchen doorway looking confused. Then her voice hardened. "You just can't stay away from other women, can you, Darlene?"

"Right!" I yelled, suddenly tired of her jealousy. "And I'll stop tomorrow night too." I slammed the refrigerator door. "I'm going back out."

"Without me?" She sounded tremulous.

"Well, do you have someone to watch Debbie?"

"No. I had planned on her being with us for dinner, not leaving her alone for the night."

"Then I guess you stay home." I picked up my jacket. "Don't wait up!"

Why did I do that? I wondered as I drove away. *She really cares about me. What am I living with her for if I don't really love her? Or is it that I can't love anyone?*

I listened to guilt all the way to the bar.

But hours later I felt fine as I fumbled my key into the lock and entered the house. Muffled sobs came from Debbie's room. I opened her door. "What's the matter, honey?"

As I lifted her petite body from the bed, she hugged me tightly and buried her face against me. "I— I don't like it when you and Mom yell at each other. I can't sleep." She spoke between sniffles and choking sobs.

I rocked her and brushed the tears from her eyes. Suddenly an old familiar pain pierced my heart. I was that little girl, listening to fighting and angry words. I remembered my vow never to grow up and have kids hate me as I hated Frank.

"Well, honey, sometimes big people don't agree about things, and yelling seems like the only way to make the other person listen. Your mom and I love each other, and we love you. I'm sorry you can't sleep."

My voice was barely a whisper as I held her close and mumbled the words into her tangled blond hair. "Why don't you lie back down and try to sleep? I promise you we won't yell anymore."

I lowered her onto the bed and pulled the blankets up around her shoulders. Leaning down to kiss her forehead, I remembered the many nights I had cried myself to sleep in the darkness. I might be twenty-two years old, but inside I was still that little girl who lay awake night after night listening to Mom and Frank fight.

9.
Breaking
Away

By the next morning I had made a decision. I called my boss at work, asking for a two-week leave of absence. Then I pulled a suitcase from under our bed and announced to Carol, "I'm going to Portland to visit some college friends."

"You mean right now?" She followed me to the closet. "What am I supposed to do?"

I shrugged as I pulled out some shirts. "I really don't care. I just need to get away from things for awhile."

"What you really mean is away from *me*, don't you?" She grabbed my arm.

"Not just you," I replied, pulling away. "I need space to think. I want to get away from the whole scene for awhile."

"Does that mean we're breaking up?"

"I don't know. I'll let you know when I get back." I folded some jeans into the suitcase, refusing to look at her.

"How are you getting there?"

"By bus. It's the cheapest. I want to see my friend Joy and also Mrs. Fuller. She's home from Beirut for a month."

"That's the woman you really love, isn't it? I'll bet she's not really straight."

I spun around, shaking my fist under Carol's nose. "Don't you ever make that accusation again! She's a Christian and one of the most loving women I've ever known. If you so much as insinuate that she's gay—"

"All right, all right." She backed away. "I'm sorry. It's just hard to imagine your loving someone so much if she's not gay."

What was so hard to understand about that? Carol and I

suddenly seemed miles apart. I finished packing in silence, then asked coldly, "Will you take me to the station, or should I call a cab?"

"I'll take you." She picked up my suitcase. "Will you call me?"

"No promises. I don't know what the next two weeks will bring." I walked stiffly to the car.

On the bus I sat in silence, watching the scenery become a faded blur as we kept pace with the freeway traffic. It had been nearly four years since I had left college, and my life seemed just like the scenery—one long blur.

I really did care about Carol and wanted us to provide a good home environment for Debbie. But sometimes I felt I was playing a role in a terrible stage play that was going on endlessly. I longed to love and be loved but continued to fight suffocating guilt every time I was with a woman, just as I had with Lois and with Barbara. I knew the Bible called it sin, but there seemed no other way for me to be close and caring with another human being.

Only drinking, although I knew it amounted to a treadmill existence, could dull my guilt and loneliness. How I longed for the relative peace I had known my first year of college when Marie and I talked and prayed together in her apartment—the time before Barbara.

As the bus approached Portland, tension and anxiety knotted my stomach. Would Marie still love me? I had never stopped loving her, although I could not change just because she wanted me to.

My conflict intensified as I walked to her house from the bus station and anticipated seeing her face-to-face. I tucked in my shirt and ran fingers through my short, wavy hair. I knew I looked different.

She opened the door as I was coming up the walk and greeted me with a warm hug. "Darlene, it's so good to see you! How was the trip?"

"Long!" I set the suitcase down on the front steps, reflecting how different Marie's hugs were from those of lesbian women. They felt safe. "It's good to see you too. A lot has happened in the four years, since you left for Lebanon."

"I know it has, dear. Oh, Darlene, I've been praying about our visit, and we're going to have a nice, relaxed time. I'm not going to tell you things you already know."

The tone in her voice wrapped me in love. She *did* still love me, and I felt more secure than I had in many months.

Over the next few days I struggled with wanting to change my life while a voice inside taunted, *You'll never change!"* I thought about Randi and others I had met at Jean's Place who had tried to go straight and ended up back in lesbian relationships. If they couldn't change, I probably couldn't either.

When it came time to leave for Joy's house, I packed reluctantly.

"It's hard to leave you, Marie," I said as she drove me to the bus depot. "I've really missed our times together."

"Just promise to write and let me know what you're doing, Darlene. I pray for you daily."

She seemed to weigh her words, wanting to say more.

Don't ask me to change, Marie. I can't stand to tell you no.

She pulled into the depot parking lot, put her arms around me, and held me close. "Jesus, I ask You to go with Darlene and draw her back to You. Don't give her one moment's peace until she is whole and complete in You."

I fought back tears as I hugged her tight, then got out of the car.

"I'll write when I get back to California," I mumbled through the open window.

The two-hour trip to Joy's town failed to dull the intensity of my inner conflict. Maybe I would never be able to love anyone. Christianity hadn't really worked for me. Maybe nothing would ever work.

Joy's husband Tim was away for a few days, and she seemed to welcome company. We talked mostly about college years and her life since getting married. Because I would not smoke in their house, we took frequent walks. Unspoken was an ever-present question about Jesus.

"Are you really happy?" Joy asked during one of our walks.

"Not right now. Things aren't too good where I live. But I'm going to make some changes soon. Things will get better." I dragged on my cigarette.

"It doesn't seem like anything has *really* changed since we left college, Darlene. Are you still mad at God over Barbara's death?" Her tone was soft and concerned.

"I try not to think about that anymore. That was a lifetime ago. I wouldn't even tell you the things that have happened since then. Let's talk about you."

"I won't pressure you, Darlene. I just want you to know I still love you and I still care." She brightened up. "Oh, you remember Sharon, my roommate from college? She still asks about you. She lives only a hundred miles down the road. Why don't you stop and visit her?"

I remembered the time Joy and Sharon prayed with me after my disappointment with Lance during my freshman year in college.

"Didn't Sharon marry a preacher?"

"Yes, and he's a great guy. You'd like him. Do you want to call and see if they're home?"

"Why not? I have a few days of vacation left. I might as well see them too." I crushed my cigarette on the sidewalk.

Sharon was home. She said she would love to have me stop and spend a few days. Joy and I reminisced late into the night. When she took me to the bus, her voice broke with emotion.

"Darlene, I want you to know I'll be praying for you more than ever. You need to get right with God."

"Hey, no sermons! We've had a good visit. Don't pressure me to make a decision I can't make right now."

"Just don't wait too long." Her eyes filled with tears. "We had a lot of good times in college before you got messed up, and I want to know I'll meet you in heaven someday."

"I'm not as concerned about the heaven up there as I am about the hell down here! Don't worry about me, Joy. I know God is still taking care of me."

I pushed from my mind the conversation with Joy as the bus sped along the interstate. That was enough God talk. Suddenly we were pulling into Sharon's town. I called her, then paced the area in front of the depot, smoking a last cigarette. I would have to take walks here, too; I couldn't smoke in a preacher's house!

A brown Fairlane pulled into the loading zone. Sharon jumped out and ran up, embracing me enthusiastically. We stumbled over our words, trying to catch up on the past few years and within minutes were turning into the parking lot of a small country church.

"This is our church," explained Sharon, "and we live in a cottage behind. Oh, Dar, wait till you meet Peter!"

She picked up my suitcase, and we headed for the white cottage tucked behind the parking lot. It was surrounded by trees and a large apple orchard.

Peter came to the door with a warm smile. "Welcome to our home, Darlene. Sharon has told me a lot about your college days."

"We've come a long way since college," I chuckled. I liked him right away. "Too bad the world isn't as protected as that small Christian campus."

He took the suitcase from Sharon and held the door for us. "Choices do seem to be a lot easier in an environment more sheltered from temptations. On the other hand, maybe that kind of environment doesn't make for real choices at all. What poet was it who said, 'I cannot praise a cloistered virtue'?"

He took my suitcase to a small bedroom off the kitchen

while I looked after him thoughtfully. I had not maintained much virtue even in a cloistered environment.

"How long can you stay, Darlene?" Sharon was already plugging in the coffeepot.

"I should be on the road tomorrow so I can have time to rest up at home before going back to work."

As the smell of freshly percolating coffee wafted through the cottage, Peter joined us at the kitchen table, where we sat for the next several hours discussing the Bible and memories from college days.

Finally I needed a cigarette. "Anybody up for a walk?"

"Sure," said Sharon. "I'll go with you." She picked up a sweater and followed me out the door.

The sky was beautiful. It looked as though someone had used a shotgun to pepper it full of brilliance. We strolled around the apple orchard as I puffed my cigarette. I could sense Sharon searching for the right phrasing of the question I knew was coming. Finally she broke the silence.

"Darlene, why don't you turn your life back to God?"

I was ready. "It just wouldn't work, Sharon. I don't want to go into it, but I've really hit rock bottom and I don't think even God can straighten out the things I've gotten involved with these past couple of years."

Her reply startled me. "There is no bottom, Darlene. I don't know about your problems, but I know about God, and nothing is too hard for Him."

No bottom?

I needed to break the tension. "What do you say we go into the church?" I said suddenly.

We crossed the parking lot and moved toward the darkened building.

Inside, Sharon flipped the auditorium lights and went immediately to the piano. "Let's sing," she said, apparently content to drop the other conversation.

I picked up a songbook and stood behind the old upright piano as Sharon played, surprised at how many of the hymns

I remembered from our days in college chapel. It was almost as though the years had not changed me. I joined my voice with Sharon's rich alto and we sang several duets. Then I bounded over to the pulpit and assumed a Billy Graham stance to silence my nagging conscience.

"The Scripture reading for tonight, ladies and gentlemen, is . . ." We both started laughing. "It's almost like old times," I said.

Sharon leaned her slender frame against the piano top as she stood to watch me. "It could be, Darlene, if you'd turn your life back to Christ." She cocked her head to one side, her long blond hair reaching almost to her waist.

"Come on, Sharon, don't start bugging me. You take away all the fun." I put the book down and headed for the door. Outside I lit another cigarette and sat on the ground staring at the sky. I avoided eye contact with Sharon as she sat on the church steps behind me.

"Darlene, you can't avoid Him forever. You know He wants you back."

I face her, prepared with a rebuttal. Tears were spilling down her cheeks.

"This could be the last chance you have," she added.

"Hey, don't pull that 'you could go out and get run over by a truck tomorrow' tactic on me, Sharon. I'm not afraid of hell or dying. I just don't know that my life could really change right now." I got up and headed back toward the house.

"All right, Darlene. Her voice was resigned. "Let me show you where you're going to sleep." She led the way to the small room off the kitchen. It was dark, with a single bed and a throw rung. "Will you at least pray with me before bed? Maybe God really is big enough to help if you ask."

"Why don't you pray and I'll listen,"I muttered.

She leaned against the door, deep in thought. "Remember that night when Lance asked you to prove your love for him and you were so upset? I've thought about our prayer time that night over the years, and how convinced we were God had a purpose for our lives. I still think He has a plan for you, Darlene."

I sat on the edge of the bed. "If He does, I'm sure I've messed it up in the last four years." I hesitated. "To tell you the truth, Sharon, I've been living a homosexual lifestyle since I left college. Things have happened I can't even talk about, but I don't think I can ever change. There's no way out."

She slipped to her knees beside the bed. "We can ask." She motioned for me to join her.

I laughed nervously as I did so. "This is a bit out of character for me, Sharon."

She spoke quietly. "We used to pray together like this in college. Jesus hasn't changed, Darlene. Just call on the name of Jesus. He can help you, but you have to ask him."

She couldn't be serious! How could I even begin to talk to God? I hadn't talked with Him in almost four years. Thoughts tumbled through my brain—the emptiness of searching for that right relationship and never finding it, mixed with words to the songs we had sung earlier—"Power in the Blood," "Victory in Jesus." I believed those words but felt chained to my life as a lesbian. God may have plans for my life, but I believed in Satan, too.

I closed my eyes to silence the refrain: "The enemy's power is broken." Nothing ever broke that power in me! My teeth bit hard into my lower lip. How did I know God even wanted to hear from me?

Then I tried to speak. A knot tightened in my throat. I couldn't speak the name of Jesus! Fear engulfed me like a shroud. I shook my head back and forth, making short gasping sounds. I could hardly breathe.

"Satan, I tell you in the name of Jesus to get out of here and release your hold on Darlene." Sharon laid her hand on my head.

I jumped at the contact. What felt like a bolt of lightning streaked through my body. My mind whirled with a dozen conversations at once as I spiraled down into a black pit. *God, help!* Suddenly I wanted to be free from homosexuality. I struggled to get the words out.

"Je—Jesus, please forgive me for leaving you. Change my life so I'm right with you. I'm sorry for my sins. Please help me to go straight."

I breathed in deeply and exhaled slowly. The tightness in my chest was gone and I felt peaceful.

"Let's call Joy," exclaimed Sharon. "She'll be thrilled to know you've come back to God."

"It's pretty late," I said.

"She'll be glad to be awakened for this news!"

We made the call, and Joy squealed with excitement, promising to drive down in the morning.

We hung up and I went back to my room, exhausted. "I'm determined to make a clean break, Sharon. Please keep praying for me." I crumpled my cigarettes and threw them in the trash. "I have some heavy changes to make when I get back to California."

"Don't worry. We've been praying for you for a long time. We won't stop now."

She turned out the nightlight and I lay in total darkness as a multitude of unresolved issues filled my thoughts. Could I really leave Carol and the whole homosexual world? Was I strong enough to stay away from the bars? Where would I find people who cared about me?

In the morning, Joy's newly arrived car looked as though it was packed for a long trip.

"I think you're going to need all the help you can get," she explained. "I'm going with you to help you move."

I gulped hard. It was so thoughtful of her. I couldn't believe she was actually ready to come. But what if I wasn't strong enough and failed?

"I appreciate your offer," I said, "but this is something I've got to do all on my own. Besides, I can't have you walking into that mess."

"I really think you need help, Darlene."

"Oh, I think I'll be all right. I love you guys, but I've got to do it my way. I'll make the break. You just keep praying for me." I picked up my suitcase. "I'd appreciate a ride to the bus, though."

Reluctantly, Sharon and Joy took me to the station. We said our good-bys and had a short time of prayer. On the bus I scribbled a note to Marie. I knew she would be happy. The rest of the trip I planned how I could move and break up with Carol without hurting her too much.

When the bus arrived in Oakland, I called her, then paced with anticipation until her car pulled into the lot. Once on the freeway, I gave her the news.

"There've been some changes," I began. "I've decided to go straight and be a Christian again. I'm leaving you and getting my own place as soon as possible."

"I knew it! I knew if you went away without me you'd do something dumb. What do you mean Christian? You are a Christian. God doesn't care who you sleep with, just that you don't hurt anyone."

"I think He's a little more concerned than that. I just know I can't be a lesbian and be a Christian, too."

She reached for a cigarette and offered me one.

"No, thanks. I've quit smoking, too."

Carol swore. "You've been gone for two weeks. You don't smoke anymore, you don't sleep with women anymore, and you're leaving me to get a place of your own. I don't believe it!"

"I don't want to hurt you, Carol, but I just can't handle this guilt anymore.

The silence was deafening.

"Don't say anything to Debbie," she said at last. I'll tell her tonight. Then she reached over and touched my arm. "Please don't leave me, Darlene. I need you."

I could tell she was fighting back tears. Something in me wanted to reach out and hold her and tell her it was all a joke; that I wasn't really leaving. Instead, I slid a little closer to the window. "I won't say anything to Debbie," I mumbled.

After dinner that evening, we sat in the front room watching television. Carol called Debbie into the room. "Debbie, I want to tell you something." She hesitated. "Darlene is going to be moving and getting her own apartment."

Debbie threw herself onto my lap and wrapped her arms tight around my neck. "I don't want you to go," she sobbed, burying her face against my chest.

I put my arms around her and held her close. "I know, honey. But it'll be all right. I'll come visit."

My memory flashed back to my own childhood. In some unexplainable way, I was the little girl again, and no one had ever come back for me just as I knew I would not come back for Debbie.

10.
I Really
Tried

I found a small studio apartment near the electronics plant where I worked, about three blocks from the cliffs along San Francisco Bay and right down the street from a large, stone, fortress-looking church. If I was going back to church, I would have to look acceptable.

Jeans and sweatshirts had become my uniform, as I molded myself to the dress style of other lesbians. In the past three years I had switched almost entirely to men's clothing, with only one skirt and blouse left from college days. Now I bought a navy blue cotton skirt and long-sleeved tailored blue blouse. To hide my mannish haircut, I purchased a medium-length wig to wear to church. Sunday morning I trailed in behind a small group of senior citizens.

At the massive stone doorway, a greeter handed me a bulletin and asked me to sign the guest book. The auditorium was massive and included a balcony to accommodate overflow crowds. The pastor was a tall stocky man with a booming voice. Although the size of the congregation provided anonymity, I decided to introduce myself to the pastor. If I was going to make it, I would need all the help I could get.

I shook hands after the service. "Hello, Pastor Stone. I'm Darlene Bogle. I just moved into the area and I'm looking for a church home."

"We hope you won't have to look any further." He smiled widely. "You'll find a welcome here and many opportunities for service."

"Thank you. I was wondering, may I talk with you some evening or Saturday?"

"Certainly. Just call my secretary and set up a time. I'll be looking forward to it."

He seemed friendly enough. I returned to my apartment with a new surge of hope. The phone was ringing as I came through the door. "Darlene, this is Carol. Would you like to spend the day with Debbie and me?"

"You know I can't see you, Carol. The two lives just don't mix. My past has to be dead!" Inside I struggled with wanting to be part of Debbie's life, and hating to live alone.

"But you said we could still be friends," she wailed.

"We can. I just can't come see you. I need time to get settled in this lifestyle."

"You don't care about us at all!" She shouted. "I just won't call anymore."

But she did—almost every night for weeks. I anguished over her plea for friendship, until I knew it was time to make that appointment with Pastor Stone. I needed help.

A Saturday afternoon meeting was set. I was nervous as I planned how to word my story. What would he think of me after I told him? In the few short weeks of my attendance at the church, I had met one family with whom I shared my background. They encouraged me to be honest with the pastor.

So now I walked into his office and sat in a large brown over-stuffed chair. I admired the wall of bookshelves and plaques that hung on the walnut paneling.

"Well, Darlene, how can I help you today?" Pastor Stone's tone was professional as he rested his arms upon the large oak desk that seemed to fill the small office. He was over six feet tall, with the build of a football running back. The desk fit him well. His gaze met mine.

I fidgeted on my seat, cleared my throat and struggled for the right words. "Well, sir, I felt I needed to spend some time with you and let you know where I'm coming from."

The expression on his face didn't change. My turmoil increased. *Should I really tell him? Maybe he already knows.*

"Perhaps where I've been is a better phrase. I attended a Christian college in Portland, where I made the discovery that I was gay. I've been away from the Lord for several years and just recently recommitted my life to Christ. I know I need all the help I can get to make it, and I wanted to tell you so I'll have a place to come for help." I stopped, took a deep breath and sank back against the chair, afraid that I had sounded too clinical.

The pastor cleared his throat. "I see. Well, I'll certainly pray for you, Darlene. But in twenty-three years of ministry, I have never yet known a homosexual to change for a prolonged period of time. I don't give you much hope. But if you are willing to keep attending this church, then I want to lay down some ground rules." He leaned back in his high-top leather chair, his tone hardening.

A mixture of emotions churned within me as he spoke. I felt angry and resentful at his words, and embarrassed that I had told him about being gay. I determined that he would never again be able to tell anyone that he never knew a homosexual who had changed. I would prove him wrong. I would make it if it was the last thing I did. My determination and pride burned more strongly than the urge to walk out of his office.

My mind again turned to the voice of the authority figure who sat before me.

" . . . and I want you to be present in every possible service. I want you to find a Sunday school class to attend and to be here on Wednesday evenings. I don't want you to do anything but listen and learn for one year. Also, I want you to stay away from children. No teaching of any kind. If you are still serving the Lord after one year, we will consider you for official membership in the church."

I was stunned. "Yes, sir," I said quietly. His comment about not working with the children cut me deeply. I would not only show him I could make it. I would be a constant reminder that he was limiting the ability of God to change people!

He intoned a professional prayer, after which, I stumbled out of his office.

Week after week I attended every service. I sat with the family that had fully accepted me. I felt locked into an invisible cage with my every move being monitored. "I just don't feel I'm part of this church," I told my special family. "But I'm glad I came, just to meet you."

Away from church my inner self was caught in a war. My only defense against loneliness was to go to bed and try to sleep the weekend away. My dreams were filled with sensual longing. Often in the middle of the night I would go for long walks around Lake Merritt, hoping to evade the demon lust that tormented my sleep. I felt more confused about my sexuality than ever, living in an environment where my only physical contact with others was an occasional handshake. I ached with wanting to be held, and told myself that in time the feelings would go away. But I couldn't stand being alone much longer.

One night I went for a walk around midnight and allowed myself to be picked up by a man walking around the lake.

Maybe I could prove I was really straight. So we went to my apartment, I pushed down all lesbian longing and Christian ideals and went to bed with him. Within minutes I became hysterical, with the familiar red lights flashing and bombs exploding in my head. "Get out, get out!" I screamed, beating my fists upon the unsuspecting stranger.

I felt corroded from the inside out by my hatred of men, while the weight of guilt sat on my chest like a cement block. Why did I even try? There was no one to talk with, no one who cared.

A letter arrived the next day from Marie Fuller. "I'm flying out by way of San Francisco," she wrote. "I can spend one night with you."

I was thrilled, although a voice inside my head mocked. Taunted, *You can't tell her about what you've done. You're a Christian and you committed sin. She'll hate you.*

After her arrival, we talked late into the night. I hinted at some of my struggles. "I don't know, Marie. I'm not drinking and smoking, and I'm not sleeping with women, but sometimes I just don't feel straight." I weighed the words carefully and watched her face.

"Darlene, I still think you need professional counseling. You've got to be realistic about your emotions. You've fed your senses with sexual perversion for years and you have a healthy appetite! You've never told yourself no. You've never tried to deny yourself. To think that you can just call a screeching halt to your sexuality without any conflicts is absurd."

"Well, if God made my sexual desires, then He ought to be able to control them!"

"And He does, dear. He does. I've been a widow over thirty years, and He is able to meet every need. You've got to work with Him, though, and it takes time!"

"I'm running out of time. I can't handle being torn apart with desire."

"Do you have a friend, someone you can pray with when the attacks come?"

"During the day, yes, but I can't call people at two and three in the morning."

"Honey, I'm going to pray that God will give you someone who will be available to you all the time. God doesn't leave us victims to our past. He'll meet your needs, I know He will."

The voices in my head mocked her. *Your sexual desire will never stop, Darlene. You'll express it with someone, or with yourself, but you will express it. God can't meet a physical need.*

Marie left the next morning, but the void inside remained, consuming almost every waking hour. I started taking pills to sleep every night. Each morning I was so exhausted I had to start the day with pep pills. Tension and stress tore at my muscles and nerves. I went to a doctor and obtained muscle relaxants. The pressure cooker inside me was about to explode.

The holiday season was getting into full swing, and I retreated more and more into the solitude of my studio apartment. No matter how much people said I was part of their family, I was always left out of holiday celebrations.

I dropped a present off for Dad and Bubba and returned to my apartment to spend Christmas Eve alone. The phone was ringing as I walked through the door.

"Merry Christmas," I gasped into the receiver, trying to catch my breath.

"Hi, Dar." Billie's familiar voice was on the other end. "I'm just calling to wish you a merry Christmas."

"Merry Christmas to you, Billie. I'm surprised to hear from you after I asked you to stay out of my life." I sank into the chair in the hall.

"Well, I thought you might like to hear a friendly voice." She paused. "And I really need someone to talk with. My life is going to pieces."

"You know I'm straight now. I don't think it's a good idea to spend time together."

It would be nice to see her.

"Darlene, I understand your religious trip, and I respect that. I just want someone to talk with. How about in broad daylight? I was in a fight last night and got arrested for drunk driving."

"Were you hurt?" Immediately my sympathy was with her.

"No, just my ego."

"All right, Billie. Tell you what. Why don't you come over about noon tomorrow? We can talk for a few hours and you'll leave before it gets dark. Fair enough?"

"Whatever you say. I just need to talk to you."

I hung up, not at all sure how I could handle being with her again. Inside I felt myself weakening. Billie did care for me, even if it was mostly sexual.

Billie kept one promise: she arrived at noon. As I listened to her story of conflict over the past several months, I found myself reaching out to her emotionally. And she responded.

"Are you *really* happy, Darlene?" she asked at length.

"Sure, I'm happy. It's not a bed of roses, but neither was being in relationships that changed with the weather and drained me emotionally. I'd be lying if I said it wasn't hard." *Too hard!*

"I know you, Darlene. I know the things you like to do. I just don't see you sitting alone night after night. She got up and walked toward me.

"Don't do that to me, Billie!" I jumped back. "You know I want to make it."

"You still have lesbian desires or I wouldn't be here today." She slipped her arms around my waist.

I didn't send Billie home that night, or the next. For the next three months she spent every weekend with me. I went to church on Sunday morning, moving farther and farther from the front. The guilt was tearing me apart, and I couldn't share my secret with anyone. I avoided direct conversations with Pastor Stone and plastered a saintly smile across my face as I pulled off my deception. My desire to prove him wrong was the only thing that still drew me to church each Sunday.

Sunday afternoons were another story: I left church and met Billie at the lesbian bar four blocks away. We shot pool and drank mixed drinks, then went out for early dinner. Then she dropped me off a block from the church and I attended evening service.

I rationalized the guilt.

One Sunday evening I arrived at the bar about a half-hour early, to see Billie wrapped in another woman's embrace. Jealousy and hurt washed over me. I walked up behind them.

"Having fun?" I snapped.

"Oh, you're here early." She pulled away from her friend.

"Apparently you weren't expecting me." The verbal battle was on. "You couldn't stand to see me go straight, and now you're cheating on me. I was better off without you." My voice trembled and I pounded my fist against the bar to keep from hitting her.

"Just calm down. I never told you I would stay forever." Her tone was hushed.

"I won't calm down!" I shouted. "In fact, as far as I'm concerned you can make it with anyone you want! I'm through." I marched out the door and walked ten blocks to Jean's Place, arguing with myself the whole way.

I don't need her. She only wanted to mess up my life. Why did I ever let her come visit. *I'll go where I'm wanted. Everyone leave me. Well, I'll get drunk and find someone else!*

I was still steaming as I walked through the door, raising my arms in mock exuberant greeting. "I'm home!"

"Darlene! What are you doing here?" Jean exclaimed.

Everyone in the bar turned toward the door. Several women came over and hugged me. "We knew you'd be back. Welcome home. What are you drinking?"

"Draft, please." I settled down on the stool, then looked around at the new faces. "Who's that?" I whispered to Jean, indicating an older masculine-looking butch sitting at the corner table.

She shrugged. "Go find out!"

"Maybe I'll change my luck if I play *femme* for awhile," I grinned. "Send her a drink on me." If I was going to turn my back on God, I might as well do it up right. And it had been a while since my stable home life with Carol.

Now I positioned myself with a view in the back bar mirror and sipped my drink. I watched the response as Jean took the blond woman a drink and said something in her ear. The jukebox music blared.

The woman smiled and lifted her bottle in a salute. I slipped off my stool and walked to her table. "Hello. I'm Darlene. You new in town?"

"I'm Pat. I don't live here. I'm on vacation and thought I'd see the sights."

"Mind if I sit down?" I pulled out the chair and joined her. "Where do you live?"

"In Monterey. And you?"

"Here in Oakland. I work for an electronics plant."

I noted with inward satisfaction that we had a branch in Monterey.

She motioned toward the table. "Do you shoot pool?"

"Sure." I stood and moved that direction.

By the time the evening was over, I felt I had known Pat for years. We spent the next three days together, and when I returned to work I filed a transfer request to our Monterey branch. The company wanted someone with knowledge in all departments, and approved the transfer.

My head spun with anticipation of the changes. Pat was a professional person, and although she was twenty years my senior, I felt our relationship could be successful.

I'll have financial stability, I reasoned. *Maybe that will keep me out of the bar scene.* So I went back to Jean's Place for a good-by party, and choked back my emotions as I bid Jean a permanent farewell.

I refused to let myself ever think about God.

11.
The
Masquerade

Pat and I began our life together with an official "marriage ceremony witnessed by several professional lesbian couples and celebrated with champagne. It was the weekend of the large parade in New York to celebrate Gay Pride week. Homosexuality was coming out of the closet on nationwide television.

I quickly discovered, however, that we were to attend only house parties and never publicize our lifestyle. Pat's friends were concerned about my openness.

"You have to quit letting people know you're gay!" someone reprimanded me at a party. "We can't afford to be guilty by association."

"Some people at the plant already know," I responded. My reputation came with me when I moved. Besides, you're deceiving yourself if you think people don't know. Not one of you looks straight with your short haircuts and masculine clothing. Even the *femmes* look out of character in skirts and blouses."

"They'll never know for sure," she retorted. "And we have too much invested in the community to be involved in a scandal. Gay liberation hasn't hit Monterey."

"If you're ashamed of your lives, then maybe you should consider changing them! I'll try, but I can't promise anything. I won't put myself in a place of hiding my feelings."

Pat was standing by helplessly. "Why don't we change the topic?" she suggested. "Darlene just needs time to adjust to this area."

"I hope I never adjust! I have to be me. I don't care if people know I'm gay. It's none of their business."

Pat put her arms around me. "It's all right, Darlene. You just have to realize that most of my friends are professionals and stand to lose a lot if it comes to light that they are lesbians. We don't go to local bars or get involved in feminist politics. It doesn't pay to be visible in such a small community."

"I can understand that," I mumbled. "It just seems that even if two women live together for years, it's no one's business what happens in their homes."

"Right—but people gossip. We are teachers, attorneys, bankers and storeowners. We lose customers if talk gets started." She paused. "Honey, you have to understand that my friends are not part of the rowdy bar crowd that you've been associating with."

"My friends may be rowdy, but at least they aren't phony! I'll try to fit into your group, but I can't make any promises."

My halfhearted resolve to remain silent was short-lived. My new office had several Christians and one homosexual man named Steven. I hadn't escaped any conflicts; instead, I'd walked right into the middle of them.

Steven was a stocky built man in his early twenties. He looked athletic and his bronzed skin and sun-bleached hair showed his love for the out-of-doors. We became friends instantly. He was not vocal about his homosexuality, but it was known among the other workers. We attended office functions together, and within weeks the questions were flying.

"Darlene, you and Steven are spending a lot of time together." Sherry eyed me with curiosity across the lunch table. "Do you know he's gay?"

I hesitated. "I had heard that. It doesn't matter to me. I like him as a person."

"You used to go to church, didn't you?" She shifted gears quickly. Sherry was one of the more outgoing Christians in the office.

"I did. God and I had some major disagreements, so we're not talking." I smiled.

"God won't change. Why don't you ask Him to change you?" she persisted.

"Tell you what, Sherry. When God accepts a gay, then I'll go back to the church." I paused. "I tried to go straight and it didn't work. I finally decided it was easier to ignore a God I can't see than to ignore the desire that is warring on the inside of me. So that's where I am. Can we still be friends?"

"We can still be friends," she said softly. "But you know what you're doing is a sin. I'll never change my viewpoint on that."

"Fair enough. You talk to God for me and if I need help I'll let you know.

Pat was furious when I told her about the lunchroom conversation. We had the first of many fights because I refused to cover up my sexuality. I soon discovered that she in turn had a problem that angered me.

We didn't go out to gay bars, but every night after work Pat had a drink. She always had one with dinner, and several in the evening as we watched television. *At least I could live without alcohol.* My resentment smoldered. Our angry pot-shots began to cut away at intimacy.

My ideal relationship was a mirage. My nerves were on edge since I wanted to make a go of the relationship and hated to see her fall into bed drunk every night. I started spending more time away in the evenings, if not at a gay bar, then with Steven. He lived alone in a double-wide mobile home overlooking the bay. Late in the evening you could hear the waves pounding against the rocky shoreline. Steven was a good listener to my tales of trying to fit into the professional class of lesbian society. Pat and I were barely surviving, not living happily ever after as I had planned.

The more time I spent away, the more Pat began to display unreasonable jealousy. "You're probably out sleeping with someone else," she charged.

"I might as well, if you keep accusing me! You're just like my stepfather. I understand my mother better all the time."

A torrent of obscenities would follow and we would retire to separate rooms for the night.

One evening Marie Fuller called.

"I'm going to be in San Francisco tomorrow," came her cheery voice, "and I wondered if we might get together."

"Sure! Hey, it's good to hear from you. The Christians haven't been taken out of the world yet. There's still hope for me." I giggled to cover up my gnawing guilt.

"Dear, there will always be hope for you, up until you breathe your very last breath. Jesus could come back for the Church at any time, though. What are you waiting for—the trumpet blast?"

Marie gave me directions to where she would be staying, and I agreed to come over the following morning.

Pat was standing in the doorway with a scowl. "Who was that?"

"Mrs. Fuller. I told you about her. She was dean of women at my college." I tucked the directions into my wallet. "I'm driving to San Francisco to visit her. She's in California just for the weekend."

"Now you're going off to visit another woman."

"She's not *another woman!* She's straight, but I happen to love her more than anyone else in the world."

"Thanks a lot! And you expect me to believe there's nothing sexual?" She sipped her gin and tonic.

My cheeks grew hot. "This is different," I said through clenched teeth.

"All right. Have it your way. But if you go see her, that means I have the right to see another woman, too!"

Arguing was useless. I slept in the spare room that night, too excited to let my visit be ruined by Pat's remarks.

I arrived midmorning at the old Victorian home where Marie was a guest. Her friends were out-of-town until that evening. She fixed a tossed green salad luncheon in the kitchen, and we talked about surface things for over an hour. After lunch we moved to the formal living area. Paintings graced the walls and Oriental rugs covered the hardwood floors. We exchanged more light talk for a few minutes, then Marie looked directly into my eyes. "Why, Darlene? What went wrong?"

Her words sank into my spirit. I lifted my gaze toward the twelve-foot ceilings. "I wish I could tell you, Marie. It was a lot of things. I never got over wanting to be with women. I got out of gay life, but it never got out of me. I know it's not God's fault. It's mine. But I really did try."

She leaned over and put her arms around me. "I know you did, honey." She began to murmur a prayer as she held me close, a prayer meant mostly for the ears of the One whom she addressed.

I buried my face against her shoulder as I caught a petition about complete wholeness being brought into my life. I fought to keep back the tears.

"Oh, Darlene," she said at last, straightening up. "You know Jesus holds onto the backslider. He has a hook in your jaw and He just won't let you go."

"I know that, Marie. But it just doesn't seem to work for me. Please don't let us end this visit on a bad note. I know you love me and pray for me. Please keep on. I count on it."

"Yes, I'll keep on. But I want you to promise me you'll get in touch with some friends of mine. They're my 'kids,' too, and they will learn to love you. They are both involved in counseling and will be able to help you. They need to learn from you, too." She handed me a slip of paper with the names and addresses of two women.

I tucked it into my wallet and stuck it in my hip pocket. "Do I have to promise?" I wanted to please Marie but felt the effort to change wasn't worth the struggle.

"No, but I'd like you to. Then I'll know you'll really do it. You might even grow to like them!"

"All right, Marie. For you I'll do it."

After a cup of tea, I headed back to Monterey. The day passed too quickly. I drove along with my mind cluttered by a thousand thoughts bumping into one another.

I wish I could have been all right with God when I saw Marie. I couldn't even pray with her, because I'm not talking to Him. Pat will be full of accusations. God! Why can't I stay straight?

When I arrived home Pat was drunk. We fought, and I slept in the spare room again. For almost a year we had waged our war. Now I knew the relationship was over.

The next morning frustration of childhood rejection came pouring out. I ignored her apology. "You're just like my mother!" "You can only tell me you love me when you're drunk. And more than that, I've just realized there's nothing wrong with me. It's with you. Your whole life is lived on alcohol courage, and I can't take it anymore." I stomped across the living room, kicking over the table and lamp. "I'm moving."

It was early November 1970. Her pleading voice followed me as I began to pack. "You can't leave me right before the holidays. Please."

But I filled a suitcase, then drove to Steven's place for the night. The next morning I rented an apartment across town.

My job transfer to Monterey had gone better than I had anticipated. I now drove a white Cadillac convertible with blue leather interior during the week and a Yamaha 250 motorcycle on the weekend. When I saw something I wanted, I charged it—or stole it. But acquiring things to fill the void in my life only increased the void. I began drinking more and many days arrived at work still high. I started taking tranquilizers and smoking a joint before going to bed so I could fall asleep at night.

In an attempt to chase away the loneliness of night time, I moved a female impersonator into my apartment. His name was Brian. Brian was slender six-foot-two and very effeminate. His tousled blond hair and boyish grin made him popular with the gay men. He had arrived in California expecting people to be more accepting of homosexuals than his home state of Michigan had been. But several months later he decided to return to Michigan, promising to look me up if he ever came back to California.

Once again my need to be needed had fallen flat. I couldn't find a long-term roommate even with a gay man.

I continued to spend every night drinking in the bar. The emptiness at home was more than I could stand, and television offered a poor substitute. My inner world felt chaotic.

One Monday Sherry went to lunch with me and pressured me gently to consider returning to church.

"I'm concerned about you, Darlene. You call yourself gay, but it's obvious to anyone who looks at you that you're not happy. Drinking every night doesn't solve anything."

"I could stop if I wanted to," I assured her. "I just go and someone always buys me a drink. You're not asking me to be rude and refuse, are you?"

"My singing group is going to be performing at a church tonight," she persisted. "It's the opening for a week of revival meetings. Will you come hear me?"

"Church? That would cut into my drinking time."

"Come on, Darlene. You can go out after the service. It only lasts until 8:30."

I hesitated. "I will if you promise not to preach at me."

"I promise." She smiled. "I'm sure you'll enjoy it."

Well, I had agreed to come, but I didn't intend to dress up for the event. Blue jeans, Western shirt and boots. I wouldn't be phony for anyone.

When I arrived, the choir was already in place. Sherry beamed as our eyes met. I hoped she didn't have great expectations for tonight. I found a seat on the aisle.

The concert was good. I recognized and avoided several people from my old church in Oakland, and wondered what Pastor Stone would say if he saw me. I hated him for his comments about never knowing a homosexual to change permanently. And how I wished he could have been wrong! Sometimes I hated me, too.

I turned my attention to the well-known evangelist who had come to the stage and was preaching a fiery sermon. If only being a Christian were as easy as he seemed to indicate.

After the service, Sherry came and sat beside me. "Darlene, do you want to pray?"

"Hey, you promised no preaching. Besides," I added, "my public is waiting at the local pub and I can't disappoint them!"

"All right, Darlene. But you can't run forever."

"I'll see you tomorrow at work. I've got to go." I made my way hurriedly out the back door, glancing back and meeting her eyes. I felt like a heel.

If I could really believe there was a chance to change and stay straight. . . .

I silenced that thought.

It won't work, persisted a deeper, nagging inner voice. *You'll never be free from the pain and conflict you try to drown with alcohol.* The nagging memory of failure reminded me of aborted efforts. And I went home later that night with a gnawing feeling of unhappiness. The pills and the booze and the dope didn't bring sleep quickly enough to drive it away.

That must have been part of the reason that at work the next morning I let Sherry talk me into attending the second of the revival meetings. Besides, nothing good happened at the bar until after nine anyhow.

All day long, however, I wished I had not committed myself to being in church. Several friends called wanting to get together for a pool tournament that night.

"Are you getting religion *again?*" exploded one friend.

Another spat out, "Church is a crutch. It's not a sin to be gay, Darlene. You don't need that!"

It seemed I couldn't win on either side.

I got to the church early and read through the hymnal, while my mind flooded with memories of a hundred other services. Inside I was being torn apart. I couldn't shake a mental picture of Jesus hanging on the cross, arms spread open. I could almost hear him saying, "I died for you, Darlene. Come, let my blood cleanse you." Then I heard a piercing screech from a bottomless pit in my mind: *You're mine; you'll never be free! You failed before. No one loves you. No one loves you.* Like a recording the words screamed inside my head.

The evangelist came to the stage and presented another salvation message. I was uncomfortable by the time he gave an altar call. I fidgeted with my papers, then took the Bible from the pew rack and pretended to read.

Suddenly the service was over and I was aware of someone beside me. Sherry knelt by my seat. "Darlene, I didn't promise for tonight. Do you really believe the Bible is true?"

"Sure I do. I know that." I laughed nervously. "Just because I'm not living it doesn't mean I don't believe it."

"Do you know what 1 John 1:9 says?" she persisted.

"Yes. 'If we confess our sins, God is faithful and just to forgive us our sins and to cleanse us from all unrighteousness.'"

"O.K. Now do me a favor. Open that Bible and read it for me."

"I just quoted it. Why should I read it?"

"I want you to really see it, Darlene." She opened the Living Bible I had removed from the rack and handed it back to me.

I read it slowly. "But if we confess our sins to him, he can be depended on to forgive us and to cleanse us from every wrong. (And it is perfectly proper for God to do this for us because Christ died to wash away our sins.)"

"If the Bible is true," Sherry interrupted, "then you need to do that right now."

"You don't understand. I've tried it already. *It doesn't work.*"

"You said you believed the Bible was true. I think God wants to prove He really means what His Word says."

"I can't argue with that," I mumbled, sinking lower in the pew.

"Then let's pray. Right here, right now. I know you want out of the life you're living. I can see it all over you."

But could it really work this time? It seemed the weight of the conflict inside would tear me apart.

Sherry prayed first. She paused, then squeezed my hand gently.

"Jesus," I began, "that verse says you'll forgive all my sins. I confess them to you right now and ask you to cleanse me. Forgive me, and help me really make it this time."

The tension flowed from my nerves and I relaxed against the seat. Suddenly I was scared. How could I handle the flak from the people at the bar? Could I stay out of the bar? Would I really be able to make it?

Almost as if Sherry were reading my mind, she spoke softly. "Darlene, there is a special woman I'd like you to meet. She teaches Bible study to the college-age group at my church. Her name is Norma. I think she would be a good person to counsel with through the rough time ahead."

I nodded. "Perhaps I should come to a Bible study. I don't know about counseling with anyone right now, though. I've got a lot to straighten out in my head."

Inside the familiar knot of tension was forming. I wished I *could* run to someone for help. But who could even understand the lifestyle I had been part of, let alone help me find the way out?

The rest of the week I attended the nightly services. Then I called Marie Fuller with the news of my recommitment.

"Oh, honey, I'm so glad that Jesus keeps drawing you. Please seek out some professional counseling this time. Will you?"

"I'll try, Marie. There are a lot of changes to make right now. Thanks for praying for me." *I'm scared. What if I can't make it?*

"I've never stopped, dear!" she chuckled. "I know He can make you whole and that's what I'm asking Him."

The concept of wholeness seemed like another illusion. By Saturday night everything in me wanted a drink. I fought the urge to go to the bar. I refused invitations from women who stopped by the plant, unaware that I had made a new commitment to Christ.

Night after night I walked almost five miles, following the path around Monterey Bay. I would walk almost to the Carmel city limits, then back to my apartment, which was in the northern section of Monterey. I found strength in the pounding of the waves. Somehow it seemed to calm the churning within me. I returned home each night and fell into bed, clutching my Bible for security.

Sleep came slowly but without pills, booze, or dope.

12.
Prayers and Parenthood

At last I kept my promise and called Elaine and Beth, Marie's friends in San Francisco. Then I spent a weekend with them, talking mostly about the confusion and inner conflicts I was experiencing.

"I don't know how long I can handle these battles," I told them. "Sometimes I feel like someone has taken spiked shoes and marched through my insides."

"Darlene, you've sown a lot of wild oats. It's going to take the Lord time to get the bad seed out and replant new!"

We prayed together several times that weekend; however, the results weren't exactly what I wanted. *No instant answers!*

When I returned to Monterey, I started attending a large church with counseling services available. I met Mr. Thomas, the staff psychologist, and committed myself to weekly appointments for six months. I also decided to check out a Bible study on Monday nights at Sherry's church, led by a dynamic believer named Norma.

I arrived at the church a little late the first night. I sat in the car for a long time, wondering how I would appear to a room of strangers. Then I tucked my cowboy shirt behind my wide leather belt, stuffed my keys into the front pocket of my black jeans, picked up my big red new Bible, and sauntered toward the building. I knocked the dust off the toes of my black cowboy boots in front of the door and rubbed them on the backs of my pantlegs. Then I stepped inside and followed the sound of voices down a long hall.

Tiptoeing into a large room, I found a chair near the back.

A tall, dark-haired woman was leading the group in prayer. *That must be Norma.* I glanced around for a moment and spotted Sherry, who smiled a silent welcome. Then the prayer ended. I must have missed the study itself.

"Let's take a short break," the leader said, "then come back and form smaller groups for a time of prayer."

Good! I can slip out.

I was headed toward the door when Sherry appeared at my side. "Come on, Darlene. I want you to meet Norma. She's the one I've been telling you about!" She grabbed my arm and propelled me toward the front of the room.

After introductions, Norma and I talked for a few minutes. She was also a counselor and offered to spend time with me if I wanted someone to talk with. I told her I would call. Sherry followed me down the hall, my boots clicking loudly as I walked back to the car.

"You will come back, won't you?" She sounded disappointed.

"Sure. I just need time to get things together." I smiled. "Thanks for inviting me, Sherry. Your friend seems nice."

I waved, then got into my car, and wondered if I would ever fit into that world. *God, please don't let me fail this time.*

At work, Steven was confused. "I just don't understand why you can't be gay and be a Christian too." He flexed his muscles and spoke in a hushed tone.

"The Bible says it's wrong to be involved in any sexual activity outside of marriage. That includes homosexuality."

"But can we still be friends?" he asked, his face lined with concern.

"We'll always be friends, Steven," I laughed. "I just can't go drinking or cruising with you. You're the safest male friend I have. I know *you* won't try to take me to bed."

Inside my head the question was far from settled. How could I give up my gay friends? I had few real Christian friends, and my gay friends didn't understand Christians.

The Christians I knew couldn't understand why I still needed gay friendships. But I couldn't be a hermit!

Finally I called Norma. After three hours of talking, she told me what I already knew: "Darlene, you need to break off all gay friendships and find some Christians you can be close to."

I agreed, but inside I was in turmoil. She didn't understand how torn I still felt.

Within the week, a new girl named Joanne started work in our department—a single Christian. We became instant friends.

Joanne had been raised in a Christian home and was naïve about life on the streets. After a couple of weeks I gulped down my apprehension and decided to tell her about my past before she heard it secondhand.

"Joanne, I've got something to tell you," I said one evening. "I don't know how you're going to react, but if we're going to be friends, there's something you need to know."

"It sounds serious." She was smiling, but a quizzical look furrowed her forehead.

"It is. I told you I came back to the Lord a few months ago?"

"Yeah. So?" She cocked her head to one side.

"Well, what I didn't tell you is the reason I was away from God so long. We had a disagreement about my sexuality. I was a lesbian." I held my breath, waiting for a response.

Her face turned crimson, clashing with her auburn hair. She laughed nervously. "I think you'd better explain. You're not now, are you?"

I chuckled. "No, I'm not now. I gave up that life when I came back to God. A lot of my friends are gay, but I don't really socialize much anymore."

"Good!" She sighed deeply. "It doesn't make any difference to me what you were. It's what you are now that counts." She paused. "But I didn't know homosexuals could change."

"A lot of people think they can't. It's not easy, and there are a lot of problems, but so far, Jesus and I have it licked."

I answered a barrage of questions for the next several hours. "One thing you have to understand, Joanne," I said, "is that you could be considered gay by association. If we were out having dinner some evening and any old friends saw us, they would assume you were my lover. It could be embarrassing for you, and I want you to know that it might happen."

"I guess I'll cross that bridge if it happens. I'm not going to worry about it. That sin isn't any worse than drunkenness or gossip, Darlene. Only man ranks degrees of sin. Besides, I can think of a few Christians who would give me more problems about being your friend than any gays." She laughed.

"Let's hope there's no problems with anyone," I agreed, as a calming warmth spread through me. She really wanted to be my friend!

Over the next few weeks the friendship with Joanne abated my loneliness, and I was growing stronger in my determination to make it this time.

The sessions with Mr. Thomas, however, seemed only to mentally rehearse my sexual behavior. I already knew that my involvement in homosexual relationships was a search for love and intimacy that I had not found in my childhood. Mr. Thomas would explain the clinical names for my behavior, and although we prayed together at the end of each session, I still felt empty.

I need answers, not descriptions, I thought. *I don't care why I do certain things; I just want to know how to stop.*

Meanwhile, the "inner me" continued to struggle with homosexual desires even though my actions had become acceptable.

I talked to Norma about this conflict at her kitchen table one evening.

"You have a lifetime of patterns to change," she said thoughtfully. "God will bring healing, but it takes time. You still seem to cling to friendships with your homosexual friends, and I don't understand that. If you really want to be clean, you have to cut them out of your life."

I gulped back my protest and sipped the cup of tea she had set in front of me, thinking about Steven.

"I don't mean to sound harsh," she continued, "but if you are going to make a break with this lifestyle once and for all, you need to do it now. You've played games long enough, thinking you could straddle the fence."

"That's not fair," I blurted out. "How can I leave my old friends when I'm not really accepted in the church? Sure, there are a few people who say they pray for me and who care, but they don't invite me home or over for lunch. I need friends, not just Sunday conversationalists!"

She leaned across the table and placed her hand on mine. "You have to give them time to accept you, Darlene. We've grown up with a lot of stories about homosexuals, and God has to work healing in us too! I'm learning from you."

I agreed to give God time to work the changes, but even prayer did not alleviate the pain of loneliness.

I stopped my sessions with Mr. Thomas and concentrated on reading the Bible and attending prayer meetings twice a week.

One weekend Beth called and invited me to spend a couple of days in San Francisco. She was easy to talk with, and I found myself again pouring out my frustrations and conflicts.

"Sometimes I feel like a powder keg about to explode," I complained. I'm reading the Bible, praying, and even staying away from my old friends, but it only feels temporary. An invisible magnet seems to draw my thoughts back constantly to old relationships."

She was sympathetic. "There is no easy way to break those patterns, Darlene. I don't know how long you'll struggle with them, but I know Jesus can help you overcome the desire and keep you free."

"But what kind of freedom is it when you never know what's around the corner? Why can't I just walk away?"

"Darlene, those people really cared for you. They weren't good for you, but their concern and love were always available. I think that until you build that same kind of support in the Christian community, you'll be tempted to return."

The weekend in San Francisco was an oasis, but what I needed was a haven. I had learned from Norma and Beth that I was in a process and that I needed to give God time. But on the long drive home I struggled with another nagging thought: *Lord, how long until something lights the fuse to my powder keg?*

A few days later my younger sister Emily called. She had just become fourteen and was having the usual teenage struggles with parental authority. She had decided that Mom's drinking was the source of her problems, so she wanted to come live with me. She threatened to run away if I didn't allow her to come to California.

I agreed to pray about it and talk to Mom on her behalf. The first thing I did was consult Norma, who advised me not to take on additional responsibilities when my own life was still so much in conflict. But I knew in my heart that I couldn't abandon Emily when she needed someone to give her guidelines and a Christian influence. Mom said that if I wanted to raise Emily, I was welcome to try. She would send her down after the semester was finished in three weeks.

As the days flew by, I secured information about schools and other necessities to provide for a teenager. I decided to buy a two-bedroom mobile home near the school that seemed to have the best reputation. And I created a mental image of myself as the perfect parent who wouldn't fail Emily the way I had been failed. I was bursting with excitement as I planned for our life together.

My dreams of perfection were shattered the first week when Emily and I had a fight over money. "If the state is providing $125 for my support," she shouted, "then I should be able to spend it the way I want!"

"I'm putting a roof over your head, buying your school clothes, and feeding you," I retorted. "I'll give you an allowance for helping around the house, but you'll earn it."

"I didn't come here to be your slave!" She turned and stomped out of the kitchen.

I didn't remember that moodiness was part of the teenage package. Resentment began to eat away at the foundation of my perfect-parent image.

Things did get better. Emily met Christians at school and began to take an interest in their activities. Giving her more freedom allowed me to become active in church Bible studies again. Emily did well in school. I attended her open house and all school functions. I got so caught up in being a parent that I began to neglect personal activities.

Then I caught her lying several times about where she went after school and who she was with. I confronted her and placed restriction on her.

She was a bundle of personality fluctuations. One day she came bursting through the front door with the announcement, "Darlene, I've decided to be a Christian. I'm not going to give you any more problems!" Two days later she screamed, "You keep closer watch on me than a jailer!"

"I just don't want you to learn things the hard way, Emily," I responded. "If you can't live the way I want you to, then I'll take you back to Mom."

"No, you won't! You love me too much and you're too much of a Christian to put me back in that environment." She sounded smug.

"Don't count on it!" I shouted. "I think we need some counseling."

"Counseling? There's nothing wrong with me."

"Well, something's wrong somewhere. This just isn't working out." I lowered my voice. "Are you willing to go with me?"

"It's your money!" She threw herself into the overstuffed chair and pouted.

I arranged a session with Norma's pastor-husband. Wes was in his late thirties and would be a neutral influence. After several hours of listening, he ventured his advice.

"You two should set aside a special time for Bible study and talk about the Scriptures and your feelings. Look for Bible answers to your problems. You both have a lot to overcome. Let's pray and ask Jesus to help."

We agreed to the plan and to work together at solving our differences. The new resolve lasted through the Christmas holidays. Emily didn't rebel as much, but she spent long blocks of time away from me.

I began to sneak an occasional drink to ease the growing tension inside me. *God, why can't you make things work out in my life?* I didn't want Emily to know I was drinking, so I hid the bottles and waited until she was in bed each night. I was losing ground on this spiritual treadmill. A recurring thought demanded my attention: *The church just isn't the answer.* I missed a few Sundays and began to visit Steven and other gay friends. Each visit with them seemed a rerun of previous conversations.

"Why are you so uptight about being gay and being a Christian?" they asked. "You can be both."

"It's a direct violation of Scripture," I said, torn inside with new uncertainty. "And no matter how you twist the words around, it still comes out sin."

My inner struggles didn't help me at home with Emily. One day just about a year after she came, she informed me she was moving in with a girl friend from school. It was the final stroke against my growing sense of parental failure.

"Where you're moving is back with Mom!" I exclaimed and began packing her things. "I'll take you out of school and drive you there myself."

"You wouldn't dare!" she challenged me.

"Go spend the weekend with your friend. It's the last you'll see her for awhile."

"You're not serious."

My face was flushed with anger. "You've made your choice and forced me to make mine."

"I'll never forgive you, Darlene. I hate you!" She ran out, slamming the door.

Tears burned my eyes.

"Now I don't have to be an example for anyone," I whispered into the air.

On the trip back to Oregon, Emily spoke only out of necessity. As we drove past Medford, a tape recorder in my mind began to play the events of my visit with Sharon and Peter a few years earlier. Those were the days of my rebellion when Sharon had confronted me with a recommitment to Christ. Here I was now, still struggling with my sexuality. Emily had been a reason to stay clean, but now. . . .

We passed Albany where Joy had lived until just two months ago. She and her husband had been called into full-time missionary service and assigned to Africa. At least I didn't have to face her with my failure.

As I headed back to California after dropping Emily off, I lost the battle with guilt. I hadn't gone a hundred miles before I pulled into a liquor store for beer and cigarettes. These two familiar friends helped to dull the ache inside and pull me closer to the past.

Once home, I called Norma to share the sense of loss and failure over my year with Emily.

"Sometimes loving people means you have to let them make their own mistakes," she consoled me. "Remember, I advised you against having her come to live with you."

"I remember. But I prayed about it. Why doesn't God make things go right for me?"

"He does things His way, Darlene, and you haven't accepted that."

"I've tried to do it His way," I snapped defensively.

"Have you quit spending time with all your gay friends?"

"I don't go to the bars with them. But you can't just throw

away years of friendships and not have anything to replace them! The only single friends I have are Sherry and Joanne. Am I supposed to spend all my time with them?"

"I'm not going to argue with you," Norma said. "I think you need to hear God tell you why you failed with Emily."

You just don't understand! I argued silently.

After several nights in the now empty mobile home, I decided to go where people listened even if they didn't understand. The noise of the gay bars drowned out the screaming accusations in my head. I drank alone, not looking for take-home companionship.

Nor did I get up early enough for church. I didn't want to hear empty platitudes from the pulpit, though I didn't agree with the answers I heard at the bar either. I decided to try talking to Norma again.

She was planting flowers along the driveway and stood up when she saw my white Cadillac.

"Hello, Darlene. What brings you out this way?" She traced the edge of the trowel in her hand. "I've missed you at church."

"I just needed a place to come and think, Norma. My life is so messed up. I can't make anything work right." I sat down in the middle of the concrete driveway. "And I've decided it just isn't possible to stop the conflict raging inside me."

"Darlene, I told you before, you need to stop seeing your old friends and stay away from the bars."

"But I can't stop seeing Steven. I work with him, and he's one of the best friends I have."

Suddenly Norma turned and walked into the garage out of sight. *Probably getting more flowers.* I waited. Ten minutes later she came back, wiping tears from her eyes.

"Darlene, I just can't take any more. You're trampling the blood of Jesus in the ground and I just can't take any more!" She turned and fled toward the garage.

I was stunned. "Do you think I'd be this way if I could help it?" I yelled.

I jumped up and ran toward my car, started the engine, and peeled rubber as I sped away. *I'll show her I can get mad too! I won't come back. I don't need her!*

For weeks I struggled; nothing worked for me. I couldn't be happy in a lesbian relationship and I wasn't happy in the church. I decided to stay drunk.

Joanne was confused about my involvements with old friends. "Darlene, I don't understand what's happening to you. If you keep coming to work drunk, they're going to find out!"

"I'll be cool!" I giggled, popping a mint to cover the odor of bourbon. "Just try to understand. I'm trying to get things together."

But silently I anguished. I wanted so badly to make it as a Christian, but the emptiness inside was swallowing up all motivation to succeed.

"I'll pray for you, Darlene, but I don't like what you're doing to yourself." Her face was stern.

"Just be my friend, O.K.?" I turned away. Did she hear the silent pleading?

I dropped out of church and prayer meetings completely and began to frequent the men's gay bar. I would go in after work and find a corner, drinking until closing. Thoughts of suicide plagued me. *As long as I don't get involved in a sexual relationship,* I thought, *I'm not really hooked! I'd rather kill myself than go through that hell again.*

The Christmas holidays were approaching again, and I was more depressed than ever. I couldn't go through another month alone! So I went to the lesbian bar.

Within a half-hour a woman named Shirley was seated at my table telling me her life's story of jilted love and lost ambitions. Her red Pendleton wool skirt and tailored black wool slacks put her a cut above the usual beer crowd. I listened for three hours, quietly begging to be needed and cared for.

Shirley was a bitter person. She had been ripped off in

every former relationship and lain awake nights planning revenge. She trusted no one and planned for the day she would own a $100,000 home and a Porsche. Shirley wanted a partner who could help her attain her goal. Shirley was a taker.

But my own needs for love and intimacy were so great that within a week we were living together at her condominium just three blocks from the ocean. I did not object when she suggested I sell my mobile home. I had determined I could make everything all right for Shirley and somehow fill the growing void in my life. God, I decided, was no longer a consideration. It would be easier to ignore an unseen being than to endure the sexual and psychological pressure that was driving me out to the bars night after night. In desperation, I embraced this relationship as permanent.

Since I was looking for fulfillment solely through my relationship with Shirley, I could not let myself fail; if I lost her, I would lose everything. So I showered her with daily gifts and pooled my finances with hers to reach *her* financial goal. Whatever she wanted I would get for her. All I wanted in return was unconditional love.

One month later, I discovered Shirley wanted something I could not give her: another relationship! She began dating a woman who made almost twice my salary. Shirley wasn't interested in love; she was interested in status and financial power.

I could hardly believe my outbursts of anger during the next couple of days. I had to strike back somehow to kill the pain of rejection.

Impulsively I bought a revolver through the black market. Rage, stemming from my desperation, began to override rational, moral thinking. *Kill her! Kill her!* The words flashed in my mind like neon signs. *Doesn't she realize I chose her instead of God? She can't abandon me! I won't let her.* Then I thought about Daddy. *Everyone walks out on me. . . .* This time I couldn't shake the compulsive thoughts of murder and self-destruction. I would kill Shirley then myself.

The next night I sat in the darkened living room waiting for Shirley to come home. I tucked the loaded gun between the cushions of the couch and waited, refusing all inclinations to turn to God. My hatred for Shirley's abandoning me blotted out all thought of Scripture. God couldn't help either of us now.

When early morning gray replaced the blackness of midnight, blinding jealousy replaced my anger. It was 5 A.M. when I heard her steps on the walkway. I clutched the bulky, unfamiliar handle of the revolver.

The door opened slowly, and Shirley entered the front room, trying not to make noise. I flipped the light with my free hand.

"Did you have a nice evening?" I asked caustically.

"Oh ... you scared me. What are you doing up?" She removed her jacket and turned to face me.

"What am I doing up?" I shouted. "What do you think? I've been waiting all night! Where have you been?"

"You'll wake the neighbors." She headed for the stairs. "I got a little tied up. We'll talk in the morning."

"It is morning, and we'll talk now! I gave up everything that was important to me just to live with you, and you think I shouldn't care if you're going out on me?"

"I'm sorry, Darlene. I thought we could make it together, but I need more than you can offer." She started up the stairs.

I swallowed hard and raised the gun toward her. "I think we'll talk now. If you're dead, you don't have any needs!" I motioned for her to move down the stairs. "You knew when I moved in with you that I was choosing you instead of God. How could you hook me on a relationship for a month and then just leave?"

"Darlene, I don't want to hurt you. Really I don't." She moved slowly down the stairs and lowered herself into the chair across from me, her eyes wide with fear. "You know how I am. I'm not capable of loving anyone."

"Yeah, and I felt sorry for you. I wanted to make all the hurts go away. But who helps my hurting? Who?" I waved the gun at her.

"Darlene, you deserve so much better than I." All the color had drained from her face. "You're the most loving person I've ever known. But it's just not there for us. I know you're hurt, but you don't really want to kill me. Besides, killing is an unforgivable sin in your religion, isn't it?"

"I don't want to talk about religion." Hot tears filled my eyes and spilled down my cheeks. "Maybe I don't really love you after all. Maybe it's hate I feel or pity. You're not worth going to jail over! Maybe I'll just kill myself. Go ahead and leave. I don't care what you do." I rested the gun on the cushion. "I'm just going to take a ride and think. If I come back at all, it'll be to pack. If I don't, find my mother's phone number and tell her to claim my things!"

I drove for hours along the rocky coast, arguing with myself for a reason to live. Then I stopped at a pull-out where the Pacific crashed against the rocks, pulled the gun from my waistband, and flung it as far as I could into the ocean.

13.
The Bottomless
Pit

I had been drinking for several hours when Colleen came on duty. I tried to order another drink but lost my balance and fell off the barstool.

Colleen rushed to my side of the bar, motioning for a couple of other women to help get me on my feet. "Darlene, you've had enough. Come on in the back and sleep it off." They carried me to a cot in the storage room.

I mumbled the story of the gun and hating Shirley. I felt like I was sinking into a bottomless pit. Then I passed out.

Several hours later Colleen came with a cup of coffee and sat on the edge of the cot.

"Here, drink this."

I held my head in my hands. "What time is it?"

"About eight. Shirley called to ask if I'd seen you. I told her to stay away."

I struggled to my feet. "I'm not going home!"

"You may not have one. She said to tell you she was moving in with some girl." She looked concerned. "What are you going to do? You've been mumbling something about killing her and killing yourself."

"Oh, I'm not going to do that now. I'll just live and make everyone else miserable." I sipped the coffee. "Besides, I threw the gun away."

"You want a night job tending bar? I need someone a couple nights a week."

"You're on! But not for a couple of days. I guess I have to find a place to live."

I drove to the condominium, where Shirley was already packing.

"You can rent this place until I sell it," she offered quietly. "Then you won't have to move."

I nodded and brushed past her to go to the spare room as tears ran down my cheeks. Would anything ever make the hurt go away? I fell asleep clutching the remains of another broken dream.

The next few weeks were an emotional disaster. I worked at the electronics plant every day, but spent my nights either tending bar or on the customer side, getting drunk.

God did not stay out of my world. Christian songs made popular by secular artists went to the top of the charts, and "Amazing Grace" and "Why Me, Lord?" were put into the bar jukebox, reminders of another love I couldn't forget.

After a few drinks, I would jump on top of the bar stool and use the broom handle like a microphone. "There's no beer in heaven, brothers and sisters, so you'd better drink up while you can!" Then I would bounce behind the bar and take orders.

"You missed your calling, Darlene," someone could call out. "You should have been a preacher!"

"Well, we could rename the bar," I would respond. "We could call it the First Church of the Thirsty!"

None of these jokes was quite as funny on the inside as it seemed on the outside.

To understand myself, I got involved in astrology charts and biorhythm schedules. Sometimes I could look into people's eyes and know what they were thinking. I developed strange powers to make spoons bend and keys curl without even touching them. I could wave my hands over the pool table when people were making a shot, say some words and cause them to miss their shot. When I shot, the balls headed for the pockets as if guided by an invisible force. I collected a shelf of trophies. When machines didn't work, all it took was for me to lay my hands on them and mumble something. Once I felt myself step out of my body and float around the room while I could see myself still lying on the bed. Nothing was too spooky to try once!

I went to bed with one of the men I worked with to see if I had changed my feelings about men. I hadn't. I justified the encounter by charging him $100, but brought home V.D. and a new resolve to stick with women. Every relationship was an effort to please, but nothing touched the throbbing pain. I wanted acceptance and approval from others, but I knew deep inside it was Daddy's love I really wanted. I may have been twenty-nine, but inside me lived a five-year-old who had never grown from the day Daddy walked out.

About that time I decided to take some time off and drive to Oregon to visit my family. Dad had moved up there the year before, an alcoholic who had lost everything he ever owned. I figured I might as well show him and the rest of the family what their lesbian daughter looked like. Maybe my white Cadillac would impress him. Then I shuddered as the familiar longing surfaced: Would Dad ever tell me that he loved me?

Why did I still care? I struggled to understand what drove me back to my roots, hoping that this time I would find Dad's acceptance. Would I ever get over his abandoning me to handle my tears?

Two days before I planned to leave I was trying to finish up some last-minute projects at the plant when I was interrupted by a telephone call.

"Darlene, this is Bubba. Are you sitting down?" His voice sounded hollow.

"What's wrong? Why are you calling in the middle of the day?" I braced myself against the desk.

"You've got to come home. Dad just died of a heart attack."

My head spun. "You're kidding! Dad can't die. I'm coming home this weekend."

"He's dead, Darlene. Get here as fast as you can."

The eleven-hour drive home was mixed with tears of frustration and angry curses. *How could you die? We never got to love each other. Now you'll never love me. What's*

*left to live for? I can't even show you I'm worth loving! I
wanted to please you so much, Daddy. I couldn't forget
you even after you left us. Did you love me, Daddy? All I
ever wanted was for you to love me.*

It was a drizzly, cold morning as I pulled into town.
Marlene was waiting for me. She told me the details of Dad's
death and outlined plans for the funeral and the handling of
his affairs. We reminisced about many of Dad's dreams that
would never have happened even if he had lived. A few hours
later we drove to the mortuary.

Marlene started to open the car door, then turned toward
me. "He'll be cremated as he requested. You'll have to carry
his ashes back to California and scatter them from the
Golden Gate Bridge. He wanted that, you know." Her voice
was matter-of-fact.

I was stunned. "I know he always said that, but I didn't
know I'd get elected." Could I even do that? I tried to silence
the objections.

We walked in silence toward the building and followed the
instructions of a somber-looking man in a black suit. I hated
mortuaries but expected to enter a small room with a nice
casket, quiet music, and flowers. Instead we found a stark
pine box sitting against the wall in a small alcove behind the
coats. I stepped closer and lifted the top sheet of plywood
that covered half the box. A pale form of a man dressed in a
black suit lay with his head on a gray-and-white striped
pillow. The thinning black hair was combed straight back.
His face was free of lines and wrinkles.

"Dad?" I breathed. Then I turned to Marlene in disbelief.
"Why an unpainted box? No pillowcase? Whoever fixed him
up didn't even know him. His glasses are wrong. Where is the
wave in his hair?" I reached down and made some adjust-
ments.

"He's going to be cremated, Darlene," she said patiently.
We told them just the necessities. It's all going up in flames,
so we kept it simple."

"You didn't even ask me!" I exploded, fighting back tears. Bits of former conversations with Dad raced through my mind.

Marlene moved closer to the box, reached out, and touched his face. "You really did it, Dad. You really killed yourself." Tears fell freely down her cheeks. She turned away. "Let's go up front until the others arrive." She started walking down the long isolated corridor to the waiting room.

I fought the urge to pound on the lifeless form in front of me. "Damn you for dying!" *Now you'll never love me!*

I reached down and touched the smooth, unnatural face of my father. "Why couldn't we tell each other we really loved one another?" I whispered in the stillness. "I really do, you know." I swallowed hard to relieve the tightness in my throat and placed the lid back on the box. "What do I do now? You can't hear me. You always leave me."

A tear slipped down my cheek as I remembered two years ago when I had last seen Dad. "I just don't understand you, Darlene," he had said. "You're the smartest kid I have and you're throwing your life away." The words echoed in my head. *The smartest kid. . . .* But he never said he loved me.

As I went to wait for the others, I glanced at my reflection in the hallway mirror. No traditional black for me. I wore a pink-flowered Western shirt, brown pants, and cowboy boots.

"Well, Dad," I whispered to my own reflection, "I guess this is really good-by. I didn't dress up for the occasion. I know you want me to be myself."

The stark pine box was moved to a small room with a half-dozen chairs for a short service. Afterward Bubba touched my arm. "Darlene, do you want to go view the body one last time?" His eyes were red; his voice was urgent.

"Yeah, sure. Why not?" I walked to the pine box, reached down and rested my hand on his shoulder. "We missed so much, Dad. It's just not fair." The tears streamed down my cheeks. "I hate you for dying. Why couldn't you live long enough for everything to be all right?" I brushed at the tears and coughed to clear my throat. I leaned down and kissed his forehead. "Bye, Dad." I straightened up, studied his still features, then turned and strode out of the chapel. Bubba was by my side a moment later as I lit a cigarette.

"The man will bring his cuff links and ring in a few minutes," Marlene said as Bubba joined us. "In four days you can pick up the ashes. It just doesn't seem real, does it?"

The man arrived with Dad's personal effects. "I'll call you when you may pick up the remains," he said. "You'll have to sign a release for interstate transportation of the deceased."

That's not the deceased. That's my father you're talking about! "O.K.," I mumbled. I turned and walked out the door, then leaned against the handrail.

Cars passed. Children played in the street, oblivious that my only reason for living was gone. *It's not fair! It's not fair! The whole world keeps moving and Daddy's dead. He'll never tell me that he loves me. No matter what I do, I'll never win his love now.* I wanted to race up and down the street yelling at cars, people, and God. *Who's going to love me now? Who?* I demanded as I walked silently to my car.

Four days later I headed home. One last act remained, but I dreaded the walk to the middle of the Golden Gate Bridge.

Marie Fuller was visiting her son in Salem. I stopped for a short visit, and she listened to my report of the last couple of weeks. We went out for coffee before I continued my trip south.

"Darlene, I want you to make me a promise," she said. "Promise me that you will have someone with you when you scatter the ashes."

"Who is going to want to walk with me to the middle of a bridge and scatter my father's ashes?" I scoffed.

"Please promise me you won't go alone," she persisted.

"Oh, all right. I'll call Steven. I really wouldn't want anyone else there."

"Good. Call me after you get home again." She hugged me and said a quick prayer for God's strength and comfort.

I called Steven from a roadside rest about an hour from San Francisco. He promised to leave then and meet me by the bridge. Sure enough, after I arrived at the north side parking area and transferred the ashes into a plastic sack, Steven pulled up beside me.

"You got here fast," he said. "How are you?" He locked the car and put his arm around my shoulder as we walked onto the bridge.

"I'm all right. I'm glad it's foggy so the men in the tower can't see us."

"They'd never be able to stop us anyway."

We walked in silence most of the way, occasionally mentioning a few of the people we knew who had jumped from the span.

Right in the middle we stopped and walked into a little alcove protected by a steel railing.

"Darlene, if you want, I'll scatter them for you."

"Thanks, Steven, but I have to do this myself."

I opened the bag. "Bye Dad," I whispered as I turned it upside down and watched a puff of white dust disappear toward the water below.

14.
The Marriage
Charade

The months after Dad's death were a blur. Every memory of that day on the bridge brought a lump in my throat. I had helped him in his final act of abandonment and made him in death as untouchable as he had been in life. Guilt worked its way deeper into my being. There wasn't even a grave to cry over—or to spit on.

As my thirtieth birthday approached, I thought a big party might fill the emptiness inside me. So I rented the local women's bar for the next Friday night.

Over a hundred lesbians and gay men came to celebrate with me. When the bar closed at 2 A.M., I was so drunk that a woman named Ramona had to drive me home. She was masculine-looking, her salt-and-pepper hair cut close to the head. Ramona spent the night and showed no intention of leaving the next morning.

Maybe it's time for another roommate. I still lived in Shirley's two-bedroom condominium and had plenty of room. I resolved not to get emotionally attached.

"Ramona, how would you like to stay here indefinitely and share the rent."

"You mean be permanent lovers?" She looked amused.

"How long is permanent? I'm available right now. We could give it a try."

"It might keep you out of the bars if you had company," she grinned. "Actually, I hoped it would come to this."

"Good." I gave her a hug. *With the extra money, I can get another car!*

I bought a blue pickup with an AM-FM stereo and a cab-over

camper. But Ramona and I had conflicts almost from the start. She didn't like men, gay or straight, whereas I had friends in both categories. Steven stopped visiting entirely when Ramona continued to glare at him and refused to join in conversations.

"I'm not anyone's property," I explained in frustration. "I have a lot of friends and I expect to share my time with them. If you can't be civil to them, then maybe we should end this arrangement."

"No, baby," she wailed. "I'll do better, I promise. I just hate having queens around."

"You'll have to do better," I responded. "I like lots of people around."

One evening after dinner the phone rang. Ramona answered, then turned to me with a scowl. "It's for you. Some queen!"

I walked to the phone.

"Hi, love. This is Brian. I'm calling from Michigan." His voice quivered with excitement.

"Brian! It's been a long time! What's happening in your world?"

"I told you if I ever came back to California, I'd look you up. Well, I'm leaving this weekend and want to know if I can stay with you until I find a place."

"Sure. You've always got a place to crash for a while. Are you coming alone?"

"Yes." His voice broke. "My lover and I just broke up. He moved out with all the furniture and left me with the bills. I'm getting stuck! Oh, well, that's life. Don't tell anyone I'm coming. See you soon!"

Ramona had been eavesdropping. "No queen is going to move in with us," she snapped as soon as I got off the phone.

"Hey, he's my friend. It's only until he gets settled." I walked out of the room. "End of discussion!"

The tension between us increased as I prepared the spare room for Brian's arrival. Ramona stormed from the house, vowing to go out and get drunk. And sure enough, at 2:30 in the morning she called from the police station. She had been nailed for drunk driving.

I couldn't believe my life was getting so complicated. I had hoped to find someone to take care of me, but instead I was rescuing her.

The next few days were anxious, filled with legal discussions. I had almost forgotten about Brian when a new LTD pulled alongside my Cadillac in the parking lot at work as I was heading home for lunch. Brian's boyish grin and tousled, blond hair brought back memories of happier days. I told him of Ramona's situation while we drove to the condominium. "Besides all that," I finished, "I wish I hadn't let myself get involved with her. You and I would make better roommates."

"Well, we'll just move her out!" He gestured breezily.

"Keep it cool. Maybe she'll go on her own accord."

I helped Brian unload his car and settle into the spare room. "I've got to get back to work. After you drop me off, get a paper and check the want ads. We'll party tonight."

He hugged me and gave me a kiss on the forehead. "I've missed your organization!"

Within a week, Ramona was packing her belongings and moving to another apartment. Brian and I seemed to charge one another with energy. We went out drinking together every night.

Within the first week I threw a party to celebrate Brian's return and new job. Steven arrived with a sandy-haired, muscular man about my age who was a prison guard at Soledad Prison. All evening I was captivated by Roy's stories of prison life.

"Would you like to write to a prisoner?" he asked me. "I have a friend who is a lifer. He's in for murder one and will probably serve five more years at least. He's nonviolent, straight, but he has a good head."

"Sure, I'll write. What's his name?"

"Toby Jackson. I'll let him know about you. He'll write first."

It was fun writing to a convict. I found out he had served twelve years already. I wrote weekly and discussed my homosexuality openly. "I'll be anything you want on paper," I told him. "But I live with women."

Toby was curious to meet me in person. I planned a trip to visit him, and immediately we became tight friends. The visit resulted in a plan to smuggle drugs to Toby, who would sell and bargain for profit on the inside. He would get cash to me through the underground, and I would increase my purchases each visit.

It didn't take long to overcome any protests from my conscience, and I justified it by reasoning that prisoners needed drugs for diversion. So Toby and I became frequent visitors. It was exciting to beat the drug regulations and reminded me of my nighttime adventures with Bubba back in Oakland.

Twice a month I drove to Soledad and played the role of girl friend as we transferred the drugs to various inmates in the visiting room. Our letters were frequent to build the illusion of a deepening emotional involvement. Then I learned from Roy that someone had tipped off the warden, and I was a prime suspect in the drug smuggling. I visited Toby that weekend but went clean.

Toby was furious that someone went to the warden and vowed to find out who it was. Then I watched his anger fade, and a strange look cross his face.

"Honey, I don't want you ever taking chances for me. I know you have your life on the outs, but you're pretty special to me. I've been thinking about you a lot. We could get married, and you could still do your thing with women."

"You're kidding! I can't marry you. I'm your lover on paper, but that's it."

"Hey, I'm a lifer! We could have a trailer visit every couple of months and. . . ."

"Sorry, Toby. It'll never work. I dig women *all* the time!" I got up and started walking toward the patio.

Toby caught up and took my hand. "All right, just thought I'd ask."

Suddenly I was aware of several guards starting toward us, trying to look routine. I clasped Toby's hand and laughed under my breath. "This is one time they can check me out. I'm so clean I squeak!"

We were watched closely the rest of the visit. I left early, happy not to pursue the marriage idea any longer.

Brian was home when I arrived. I told him about the guards and the marriage proposal.

"We make a better couple than you two," he said. "I can keep house, and you can pay the rent."

"Oh, sure," I laughed. "Wouldn't we make a pair!"

Then the same idea occurred to us at the same time. "Let's really do it!"

Within a few days, plans were almost completed for a trip to Reno. I took off two days for my marriage plans and kept the women at the plant wondering what the real story was.

Joanne was horrified. "Darlene, how can you do this? You might not be living like it, but you're a Christian. You're making a mockery out of something sacred!"

"It's not that big of a deal," I retorted. "It's not a real marriage, just some words on a piece of paper for our convenience."

Inside, however, it was a big deal. I knew the ordinance of marriage was sacred and felt guilty when I thought about God's plan for men and women. Maybe I would just forge the signatures on the license and *tell* people we got married. I seemed to be riding a merry-go-round of fantasy, acting out every thought that entered my mind, helpless to stop myself no matter what the consequences. Though I had been killing my conscience by degrees for years, I knew something important had died with Dad, and I had no idea how to find a new reason to live.

Joanne cried freely. "You're going to ruin your life!"

"Does this mean you won't come to our reception?" I tried to make her laugh, uncomfortable at her display of emotion.

"I won't be a party to this in any way. Please change your mind, Darlene. Please!"

"Can't. I don't have any vacation left and I want to go gamble." I turned and left the room to cover my feelings of guilt.

God doesn't count! And so what if she won't come to my reception. I don't need Christians there to spoil my fun. I ignored the memory of Joanne's pleading—and tears.

On the trip to Reno, Brian and I talked about notifying his parents and my family.

"We could just tell people we got married and not really do it," I suggested. "I could forge the signatures."

"No." He was firm. "I want it to be legal. It makes no difference as far as our relationship goes, but I want the paper to be legal."

Nervous excitement grew as we found the courthouse and became Mr. and Mrs. Mainer. Why was I so nervous? I was thirty-one and this was just a charade even with the license, matching rings, and the right words sealed with a kiss in front of two witnesses. At my age I didn't need anyone's approval, but deep inside I knew I didn't even have *my* approval or God's. Why was I doing this?

"Just don't get any funny ideas about *really* being my husband, Brian." I jabbed him playfully in the ribs. "You might be bisexual, but I'm not. Let's call your folks, then party!" I ignored my discomfort.

"Whatever you say, Mrs. Mainer."

I laughed. It sounded strange to be called Mrs. even though I had decided to keep my maiden name and was not legally Mrs. Mainer at all.

Somehow we made it back to Monterey. On Monday morning everyone at work was waiting to hear if I had really gotten married. I waltzed through the office with marriage license in hand and invited everyone to a reception Friday night at the condominium. Only Joanne avoided me.

We had all the right props the night of our reception: the

cake, the guest book, affectionate hugs for the photographer, and plenty of champagne. Brian wore a new shirt and pants outfit, and I wore white jeans, a white turtleneck, and a black vest.

People came because of curiosity more than devotion. We snickered as people toured the house and commented about the use of two bedrooms. I collected the gifts and stacked them in a corner.

After several glasses of champagne, I made an announcement: "Ladies and gentlemen, Brian and I want you to know you're welcome in our house anytime. Our marriage is unusual. Some of you know and most of you have guessed that we're both gay. I don't think society should discriminate against us as far as taxes and social acceptance. We've beat the system! Our friendship became a marriage, and we welcome you to be part of our lives."

Applause filled the room. A co-worker stood. "I propose a toast to Mr. & Mrs. Brian Mainer. They have more guts than anyone I know!"

The next three months were filled with a succession of similar parties and nameless faces that spent the night in Brian's room. I grew increasingly concerned about the safety of my belongings and who might wander into my room at night.

"Brian, I'd like some new rules for this household," I said one evening. "I don't want strangers in the house at night. If you're going to turn a trick, I want you to go to their place."

"That's not always possible," he said defiantly. "It's my house too."

"Right! But almost everything here is mine. I don't want any more strange people here. I need a place to feel secure."

"All right," he muttered. He walked out the door, slamming it behind him.

Brian began avoiding me, coming home only to change clothes. When we met at the bar, we were friendly but cool. The thought of divorce crossed my mind.

One Saturday morning Brian knocked on my bedroom door. "Can we talk?" he asked.

I opened the door. "Sure, come in. What's on your mind?"

"A couple of things. Are you mad at me?"

"Not really. I just can't take a steady flow of traffic. I notice you seem to be settling down these days."

"I met this neat guy. He wants me to move to Los Angeles with him. I'd like to, but what if Mom called?"

"Well, you could just leave me a number. If she called, I'd say you were out and would call her back. That's no problem." *Maybe I can get him to agree to a divorce.*

"Would you really do that? I thought you'd be glad to get rid of me."

I tapped him on the shoulder with my fist. "You're my hubby! I wouldn't desert you." I paused. "You know, though, if you're in L.A., perhaps we should make one change. You're still legally responsible for my debts."

"Yeah?" He looked puzzled.

"Well, we could get a divorce and not tell anyone. Legally, you wouldn't have to pay my debts, but as far as the world is concerned we're still married." I held my breath.

He looked thoughtful. "Can you do the paperwork?"

"I think so. I can get a book about how to do it. I'll pay for it."

"All right. I don't want Mom and Dad to find out though."

"Great!" I hugged him. "When do I get to meet your new friend?"

"He's a salesman from San Jose. He said he'd meet me at the bar later today."

"May I join you?"

"Of course."

But Erick didn't come that night, so Brian spent the evening with a stranger at a corner table. I spent the evening shooting pool and listening to some troubling news. A homosexual we all knew had been murdered the night before by a bisexual he had taken home as a trick. It was the third death in the gay community that month.

It didn't make me any happier when, at "last call" around 2 A.M., I strolled over and discovered Brian's plans for the night.

"Are you going home or what?" I asked, eyeing his companion.

"Darlene, this is Roger."

"Hi. How you doing?" I extended my hand.

"All right." He giggled as he tried to stand, and slipped off the chair. Brian helped him to his feet.

"I think we're going out for a bite to eat. I'll drive Roger's car and be home later." He tried to support his obviously intoxicated friend.

"All right. Just be careful!" I watched them leave, hesitated, then walked to my truck. *Wonder what happened to Erick? I'll be glad when I'm not legally responsible for Brian! He'll never learn.*

Our charade would become more complicated. Although we would not be married legally, we would still pretend that we were. If anyone saw it in the paper, we agreed to admit we were divorced; otherwise, it would be our secret.

I did the paperwork and filed it with the court. A mutual friend served Brian the papers. We had been married just over three months, and it would be six months before the marriage would be legally terminated.

I wrote to Brian's parents weekly, sending pictures and making all the right small talk. After one call from his mother, I commented, "Brian, our lives should be a soap opera!"

He grinned. "This star is about to leave the show. Erick has told me he has to be more discreet while he lives in Monterey. But next month we're moving to Los Angeles, where he'll feel freer to visit the gay bars. It should be one big party." He laughed. "Maybe Hollywood will discover me yet!"

15.
My New
Wife

One night I went out drinking to celebrate my upcoming freedom. The bar was filled with members of the girls' county softball team. I walked over to talk to a couple of women I knew.

Suddenly I noticed a woman I didn't know, sitting next to my friend Liz. She was tall and slender with short, brown curly hair. "Hello," I greeted Liz as I gazed at the new woman. She had sparkling brown eyes and a soft, seductive half-smile. "Who is your friend?"

"Hi, Darlene. This is Rebecca. She's new to the team."

I sat down at their booth. "Hi Rebecca. Do you shoot pool?"

"No, but I'm willing to learn." She scooted out of the booth and followed me across the room to an empty table.

I picked up a pool cue and leaned against the table. "So tell me about yourself. Where did you come from, and why haven't I seen you before?"

Her tone was low, almost secretive. "I've been here a few months from southern California. I've seen you before, but you were always with someone. My son and I are making a new home for ourselves."

"Your son? How old?"

Randy is five. I've been divorced almost three years." She picked up a pool stick. Now, how do you play this game?"

I talked as I racked the balls. "How old are you?"

"Twenty-four. Is that all right?" She was smiling again.

"Yeah, that's all right. It sounds like you've had a rough time."

She leaned closer. "He abused the baby and knocked me around one time too many. I decided I was better off without him."

"I'm sorry."

Turning back to the pool table, I gave her some instructions. I watched her graceful movements. She had a naïveté that was missing in most of the women who frequented the bar. I was overwhelmed with emotion. I wanted to preserve her innocence and take care of her and Randy yet I had only just met her! I always struggled to find that "perfect" relationship, the person who would love me not reject me.

She's the right one I thought. It could work with her. I know it could!

I kept my thoughts to myself as we played several games. I quizzed her about her background. Then I noticed Liz looking our way.

"Say, I know you came with someone else tonight," I said, "but could I have your phone number and call you tomorrow?"

She spoke seductively. "I was hoping you would ask."

I wrote her phone number on a napkin and stuck it in my wallet.

The next morning I reached for the phone even before I got out of bed. A child's voice answered after the second ring.

"Hi, Randy," I said. "Is your mother there?"

"Just a minute." The voice faded. "Mom, phone for you. I don't know who it is."

When I heard Rebecca's voice, a magical quality captivated me. I *knew* she was the right one.

"Hi. This is Darlene. I wondered if you'd like to go to the movies tonight." I held my breath, fearing she might say no. "You remember who I am, don't you?"

She laughed. "Of course I remember. I don't have a baby-sitter for tonight. We'd have to take Randy along."

"That's fine with me. Give me your address. I'll pick you up at 7:30."

I saw Rebecca that night and every night for a week. We decided to become roommates. I was on an emotional high when I burst through the front door of the condominium to tell Brian the good news. I stopped in midstride. Brian was in tears.

"What's wrong?"

"We broke up! I really loved him." Brian's voice broke. He cupped his face in his hands and his shoulders shook with compulsive sobs. Finally he wiped the tears away. "Erick wants to live by himself."

"I'm really sorry, Brian, I said, putting my arm around his shoulder. "It seemed so perfect. I was just coming to tell you I'm moving in with Rebecca. I've finally found the right wife."

"Well, I hope your plans work out better than mine," he said bitterly. "I don't know what to do now."

"You can keep this place. I'm paying the rent for another month so I can take my time moving."

He shook his head in despair. "I can't afford it. I'll have to find another place to live." Then he squared his shoulders and faced me. "Well, since I'm not going to L.A., I don't want a divorce. I just can't handle losing everything at once." He sighed. "You won't leave me, will you?"

My heart sank. "Oh, Brian, of course not! I'll cancel the paperwork."

My thoughts went wild. *At least, as far as you'll ever know. I'll hold your papers and just let it become final. If you ever inherit money, maybe you'll split it with me!* I could hardly believe my deceitfulness.

"Oh, there was a letter for you in today's mail." He reached on top of the refrigerator and handed me an envelope.

"Oh, good. It's from Marie!" I tore it open and read silently. My eyes smarted. "Mrs. Fuller always made me feel bad and good at the same time."

"What does she say?"

I scanned the letter. "She says she hasn't known how to respond to our marriage. She says she still loves me and will put you on her prayer list too and to give you a hug for her.

Then she adds that I'm still accountable for the truth that I know from the Bible and that if you don't know Jesus, it's my responsibility to tell you."

"Well, I'm glad she's praying for me. I need all the help I can get!" He smiled. "She sounds like a special person, Darlene. She must really love you."

"She does. I've counted on her love for a long time. Now I need to figure out how to tell her about Rebecca and Randy. It's hard for her to keep track of my activities!"

"Maybe the less you tell her, the better."

"I've always been honest with her, Brian. No matter what, I won't ever change that." I paused. "Where will you go when the rent is due?"

"I'll check into a room downtown. Let's give my mom your number and make sure we call her frequently so she doesn't know we're not together."

"Sounds good. I'll tell Rebecca what to say if we get any calls. I feel like I'm leading several lives!"

I moved my belongings to Rebecca's two-bedroom apartment the next weekend. It was on the other side of town in a hilly area bordering Carmel. The ocean was now a late-night background sound rather than a three-block jaunt.

The first week I was there, Randy was sick every night. He came into our room during the night and would be comforted only by falling asleep in Rebecca's arms. I thought he was feeling threatened because I occupied so much of Rebecca's time. I allowed him to stay, hoping to reassure him.

When I decided to sell the Cadillac and the blue truck to buy a new white Datsun King Cab truck, Randy helped Rebecca and me pick out a fancy camper shell with carpeting, shelves, and a bed. It was the first brand-new vehicle I had purchased, and Randy was elated that he could help.

"I want to make sure we do things that include Randy," I told Rebecca. "Now we can go on weekend trips to the mountains or to the beach. We're a family and I want him to know that."

"I attend a lesbian mother's group that has activities for couples with children. We can check that out."

I was intrigued. "Do they teach kids to grow up gay?"

She laughed. "No, they just have activities where you can do things as family units and get counseling if the kids want to discuss their sexuality."

"From all the women I've known, their kids usually grow up gay or with a lot of problems adjusting to their sexual roles."

"That's why there's counseling. They're given the facts, and if they want to pursue that lifestyle, they are encouraged to do so. No one is forced into being straight or gay."

"And what about Randy?"

"I think he already has gay tendencies. He has no male role models, and I certainly wouldn't trust him with any gay men!"

"I agree. He's only five, but I know too many chicken hawks to let him out of our sight."

"I can't stand straight men either. I won't let him spend time with his father. He was violent and mean. Randy is a gentle, sensitive boy, and I don't care if he grows up gay. I just want him to be caring."

"And I want him to know we both love him. He's the son I never had."

That summer was an endless succession of camping trips to the mountains, visits to the zoo, and a week-long trip to Southern California to visit Disneyland. My love for Randy could not have been more real if he had been my very own. Rebecca suggested I make time to do things alone with him, and I readily agreed. Then I found out her real motive.

Rebecca wanted Saturday nights to be her one night *away* from Randy and me. She was tired of "playing mother," and now that she had someone she could trust, she turned that responsibility over to me. Her lack of parenting began to trigger memories of my own neglected childhood. Late one night about six months after I moved in, I telephoned the bar to talk to her.

"Rebecca, I want you to come home."

"This is my only night out! Why don't you come down for a couple of drinks?"

"I'm not leaving Randy alone. He could wake up and be scared, or a fire could start. I want you to get home now. I'm not your built-in baby-sitter."

I could hardly hear her voice above the noise of the bar. "I don't want to come home from the office and spend time only with you, Darlene. I need more people in my life. You can't meet all my needs."

I was stunned. "What do you mean by that?" I screamed. "It sounds like you're saying you want out."

"No, I don't want out! Just calm down. I'll come home and we can talk." She hung up the phone.

She can't leave me! I won't let her. I paced in the front room, puffing on a cigarette. Minutes passed. Then I heard her Volkswagen outside the house. I opened the front door and positioned myself, hands on hips. "You want to explain why I'm not enough?" I challenged her as she came closer to the door.

"You know how I am, Darlene. It's not that I don't want a family, I do. I also want the freedom to come and go ... to spend time with other women." She slipped through the doorway and kicked the door shut. "Let's not have the neighbors listen to this."

I shook my head. "I know I'm older, Rebecca, but to me a relationship is a commitment to one person. Either you want me or you want someone else. It's that simple."

"Please hear me out! If I promise not to be sexually involved with anyone, why can't you let me have one night out without you?"

"How can I trust you not to sleep with someone else? I can't handle the thought of you with anyone else." *I love you too much! I'll do anything to keep you.* My inner conflict raged. *This is my last relationship! If it doesn't work, I'll kill myself!*

Our argument continued into early morning, ending only

when I promised to try not to be jealous and to give her one night out away from me. My underlying tension was pushed away but not forgotten.

To attempt to satisfy Rebecca's sensual desires, we subscribed to *Penthouse* and other pornographic magazines. We built a library of sexual books, records, and movies to feed our appetite. The more we tried to satisfy our lust, the more lust we seemed to have. We tried every sexual act we read about or viewed on the screen, never satisfying the lust only arousing deeper cravings. Our bedroom wall was a mural of lesbian centerfolds. I acquired photo albums of Polaroid pictures from our sexual orgies with free-thinking friends. Whatever our minds imagined, we experienced, and often Randy was allowed to sleep in the room. I hated exposing him to sexual activity, but Rebecca wanted to be "free" and have him comfortable with touching and other expressions of affection. I began to drink more and smoke a few joints before we went to bed. I couldn't handle the influence we were making on this six-year-old life, but Rebecca insisted.

Then something snapped. My body went along with everything Rebecca suggested during these times, but I found myself able to step outside my body and float to the ceiling. I viewed the events like watching a movie, except I was one of the actors. I could leave my body at will and return, convinced that the real me had not been involved with influencing Randy. Astral projection was my thin lifeline to sanity.

One evening I came home from the plant and heard children's voices coming from our bedroom. "How come they're all ladies?"

"Cause Mom and Dar like them." Giggles.

I cleared my throat and made heavy footsteps across the wooden floor.

"Let's get out of here!" Three neighborhood boys tore out of the room with Randy trailing.

"What are you boys doing?" I asked.

"Nothing, Dar. I was just showing them the pictures on our wall."

"You were, huh? You boys go on home. Randy, we need to talk."

The boys ran out the door. "Are you mad?" asked Randy. "I'm sorry, I won't do it again." He cowered just out of reach.

"Hey, don't be upset, son. I'm not mad." I walked over and scooped him into my arms. "You need to understand that those boys' moms might not like them looking at pictures like that. What we let you do is one thing, but don't you bring kids into our room anymore. All right?" I gritted my teeth. Rebecca had to make him part of our sex life!

"O.K., Dar." He relaxed and hugged me. "I'm glad you're not mad. Can I go play?"

"Sure." I swung him to the floor. "Be home in an hour."

I flipped on the television just as the phone rang.

"Hi love. It's me." Brian's high-pitched voice was cheery. "How are things?"

"All right. What's up?" I lit a cigarette.

"Well, I have a request. How would you like to play Mrs. Mainer for the benefit of my parents?"

"Are they coming out?"

"No. Mom wants us to come for her birthday in two weeks. She wants to throw us a belated reception."

"We would deserve an Academy Award for that production! Well, I've never been to Michigan. Why not?"

"You'll do it?"

"Sure, tell your mom we'll be there." I turned to see Rebecca in the doorway.

"Be where?" she asked as I hung up.

"We're going to Michigan for a few days with Brian's parents. I need a vacation, and they want to give us a reception."

"While you're off playing wife, do I get to play here?"

My stomach lurched. "I don't want you to. But being two thousand miles away, I can't stop you. Just don't tell me."

"I was only joking. Where's Randy?"

"Outside." I related the event with the neighbor boys.

"Just what we need," she responded. "I hope they don't tell their mothers. We'd get arrested for corrupting minors."

"I didn't think you were concerned about corrupting anyone," I said caustically.

"They have to be the age of consent, at least!"

"Is Randy?"

"That's different," she snapped. "He's my son!"

"All right. Let's drop it. I'll put a lock on the door so it doesn't happen again."

Now I insisted that Randy sleep in his own room and that we be more selective in our display of affection. But fear had my stomach tied in knots when it was time to leave for Michigan. *Would Rebecca go out with someone while I was gone?* She drove Brian and me to the airport.

"I'll miss you," I whispered, freely embracing her. *Please don't hurt me.* I turned quickly; Brian and I strode into the terminal to play Mr. and Mrs. Mainer. I had changed my hairstyle to soft curls for the occasion and brought what few women's slacks and blouses I had in my closet.

Six hours later we walked into the welcoming arms of a short, pudgy woman with graying hair. Silver-framed glasses magnified bright blue eyes. "You're just as I pictured!" she bubbled.

Brian's dad was a tall, outdoors type. A deep tan crept into his receding hairline. Blue eyes sparkled along with his lopsided grin. "Welcome home!" He draped his arm around my shoulder and squeezed lightly.

The next five days were a three-ring circus of aunts, uncles, cousins, and friends from the small country town. We played the devoted newlyweds in public and snickered privately at our successful deception. At the end of the week, we left empty promises of future grandchildren and brought gifts home to divide.

Rebecca met us at the airport. Too anxious to talk much about our week, I asked the question foremost on my mind. "Did you go out with anyone while I was gone?" I held my breath. *Please say no.!*

"I went to the bar a couple of times but not with anyone special." She seemed to be hedging.

"Did you come home alone?" I asked accusingly.

"I thought you didn't want to know."

My heart sank. "You just answered my question."

We rode in silence the rest of the trip home.

As the weeks slipped into months, there was a growing deadness inside me. How could I have lived almost thirty-two years and be so insecure? The tighter I held her, the farther away she felt! I needed to give her space. Then I thought of a solution.

"One of the guys at work just got a second job two nights a week," I commented over dinner. "It's at a Thriftway Mart across town. I'm thinking of applying there too. It would give us time apart and extra money for a special vacation."

"Would you work weekends?" Rebecca asked. "We'd never be able to leave town if you did."

"I'll check into it tomorrow and see what's available."

The store hired me immediately for two nights a week from six until two. Rebecca was happy. My two nights away provided more money for us and more freedom for her.

There was another advantage I hadn't considered. It was convenient for Rebecca to stop by the store and pick up whatever we needed at home. I was the only clerk on duty and could bag up whatever we needed at no cost.

The weeks and months rolled by while I saved my extra paychecks for a cross-country vacation. Our unresolved conflicts, my jealousy and her restlessness, were put on hold, while a plot began to unfold that would eventually prove my undoing.

16.
Grand Theft
and Murder

When Bubba left his wife, he needed a place to stay for a while.

"Your brother isn't going to live with us," Rebecca protested. "We wouldn't have any privacy, and he's straight."

"He knows we're gay, honey, and it's no problem. We keep our door closed anyway because of Randy. Besides it won't be forever just until Bubba finds a job."

"This is just a two-bedroom apartment, and I don't want a man living here!" she yelled.

"That man is my brother, and I won't leave him out in the street. He stays."

Rebecca was cool toward Bubba when he arrived a few days later. "It's just temporary until he's on his feet," I reassured her. "Shouldn't be more than month. Just be yourself and don't worry about Bubba. I'll make sure he understands our need for privacy."

Within the week, Bubba had a job working with Brian at the hospital. He came home only to sleep on the sofa and pay his share of the rent and food when his paycheck came each week. Rebecca stopped complaining about another person sharing our place. When I found a nice three-bedroom house for a reasonable rent nearer to downtown Carmel, we moved two weeks later.

My second job expanded to four nights a week, and my boss approached me about working Saturdays from six in the morning till one in the afternoon. The hours would have exhausted me, except I found the material benefits exhilarating.

During the months of working at Thriftway, I had devised numerous ways to embezzle money and rip off merchandise. All our booze, paper products, and cigarettes were free. Bubba or Rebecca would come in right before closing and pick up what we needed. And because I could pick the lock to the floor safe, my shift was always balanced to the penny while other shifts came up short.

One Saturday morning I arrived at 5:30. I scanned the building, then read the store log from the night shift in which Tommy, the clerk on duty, reported an unknown male who had entered the store while he was stocking the cold room and then sped off without payment. I folded the log and started to place it along the magazine rack behind the counter when I noticed a brown paper bag on the floor in the corner. I reached down and opened it. I became flushed and light-headed when I saw a stack of green bills and several rolls of coins.

The tag was initialed by Jim. That meant this was yesterday's money and had been here all night! Jim had apparently forgotten to put it in the safe, and Tommy must not have seen it. His entry into the log the night before would be the perfect alibi for the disappearance of the money.

I flipped through the stack of bills again. There was well over a thousand dollars. I bundled the sack quickly with rubberbands and stowed it under the driver's seat of my truck. It was time to open. If I could get the money home, they would never catch me.

The morning dragged. Then, with about an hour remaining on the shift, Jim came in to complete the week's paper work. He started with the night shifts. I held my breath each time he came near the safe. The minutes ticked by, and my heart pounded harder. Then the gas truck arrived with a delivery and took Jim away from the books. I breathed a sigh of relief. I finished my work and balanced out, dropping my cash on the desk for Jim to prepare with the deposit.

Fighting the urge to run, I strode casually toward my truck. *Once I get this money home, they can never prove a thing!*

I pulled into the driveway and ran into the house squealing with laughter. "I did it! I did it!"

Rebecca appeared in the kitchen doorway. "Did what?"

I dumped the bag on the sofa, and money flew everywhere. "Ripped them off!"

"Where did you get that?" she gasped.

I explained, then started collecting the money efficiently. "Separate all the checks," I said. "I'll burn those in the sink, and let's get these food stamps hidden. I don't want anything that can connect this money to the store."

I took several stacks of bills and hid them around the house. "There are too many one dollar bills. I'm going shopping at a couple of stores and get rid of them. Be back in an hour." I breezed out the door and was gone before she could object.

When I returned, Rebecca's face was ashen. "Your boss called. He wants you to call immediately. Why did you do it?"

"You're asking *me* why? You and Randy have everything you need, and we go on trips every weekend that I'm not working. That all takes money! Relax Rebecca. They'll never catch me. I could lie my way out of jail if I had to."

I could hardly believe how callous I had become. Even knowing that Scripture says thieves and liars have no part in the kingdom of God didn't phase me. My conscience seemed petrified.

"I'm missing some money," Jim told me when I called. "Did you see a paper bag when you opened this morning?"

"No. Where was it?"

"I think I left it behind the counter." His voice broke with emotion. "I've got to find it! There was over a grand from my day shift."

"Wow," I whistled. "Have you checked with Tommy? He worked last night."

"I'll try him next. If I can't find it, we'll all have to take lie detector tests."

"It'll turn up. Tommy probably put it someplace safe." I tried to sound encouraging. When I hung up, I was relieved. I rationalized that Jim deserved to lose the money because he left it out. Besides, the store overcharged people every time a product was sold. Thieves got caught only when they kept guilt inside. I intended neither to feel guilty nor get caught.

Tommy had not set the money "someplace safe," and we were all required to show up for a polygraph test the following day. I arrived on time with no feelings of fear or remorse. The questions were direct once I was hooked to the machine.

"Have you ever stolen anything from the store?"

"No."

"Did you take the money?"

"No."

"Do you know who did?"

"No."

The test took fifteen minutes. Several questions were repeated. My graph was steady across the board.

"At least I know who didn't do it." The officer smiled as he unhooked the machine.

I laughed under my breath. "I hope you find out who did, sir. This machine should do it."

I walked out with top grades for honesty while Tommy, Jim, and one other clerk were all fired.

I decided to change my work schedule and keep weekends free to spend more time with Rebecca and Randy. After nearly two years, I was afraid we were drifting apart. We busied ourselves with activities in the gay community. San Francisco was preparing for their annual Gay Parade, and Rebecca wanted us all to attend as a family this year.

It was impossible to find parking within a mile of the starting place. I parked near the end of the route. We pushed our way through the masses of people who lined the streets for the well-publicized march. I hoisted Randy to my shoulders to keep him from being stepped on.

"I've never seen so many homosexuals in one place," I whispered.

Decorative floats bore signs from all major California cities and a few from out-of-state. Men in full drag, decked out in miniskirts and heels, were being escorted by lesbians in tuxedos. The parade also included clowns on roller skates, "Dykes on Bikes" displaying nude bodies on motorcycles, disco dancers wearing only body paint, and two gay city supervisors to represent the political stratum.

When I noticed some straights mingling and passing out tracts, Rebecca poked me in the ribs. "Wouldn't you just know the Jesus freaks would show up?"

But something about the parade troubled me. "It's a good mission field," I said curtly. I watched the straights move through the crowd, talking with anyone who would listen. I was a long way from my days with Teen Challenge. For a fleeting moment the longing for peace almost overwhelmed me. *Why were God and I never on the same wavelength?*

"Hey, I was only joking. Don't take it personally."

"Some things are serious, Rebecca. Let's drop it. I don't need a fight today." I pushed forward in the crowd, but my mind could not quite shake the memory of when I was right with God. It seemed like a lifetime ago. Although I was only thirty-two, today I felt old, very old.

We were almost at the starting point. Policemen had set up blockades allowing only pedestrian traffic. Television cameras captured footage of more than a hundred thousand homosexuals. Men walked arm in arm. T-shirts read *I'm His* with arrows pointing to the partner. Signs danced in the air above the heads of the crowd. *Gay Rights Are Human Rights* and *Say It Far: Say It Loud, We Are Gay and We Are Proud!*

We passed two twenty-foot banners, *Lesbian Mothers for Freedom* and *Gay Democrats for Gay Rights.*

Each of the more than fifty gay bars in San Francisco decked a float with its name and the clientele to whom they catered.

Rebecca turned to me. "Who do you want to march with?"

"I don't know. Lesbian mothers, I guess. We really don't have to be with anyone."

"We could ride on that one." She pointed to a large, twenty-foot float made into the image of a church. An open Bible of flowers was spread across the front. Two verses, "Thou shalt love thy neighbor" and "Thou shalt not judge," were written in dark flowers. A banner waving from the top read *Metropolitan Community Church—Everyone welcome.*

"Don't you want to ride on it?" Rebecca persisted. "You're religious. It's right down our alley."

My face flushed. "I don't want anything to do with that float. I won't even walk near it. It's a mockery! They took those Bible verses out of context." I felt I had been slapped in the face with the deception of our lifestyle and turned away, hoping Rebecca wouldn't notice my conflict. We joined the lesbian mothers.

The parade lasted more than three hours. Booze flowed freely; couples hugged, kissed, and performed for the onlookers and the cameras. The last float had an effigy of Anita Bryant, the well-known Christian crusader against homosexuality, hanging by the neck. The effigy was set ablaze as the parade ended while the crowd yelled, chanted, and sang into the cameras of the newsmen. I felt sick to my stomach.

My time with Rebecca and Randy decreased as I began to work more hours at the store. My recent promotion to shift supervisor at the electronics plant provided an adequate income for us, but the month-long vacation that Rebecca wanted would require several thousand dollars extra in savings.

I was working one Friday evening when Brian came by the store.

"What's going on with you and Rebecca?" he asked.

"What do you mean?"

"I just saw her down at the bar with some woman named Jan. They were hanging all over each other. I thought you two broke up or something."

The heat rose to my cheeks. "I hate it when Rebecca leaves Randy alone at night. He must be alone now. And she must think I'll never find out that she's at the bar."

"I love you too much to see you hurt, Dar." He gave me a hug. "I have a favor to ask, which is the other reason I came."

"What's that?"

"I owe some money for some dope. Can you help me?"

"I don't have much on me." I hesitated. "I could borrow from my savings."

"I have a better idea." He leaned over the counter. "We could fake a robbery here—tonight!"

I giggled. "On one condition. You split the take with me. I'll meet you at the bar right before closing."

"It's a deal!" He reached out and clasped my hand.

I opened the register and put the money in a small bag. "Get out of here. I'll call the police and report it in about five minutes."

Brian grinned. "We're some team, Mrs. Mainer!"

If you only knew. You're a divorced man.

Minutes after I phoned the police with a description of a black man carrying a gun, patrol cars lined up outside with flashing lights. I called Mr. Whirtley, the regional manager of Thriftway Mart, who arrived just after the police.

"The description matches one from several robberies this past month," the officer said. "You're lucky. He shot the last clerk."

We balanced out the register. "He got around seven hundred," Mr. Whirtley told the officer. Then he turned to me. "Are you going to be all right?"

"I guess. I'm really trembling inside. I've never looked down the barrel of a gun before."

"Let's close early. I'll help you with the paperwork."

We finished in about fifteen minutes. I drove to the lesbian bar looking for Rebecca. Her car was parked behind, but she wasn't inside. No one seemed to know where she was. So I drove to the men's bar and met with Brian in a booth.

"I divided the money in half," he said slipping me a stack of bills and some rolled coins. "Thanks, Darlene. It pulls me out of a mess."

"Any time," I smiled, lifting my drink in a toast. "I'm not going to tell Rebecca about this money. *This* is mine to spend as I please."

At that moment Rebecca walked toward us. "Hi. I heard you were in the bar looking for me. You get off early?"

"Uh-huh. Where were you? Is anyone with Randy?"

She avoided my second question. "I went out for pizza with some of the girls."

"Are you heading home now?" I gritted my teeth. *You're lying.*

"I don't have my car. I'll go back to the bar until closing, then be home."

I took a long draught of beer. "I think we need to talk when you get home."

"All right." She turned without further comment and left.

I left soon after she did and drove home, where I alternated between watching the late show and the wall clock. Bubba wasn't home, and all was quiet from Randy's room. I paced the floor, trying to separate my concern for his mother from my anger. A growing pile of cigarette butts betrayed my anxiety. I dozed as the movies changed from night owl to early morning. Then I heard the Volkswagen engine in the driveway.

I flung open the door. "Did you enjoy yourself?"

"As a matter of fact, I did!" She shoved past me into the front room.

Our angry voices broke the early morning stillness. "I'm not accountable to you!" she yelled as she ran into the bathroom and locked the door.

I bounded after her, ordering, "Open this door or I'll break it down." Without waiting for a reply, I kicked full-force with my boot. The door splintered.

Suddenly Randy was in the hall, crying as he watched the scene. I turned.

"Hey there, what are these tears for?" I wiped them away with my sleeve and spoke soothingly to him.

"You and Mama are hurting each other," he sobbed.

"It's all right," I crooned, patting his back. How I hated myself when I got violent! It was bad enough that I had allowed the child to witness our sexual behavior without having him be afraid of me too.

I kept my voice firm but controlled. "Rebecca, come out here and let your son know you're all right. I stood up and grabbed my jacket. "I'm leaving."

I drove down the Pacific coast for over an hour. Finally I parked and walked along a secluded section of beach. The waves smashed against the rocks like my succession of "forever" relationships.

Apparently I cared for Rebecca too much. I couldn't let her leave me. Nor could I go on living like this. Every relationship I had had was destroyed. Where was God? I never had been able to love Him right either or find from Him the love that I sought so desperately.

Late the following day, Saturday, I decided to move into the spare room. Bubba and Randy had been sharing the large second bedroom so we could use the smaller one in the back for storage. On impulse I stopped by a furniture store and bought a new twin bed. Groaning under the weight of the box spring, I maneuvered it through the house to the back bedroom.

Rebecca sat at the kitchen table. "What's that for? Are we having company?"

I rested the load against the doorjamb. "I'm moving into this bedroom and I wanted a new bed."

A puzzled expression lined her face. "Are you sleeping with someone else now?"

"No such luck," I retorted. "Actually, I'm still hoping that we can put our relationship back together. But I know I can't keep sleeping in the same bed. I haven't learned to share my lover with half the town." I picked up the box spring and moved it into the bedroom.

Rebecca followed. "You're not sharing me with half the town. You know I love you more than anyone else. I just need more than you can give me."

I arranged the frame supports, avoiding direct eye contact. "Even one other person is too many!"

I pushed past Rebecca to bring in the top mattress from the truck. She reached out and grabbed my arm. "We need to talk about last night."

I pried her fingers from my arm. "Talking won't solve the problem. When my friends come to tell me you're out running around on me, the time for talking is over." I raised my voice. "And just for the record, you tell your new friends if I ever catch them with you or in my house, I'll kill them." I pulled away and went after the mattress.

Moments later I lugged it into the bedroom, collapsing in a heap on the bare mattress. Rebecca had apparently gone into her room. Did I have the strength to stay away from her? I wanted to kill her for being with someone else.

My thoughts were interrupted by a loud knocking on the front door. *Rebecca can get it!* I lay with my eyes closed. Rational thoughts tumbled with irrational emotions of love-hate for my lesbian wife of two years. *This was supposed to last forever! I can't live without her, and I don't want to live with her.*

"It's for you." Rebecca's head popped through the door-way. "It's your drag-queen husband!"

I walked into the front room. Brian was standing just inside the door. He shifted his weight nervously from side to side. His six-foot-two frame was hunched forward as he lifted the shade and checked outside. He tried the lock on the door, confirming it was secured.

"Who are you running from now?" I asked curiously.

"Oh, hi." He walked over and kissed me on the cheek. "You got a couple of minutes to talk?" He glanced at Rebecca standing in the doorway, her arms folded across her chest.

"Sure, Brian." I moved toward the couch. "What's happening?"

"Uh . . . can we talk privately?"

"Don't worry about me!" Rebecca stomped into her bedroom and slammed the door.

I smiled. "Come on." I nodded toward the back bedroom.

Brian was right on my heels. "You still fighting?" he whispered.

"Yes, but that's nothing new. Actually, I think things are about to end. I'm moving into this room until I get my head together." I clenched my teeth to stop the heat of anger rising to my face. "I went through her drawer last night and read her journal. She's been planning for months to get me so mad that I'll leave. I might have, if I hadn't found the journal. She and Randy need a place to live, but I'd die before I'd move out and let Jan move into my house with my family!"

"Good for you." Brian's strong arm dropped around my shoulder protectively. "It's about time you stopped letting her take advantage of you." He pulled a cigarette from his coat pocket, offered me one, and glanced nervously out the window.

"Thanks." I leaned against the wall. "Hey, what's making you so paranoid?"

"Can she hear?" He pointed through the wall toward Rebecca. "She's always resented me because you and I are married."

"It's not just you. She hates all men. It's only a few short years until Randy will be a man, so I guess she'll hate her son too. Anyway, if we talk low, she can't hear. What's the secret?"

Brian took a long drag before he began. "Well, you know that I'm into some big people for a lot of bucks."

"I know," I said as I sat on the bed. "But I can't help you right now. If Rebecca and I break up, I've got to pay all the bills here, and I have a year's lease."

"No, you don't understand." He joined me on the bed and tapped my knee. "In fact, this time I can help you."

I sat up straight. "How?"

"It's a business proposition." He moved closer and continued in a hoarse whisper. "I can make five grand but I need your help." His eyes locked mine.

"Five grand! What do you want to do—kill somebody?"

"Exactly."

I listened carefully as Brian outlined his act of revenge against a dealer who had burned him in a drug deal. "I'll cut you in a grand just to be my alibi for the night."

"I think I can handle that. I'm pretty good at convincing the police that I'm telling the truth. I beat the system, remember?"

"Of course I remember. Anyone who can pass a lie detector test can be on my team anytime!" Then his face grew serious. "I hope you and Rebecca can work things out, Darlene. You have made it longer than most couples in this lifestyle." His face brightened.

"I have a new lover each week!"

I patted his leg. "Well, don't try to convince me that you really want it that way. I know you'd like to settle down someday too."

He jumped to his feet. "Never happen. Want to come have a drink with me?"

"Sure. I stood and looked at the mess of bedding and clothing removed hastily from our bedroom. "This can wait. I need a break from her. It's my turn to stay out all night!"

17.
Who
Needs It?

Unlike Rebecca, I didn't enjoy being away from home all night. The bar had closed, and I had turned down several offers to go out to Sunday morning breakfast with the boys. I sat in my truck smoking a cigarette. *I wonder if Rebecca's home. I won't give in to her. No more orgies. No more one-night affairs with strangers. It's either me or nothing.* I started the engine and pulled out of the parking lot.

Rebecca's car was in the driveway when I arrived home. All the lights were off except the front porch. I fumbled for the house key and opened the door slowly. As I turned to close the door and bolt it, Rebecca's voice made me jump.

"Did you have a nice time?" she asked softly.

"Yeah. What are you doing sitting here in the dark?" I could barely see her form on the couch.

"I was waiting for you to come home." She switched on the hurricane lamp. "I've been doing a lot of thinking, Darlene, and I've decided that I want you more than anyone else. I don't know how I'll be able to handle it, but I'm willing to give it another try." She stood and walked over to where I was leaning against the door. "Are you?"

I shook my head to clear it. "That's a switch. I honestly don't know. You know I love Randy as if he were my own son. I've given you everything you wanted, and you say it's not enough. I don't know how much more hurt I can take." I lit a cigarette and took a long drag.

"I want us to be a family, Darlene. I know we can make it. I just need space to be me. I promise you I won't cheat on you again. If we can't work things out, then we'll split, but it won't be for another person."

"You really mean it?" My heart beat faster. "What about your new friend?"

"I called her tonight and told her it was over. I want to have a home, not just sex." She moved closer. "Want to give it another try?"

"You're my last chance. If it doesn't work with you, I'm checking out! Let's go for broke." We joined hands and walked toward the bedroom. "Well, we have a new bed for the guestroom! You can help me move my stuff back into our room tomorrow."

"I already have." She squeezed my hand.

I lay awake long after her deep breathing told me she was totally relaxed and asleep. Doubts and questions floated in my mind. Would any relationship work when it was a sin? Gay lovers and Christianity would never mix. So why do I keep on trying?

Several uneventful weeks passed as I worked at rebuilding our relationship. Bubba gave us plenty of time alone, staying out until after two each night and leaving for work before eight each morning. We replaced our nights out with house parties, hoping that time out of the bar would lessen our conflicts. Every night our house was full of women, listening to rock music, smoking dope, and telling fortunes with Tarot cards. The house reeked of incense and stale booze.

But Rebecca played seduction games with our house-guests, thinking I wouldn't notice. Finally one night I called her aside and ordered a halt to the party. "I'm going to the bar for a drink." I said icily. "When I come home, I want everyone out of my house."

"What do you mean, your house? It's my house too."

"Not for long. The only thing we've changed is the price of the drinks. I'm too angry to talk now, but tonight is the last house party. I'm not sure keeping you is worth the price." I picked up my jacket and left by the back door.

The bar was crowded with a lot of young faces I hadn't seen before. I ordered a drink, then moved to a bench in the rear to watch the pool games. A voice startled me.

"Hi. My name's Penny. Mind if I sit down?"

A shiny brass buckle sporting a large marajuana leaf greeted me. I looked up into the eyes of a short, stocky girl with curly black hair. Her blue-flowered man's shirt was tucked neatly into the waistband of her black jeans. She looked like me fifteen years ago. I nodded for her to have a seat.

"You alone?" she asked quietly.

"Yes. I'm Darlene. You hardly look old enough to be in here."

A grin told me I was right. "My I.D. says I am."

"So did mine before I was old enough." I watched her intently. "How long have you been gay?"

"All my life."

"That's a cop-out! Have you ever been with anyone?"

Her face flushed. "Not yet."

"Look, Penny, I'm going to tell you how gay life really is." I waved my hand around the room. "See these people? They're all empty. They come here searching for the perfect lover and spend years in bars only to wake up and discover they're alcoholics." My voice broke. "No matter how much you give to people, it's never enough. They'll find someone else. Possessions can't hold them, and love can't either. No one really knows what love is because God is love, and being gay is against God's love." I paused. "Gay love is temporary commitment, kid. There's no *right* relationship. You'll live to regret it, and if the booze and drugs don't kill you, you'll die of a broken heart."

"You sound bitter. Maybe you never found the right one. I'm not like everyone else," she added with a seductive smile.

"I said those same words myself. I've made so many compromises in the last fifteen years that I hate myself." I ordered another drink.

"Maybe things will be better tomorrow," she said softly. "You should stop drinking so much or you'll be sick in the morning."

I struggled to my feet. "It'll never get better. But you keep hoping it will. You go from lover to lover year after year, thinking this time it's right. It's all a lie. If I could talk you out of that first experience, I'd do it."

"Why don't you let me decide for myself?" She slipped her arm through mine. "Take me home?"

I reeled with the effects of the alcohol. Rebecca had probably gone out with one of her friends. "Are you old enough to drive? I'll leave my car here." I bought a six-pack and headed for the door. "Come on, kid. Maybe it's time you grew up."

We pulled into my driveway, and I opened a beer. I got out and leaned against the car, looking at the sky. Suddenly I remembered Barbara many years before. Could I now live with the guilt of bringing someone into gay life? "Do you know what, kid? No matter how much you drink, the hurting never stops." I downed the drink, then flung the bottle against the concrete wall at the end of the driveway. "Broken bottle, broken promises. That's the bottom line." I turned to face Penny, steadying myself on her arm.

Suddenly a dam burst deep inside me. I leaned my head against her shoulder and burst into racking sobs.

Penny put her arms around me and held me. "Go ahead and cry," she said quietly. "It'll be all right."

Several minutes later I regained composure, brushing the tears from my face. "I need to go to bed, kid. You get out of here. I hope to hell you never have that first experience."

"I'd like to stay," she persisted.

"No. Go home! I don't need one more thing to feel guilty about." I staggered to the door without looking back. Once inside, I passed out.

It was late afternoon when Rebecca returned home. I had called in sick that morning with what seemed like the flu, and now her footsteps on the porch awakened me. I leaned back on the couch and lit a cigarette. My stomach hurt, and my nerves quivered at the slightest movement.

Rebecca came in and sat in the chair across from me. "I'm sorry about last night, Darlene. I've really tried to do things your way. I just need more people in my life." She hesitated. "I'll be leaving for Oregon at the end of the month."

I shook my head to make sure I had heard right. "You're leaving me?"

"I have to, Darlene. I do love you, but we're no good together. This thing just isn't working."

Stunned, I stood up, supporting myself with the couch. "We'll talk later," I said and rushed to the bathroom to vomit.

I kept hoping in the next few days that if we didn't talk, somehow Rebecca's leaving would not be real. I had no alternative plan. I threw myself into work at both jobs and avoided a confrontation, still feeling ill physically as well as emotionally.

Then on a Tuesday morning, I began hemorrhaging. Scared, I went to the medical clinic for an examination. Dr. Swensen told me to call him the first of the week for the results.

Meanwhile, Rebecca was gone almost every night with Jan. My sense of isolation was overwhelming. It tore me up to realize she was out with someone else, even though I tried to convince myself that I could do better than her.

On Thursday morning just after I arrived at work, I was paged for a call. It was Dr. Swensen's nurse asking if I could come in for an 11:30 appointment. The doctor needed to do some further tests.

Just outside the main entryway to the clinic I glanced at my reflection in the double glass doors. I tucked my shirt into my wide leather belt, ran my fingers through my hair, threw my shoulders back, and walked with a steady stride into the waiting room. Doctor's offices made me nervous.

The nurse met me immediately. "I know you're on your lunch hour, so we'll get you right in." She led the way to Dr. Swensen's office rather than an examination room. "Just have a seat. Doctor will be with you in a moment."

I stared at the cluttered desk with a picture of his family tucked in the corner. The wall was filled with framed credentials and shelves of books.

The door opened. "How are you feeling today?" Dr. Swenson flipped through a medical file.

"Pretty good." I paused. "Your nurse said we needed more tests?"

"Has the bleeding stopped?" His tone was clinical.

"Not entirely. Is something wrong?"

He began a long explanation, using terms I couldn't pronounce or understand. Then I interrupted him. "Are you saying I have cancer?"

"For a woman, it's the best kind. We can remove it with an operation. It's localized. You're still young. If you want children, we could put if off for awhile, but that would increase the chances of its spreading. I could set up some counseling."

My brain struggled to process his words, as I pushed down the strong maternal feelings I felt for Randy. *Counseling? Children?* My voice sounded miles away. "Doc, you're honest with me; I'll be honest with you. I'm a lesbian, so take it all out. And don't worry about the counseling."

He stuttered, "Oh, I see. Well, in that case, when can you arrange to be off work for six weeks?"

"Next month, maybe."

"You don't understand. I mean tomorrow or the first of the week at the latest."

I was stunned. "I'll have to work things out with two jobs. I'll call back this afternoon."

I stumbled out of the office, glancing at my watch. Fifteen minutes had passed—fifteen minutes that changed my life. *Cancer? How could I have cancer? What if I died?*

I went home and called people who I knew were talking to God, requesting prayer for my surgery the following Monday. Marie Fuller was at the top of the list.

Her voice sounded weak. "I'm recovering well, Darlene. I

haven't had time to tell you. They found breast cancer and had to operate."

Suddenly I was scared. "Are you going to be O.K.?"

"I'm sure I am. They think they got it all in plenty of time. How are you doing?"

"That's why I'm calling you, Marie. I have to go in for a hysterectomy. Cancer. I want you to pray so I wake up."

"I will, honey. You're in the very best hands with Jesus. He has all our tomorrows planned, even yours." Then she chuckled. "You could talk to Him yourself, you know."

"Maybe next year." I sighed. "Marie, what if you had died? No one would know to tell me."

"Someone would let you know, Darlene. Besides, I'm ready. You would just have to straighten a few things out with Him so we'd see each other again. Jesus is the only one who can give us the grace to accept death, honey. And it's only by His grace we ever learn how to live."

"Are you preaching at me, Marie?"

"Well, who called whom?" She laughed lightly. "I just love the way you walk right into it, dear. And I'm going to be faithful to uplift Him.

"Well, you'll pray for me next Monday, right?"

"I pray for you every day. But I'll be especially asking Him to make you whole. He is the great Physician!"

After talking with Marie, I telephoned Norma, who had just moved to southern California, and Beth, Marie's friend from San Francisco who had just married and moved to Los Gatos. It had been almost two years since I had contacted either of them.

Beth surprised me. "I'll not only pray on Monday," she said, "I'll drive down and be in the room when you come out of surgery."

"You would do that for me? I just needed you to pray!"

"I'll bet you're frightened under that rough exterior. Anyone facing major surgery would be. Just know that when they bring you out of recovery, I'll be waiting—and praying."

"Thank you, Beth. You'll never know how much that means to me."

After several more phone calls, I went to bed and tossed all night. I believed in the prayers of the people I had called, but what if the prayers were not enough?

Rebecca didn't come home that night. Bubba knocked on the bedroom door about six the next morning. "I'm leaving for work, but I wanted you to know I'll take you to the hospital on Sunday." He indicated the empty space beside me. "She didn't come home?"

"No, she must be with Jan." Hurt masqueraded as humor. "It's ironic. I'm always what everyone else needs, but when I need, everyone disappears."

"I'm here, Sis." His voice was gruff. "I'll take care of you."

"Thanks Bubba."

All day long I ran errands and made phone calls, trying to get things organized. I also decided to find Rebecca and have her move her things by the time I was home from the hospital.

That night I found her car parked behind the girls' bar. I blocked her car with mine, then walked to the front of the bar. As I stepped through the doorway, couples poked one another and lips moved. Only the blaring jukebox failed to heed my entrance.

I moved slowly to the back of the bar where Rebecca leaned against a pool stick, watching with a smirk. Jan stood off to the side, a cigarette hanging from the corner of her lips. I'd heard enough about her to recognize her without an introduction. She reminded me of a hoodlum from the fifties. She wore a brown striped tank top, displaying muscular arms covered with tattoos. A package of cigarettes was tucked in her waistband. She eyed me with suspicion, holding tight to the cue stick.

I concentrated on keeping my voice steady. "Rebecca, I want to talk to you." I motioned toward the back door.

"Go ahead, honey," Jan said. "If you need help, just holler."

I moved toward the door. "I wouldn't step outside the door if I were you, Jan. Rebecca is safe; I can guarantee that you would not be." I glanced back, feeling hatred ooze from my soul and out my eyes. I stepped into the blackness, holding the door for Rebecca.

"I know you've heard by now that I'm having surgery." I clenched my fist. "I just want to thank you for being there when I needed you." The sarcasm stung in my mouth.

"That's not fair," she objected.

"Not fair?" My voice rose a fraction. "You never bothered to find out if I was alive or dead for the past three days. No matter. What I really want to say is, I want all your things out of the house by the time I return from the hospital. I'm sorry I ever loved you." I felt like the words were being ripped from the depths of my heart, a tear trickled down my cheek.

"I know you don't believe it, Dar, but I do love you—"

"Don't!" I raised my hand, remembering her smirk in the bar. "Don't bother. Just be gone when I get home in a week." I wanted to be tough, uncaring, and strong but inside I was trembling.

"Don't you want to tell Randy good-by?" she asked softly.

I felt a painful twinge. "Well, maybe. But I don't want to see you again ever." I turned to leave. "And if I see Jan at my house, even if I'm on my deathbed, I'll kill her. So help me, I'll kill her!"

I stomped off into the night. *I wish I didn't care. Why did I ever let you get close enough to hurt me?* Hours later in the darkness of my room, I tried to erase the memory of the conversation. *"I love you...."* echoed in the painful space that she alone occupied in my heart. Tears scorched the sides of my face and filled my ears as I lay on my back, staring at the ceiling.

Then why aren't you here? I whispered into the stillness. *Why aren't you here?*

18.
Time
to Remember

I was wrapped in a cocoon of pain. Voices in the hospital were muffled and far away, and it seemed I was in motion. Then a cool hand reached around my fingertips. "Darlene, I'm here. It's Beth."

I tried to smile. "Thanks. . . ." Then I was asleep again.

A noise jarred me to consciousness. *Where is everyone?* I saw a note on my nightstand.

"We'll see you tomorrow. Remember we love you. These people called. [A list followed.] Here's a book for you to read. Love, Beth."

I glanced at the book. It seemed to be a Christian testimony. Then a nurse entered the room and gave me a shot. I lapsed into unconsciousness again.

My room soon filled with plants and cards from friends. With the exception of Bubba and Beth, all my visitors were lesbians.

The third day, I heard a tapping noise at the window. Randy was grinning from ear to ear. "Hi, Dar!" he yelled through the glass.

A voice by the door startled me. "They wouldn't let him come in because he's a kid." Rebecca walked to the window and opened it slightly.

I ignored her. "Hi, Randy. How's it going?"

"O.K. We're moving to Oregon." His smile faded. "I wish you were coming too, Dar."

"I have to get well, Randy. You can come see me sometime on vacation. All right?"

"Sure!" He looked at Rebecca. "We can, can't we, Mom?"

"We'll see. Go back to the car now. I'll be there in a minute." She turned to me. "I just wanted to tell you good-by." She bent down and kissed my forehead. "I do love you."

I turned my face away. It hurt to move but it hurt even more to see her.

The phone rang. It was Beth, checking on me. When the call was finished, Rebecca was gone.

Several days later I had mended enough to go home. Bubba had asked a bisexual girl named Sandy to move in and help me around the house. But once home, I discovered the last roommate hadn't really left. All of her belongings were still there.

"Rebecca said she'd come for her things when they had enough money," Bubba explained. "What could I do?"

"Well, at least rip that down!" I pointed to the mural of centerfolds. "I'll pack the rest of this and drive it to Oregon myself as soon as I'm able.

For three weeks Sandy kept me company and helped around the house. My physical pain couldn't begin to match the emotional pain from the daily reminders of Rebecca and Randy. I still cared deeply for Rebecca, and although I wanted her out of my life, I couldn't make the emotional break while the house was full of her belongings. I rejected Bubba's suggestion to hold a yard sale and instead had him pack everything in a U-Haul trailer. Although physically I was not well enough to make the trip, emotionally I was cracking up. I was determined to drive her things to Oregon and be free once and for all. Bubba had accepted a construction job near Tahoe and would be leaving the next night.

The twelve-hour drive left me physically drained. I arrived at four in the morning, demanding that Rebecca and Jan unload the truck and trailer.

"I couldn't help even if I wanted to," I said, sprawling out on the couch. "I want fifty dollars for my gas, then I'll be on my way."

"Don't you want to wait for morning and see Randy?" Rebecca offered.

"I *am* tired. . . . All right. I'll wait until morning." My recent surgery had affected me more than I was admitting. I didn't know how I could even make the return trip. Somehow I thought that if I saw her a little longer, we could start over. I wanted things to be as they were when we first met. The past year and a half had changed many things, but not the inevitable termination of my "forever" relationship.

Randy came bounding into the front room early the next morning. "Dar! Are you gonna stay with us?" He threw his arms around my neck.

"I wish I could, honey. I have to go home today." I hugged him gingerly, careful of my incision. "I just wanted to bring your things up to you."

He had to leave for school. "I sure miss you, Dar," he said as he stood in the doorway.

A lump formed in my throat. "Yeah, me too, kid. I'll see you soon."

Rebecca came in and stood by the couch. "I know you still care about us, or you wouldn't have brought the furniture all the way here."

"Caring has nothing to do with it. I just want this chapter closed." My resentment grew. "If Jan loves you so much, why didn't *she* see that you had what you needed?"

"Don't hate her. I'm the one who left." She spoke softly. "You knew it couldn't last forever."

"Right! Nothing does, does it? Well, thanks for the memories." I picked up my jacket and ran to the truck.

I drove twelve hours straight, arriving home about nine o'clock. I had told Sandy before leaving that I would not need her anymore, because I didn't want anything to remind me of gay bars or Rebecca.

I collapsed in bed and could not move without pain for three days. I spent the time reading the book Beth had brought me and even began to read the Bible again. A nagging thought persisted in those long hours of silent reflection: *Can I change? Do I want to?*

Beth and Matt called several times a week and invited me to their home for dinner at least once a week. Time spent with them was comfortable. We discussed religion, certain points from the Bible, and what was left of my faith, but they never pushed me into defending my lifestyle.

"Darlene, we love you and pray for you," Beth assured me one evening. "We're here to listen whenever you want to talk. I know you know that Jesus has a better plan."

I smiled. "Yeah. I've just never figured out how to make it work."

When I returned home after one of our dinner talks, the phone was ringing. "Dar, it's me." Someone was sobbing so intensely that the words were almost incoherent. "I know you hate me, but you're the only one I can turn to."

"Rebecca? Where are you? What's happening?"

"Jan and I broke up. I don't know what to do. If I come back to California, can I live at your house? It would be strictly—you know, as roommates."

I fought the urge to say yes. "Forget it, Rebecca. I can't have you here. It can never be as it was." My voice trailed off. "But I *will* help you find a place to live if you move back here. Just make sure it's what you want to do."

She perked up. "I'll call you later this week."

Now I plunged into depression. Removing Rebecca's things from the house had not removed her memory from my heart. In one week I would turn thirty-three, and my aloneness was overwhelming.

When Beth called to invite me to dinner for my birthday, I shared the phone call from Rebecca. As I might have expected, Beth warned me that Rebecca, sensing that I still cared deeply for her, was probably only using me, and she urged me not to let Rebecca back into my life. But I didn't know what to do; I still had a year's lease on the house, and I just couldn't handle being alone.

It was mid-September; I had been off work five weeks. After a good checkup the doctor estimated that I would be able to return to light work in two more weeks, I left his office and went to the store immediately to be put on the schedule. Mr. Whirtley sent me to a business office downtown for a current polygraph test, which Thriftway now required every three months.

It was not a standard polygraph. It was a new machine called a voice stress analyzer, highly perfected and accurate. Only one in twelve thousand, the administrator told me with pride, could lie to this machine and pass.

The procedure was much the same as the first test. "There are twenty questions. I want you to answer one of them incorrectly."

"You want me to lie?"

"Just on one question. Don't tell me which one until after the test."

I kept my thoughts on other subjects as the administrator asked the questions. *I never stole anything from anyone. I don't feel guilty.*

"Hmm," he said. "I would say you lied on number seven."

"What was the question?"

"Have you ever taken anything from Thriftway?"

"Right. I lied when I said no."

"What did you take?" he asked suspiciously.

"If you'd check the last test, you'd see I told them I took a Coke a couple of times when I first started working and didn't have cash with me. My boss told me it was all right if I paid it back the next shift."

"I see." He looked at the chart and compared some numbers. "The test is perfect, Darlene. I can assure them of an honest employee."

"Thank you, sir."

You just met one in twelve thousand.

Returning to work did not lessen my depression. I began to spend almost every weekend with Beth and Matt just to flee thoughts of suicide. As much as I tried to push away feelings of guilt and conviction, they kept rising to the surface. I felt like a failure with no chance of making life work right.

Beth called midweek. "There's a sexuality seminar at a church in Palo Alto. Elaine will be one of the speakers. Would you like to come with me?"

"I don't know if I'm ready to go to a church service. It's been a few years."

"It's not a regular service. And besides, I don't want to drive there alone. Please come."

"All right, Beth, . . . although I'm not sure I'll feel comfortable."

The next day at work I began to harass Julie. She was a new employee whom I had heard was a Christian. "Do you pray for me, Julie?"

She broke into a smile. "Why do you want to know?"

"Because you never witness to me. Christians are supposed to witness to others, especially to backsliders."

Julie wasn't intimidated. "Why should I witness to you? You seem to know the Scriptures better than I do. But to answer your question, Darlene, you'd be surprised who is praying for you!" Her eyes twinkled as she returned to her paperwork.

I laughed. "In that case, I thought you might like to know I'm going to church this weekend."

She looked up, surprised. "Really? Where?"

"In Palo Alto, with a friend. I'll let you know how it turns out."

She nodded. "I don't think God has given up on you, Darlene."

"I'm not so sure. But even if He hasn't, I'm not going to change. I've tried all that before, and it just doesn't work."

"Your way hasn't worked either, has it?"

"Enough! End of conversation. I'm not getting caught in this trap." I walked away in mock disgust, asking myself why I had initiated that conversation. Was it possible that deep down inside I really did have a desire to change, and that there really might be hope?

Rebecca called twice during the week to say that she had decided to stay in Oregon but that she loved and missed me. Maybe all this would turn out to be a bad dream. Maybe she would show up at my door, and things would be as they had been those first months of our relationship.

Then reality struck me; it would never happen. Even if Rebecca came back, I would not let myself love her. I would not be hurt like that ever again, nor would I even cry. Big girls did not cry.

That same week while waiting for the sexuality seminar to start, I was asked to read some of my poetry in a feminist rally at the college in Santa Cruz. The platform was shared by several local artists, emphasizing the National Organization of Women, the Equal Rights Amendment, and lesbian organizations around the state.

I selected poems depicting new love, frustrated love, and broken relationships. And as I had hoped, my graphic portrayals of lesbian love affairs won me a burst of applause as I stepped from the stage. But I could not help remembering the poem I had prepared as a high school senior to present on graduation night, which neither my father nor my mother had attended. Pain dulled my ears.

I went to the bar on Thursday night, trying to ease that pain with alcohol.

On Friday evening I clumped into Beth's house wearing jeans, cowboy boots, and a Western shirt. "I could have worn girl things," I explained, "but I didn't want to. Still want me to go to church?"

"Of course I do," she smiled. "Bet you thought I'd say no, didn't you?"

We sat through the seminar, which was interesting but offered nothing I had not known before. Driving home, Beth was quieter than usual. I suspected a sermon was coming.

"Darlene—" She paused. "I won't press you about Christ, but try to verbalize in one sentence what keeps you from recommitting your life to Him?"

"I knew that was coming! Beth, you know I've tried before. The Christian life just doesn't work for me. And I'm tired of answers that don't work."

"Couldn't you give God one more chance?"

"Sure, I could give Him one more chance. I could leave gay life. I could quit drinking, smoking, and swearing. I've been in this struggle since I was seventeen and I've given it all up twice already. But this time it's different. I've screwed up my life so much, I don't know if even God could fix it.

"There's another big problem too," I added after a silent struggle with myself. "I'd have to confess to several counts of grand theft, and I'm not about to go to jail for God or for anybody!"

"Tell me about it," she said softly.

"What's to tell? I've ripped off the store where I work nights. I've taken two lie detector tests and passed. I don't seem to have a conscience anymore. I don't even feel bad most of the time. And if I gave my life back to God, I know He would make me confess." Then I chuckled in spite of myself. "I wouldn't do too well in a woman's prison, even if I were a Christian."

Beth did not smile. "Don't you think God could work it out?" she persisted.

"No, I'm not really sure He could. Besides that—" I gazed intently at her. "I'm also involved in a murder plot. Tell me how God could fix *that!*"

It sounded unreal even as I said it. What in the world was I doing with my life?

But Beth never flinched. "Do you want to talk about it?"

"I can't give you details, but I'm supposed to be an alibi for someone. I'm such a good liar, it's no problem. I'm really agreeing that a person's life is worth a thousand dollars. I've sunk to the lowest level I can imagine. I don't seem to care about anything anymore. A lot of the time I don't even want to live!" I leaned my head against the seat, turning to look at her face. "Do you still like me?" *Please say that you do.*

"Darlene, you are a special person to God." I could tell she was choosing her words carefully. "And He has the answers. I don't know how, but I know He'll work it out if you let Him."

"It would take a major miracle, Beth. I told you I have no intention of going to jail." However, a spark of hope ignited. *Could He?*

We stopped in front of her apartment. "Do you mind if I pray?" she asked.

I laughed. "I think you'd pray even if I did mind!"

She reached over and took my hand. "Father, thank You for sending Jesus. You are the God of miracles. I don't know how to pray, but I ask You to work another miracle now and bring Darlene back to You. I commit her situation into Your hands. Do what You must. In Jesus' name, Amen."

She squeezed my hand. "I love you, Darlene, and so does He."

"I know it," I muttered, trying to swallow the lump in my throat. "I'll call you tomorrow."

There was plenty of time to reflect as I drove my truck back to Monterey. I wasn't wild about Beth's prayer that God "do what He must" to bring me back to Him. But before I could begin to think about it, an inner voice began to speak.

Darlene, give Me the chance to work a miracle. Just ask!

I reached for a cigarette.

Darlene, do you remember how good it was?

In my mind flashed an image of me as a college student in devotional time alone with God.

"But it didn't work!" I yelled. "I always fail!"

Darlene, I never fail. Give Me another chance. I will take care of you.

I agonized for one long moment. Was I actually considering giving my life back to God? Wasn't this turning into one lifelong charade, first giving myself to Him, then taking myself back? What would make it any different this time than it had been the other times? And besides when God required me to confess my crime of embezzling, which I knew He would, I would end up in some women's prison somewhere. There I would pay retribution for my sin and be forced to participate unwillingly if not willingly in the sexual whims of the other inmates?

Suddenly, more out of frustration than spiritual resolve, I consented.

"All right, God. Let's see You work a miracle. I'll give You another chance right now." I reached for my pack of Kools and threw them out the window. "Show me!"

19.
The Price
of Confession

I spent the rest of the trip home in dialogue with God.

What if I go to jail? Can't I sneak the money back into the till? What if I can't stop smoking? How can I give up all sex?

"God, I don't feel any different," I said aloud. "But I'm asking You to cleanse me from all my sins. I can't name them all, so please just remind me." *I won't tell anyone until I'm sure I can make it.* "And if You want me to confess all this, then You're going to have to show me how."

I slept more soundly than I had in months. It was after nine on Saturday morning when I rolled over in bed and reached for my cigarettes. *Oh, yeah, I threw them out.* I flopped back against the pillow and stared at the ceiling. "Well, Lord, this is the first day of miracles. What next?"

I jumped out of bed and into the shower, where a nagging voice followed me. *You'll never make it, Darlene. You've tried before and failed. God let you down. You don't want to quit smoking. And you're going to end up in prison if you don't end up in the loony bin first.*

Every fear I had ever known attacked me.

"I don't care how I feel," I insisted staunchly. "I've made a choice. God, You've got to help me!"

I finished my shower and pulled on my clothes.

"Right, Bible!" With sudden recall of familiar patterns, I took my worn King James from the bookshelf. It had been my high school graduation present, and I had particularly loved the Psalms. Today especially I needed those words of hope and comfort.

I read, cleaned house, read some more, then paced the floor. I needed to talk to someone. When there was no answer at Beth's house, I dialed Julie.

"Do you have a few minutes?" I asked, curling up on the couch.

"Sure! How did things go last night?"

"I don't know if you're ready for this, Julie, but here goes." And without answering her question directly, I launched into a half-hour account of embezzling from Thriftway, staging a fake robbery, smuggling dope in to Toby, and every other sin I could think of over the last few years.

"I'm not sure why I'm telling you all this," I concluded. "But I needed to get the real story out." A weight had already lifted from my shoulders. "Julie, are you still there?"

"Yes, I'm here. Why are you telling *me* these things?"

"I just needed someone to talk to. Since Sherry graduated from college and moved away, I haven't known anyone willing to listen."

"What I mean is, you could confess to Christ and He could forgive you."

I realized that I had not told Julie about my renewed contact with God; even so, maybe talking with her was part of God's answer to my question about how to confess all my sins. At least it was a beginning.

"Maybe He already *has* forgiven me," I said. "In fact, I'm planning on going to church tomorrow."

"Really?" Julie sounded genuinely surprised. "My prayers are apparently working!"

"I'll give you a progress report on Monday. Thanks for listening, Julie."

I hung up and flipped through the yellow pages. I would choose a church whose pastor I did not know. Suddenly I threw myself on the couch, laughing hysterically. Going to church meant I would have to wear a dress! I rushed to the closet and flipped through the hangers of men's shirts, jeans, and suits. In the back I found my only dress, an outdated A-line in gold print. It had been five years since I had worn it! *Now, shoes . . . I must have some.* I located a pair of beige patent-leather pumps, outdated but hardly worn.

I was pressing the dress when I had another thought: I would need nylons. I would also need to shave my legs! It was good that it was Saturday, and I had plenty of time. After ironing the dress, I marched into the bathroom and shaved my legs. It took two blades.

Finally I had assembled the proper attire for my first day at church, including my Bible and an old purse that was much too large for simply my wallet and keys. What else did women put in those things, anyway?

I awakened Sunday morning with at least a hundred reasons not to go to church. Then I stared at my legs, unexpectedly clean-shaven. Well, I had already gotten everything ready; I might as well go. Once dressed, however, I felt as though I were in drag. Nothing felt comfortable or familiar. The air around my legs added to my sense of exposure.

I had selected a church I passed every day on my way to work. But I had not remembered its being so big! I clutched my Bible and purse for security and strode toward the front door.

I was greeted by an older woman with graying hair. "Hello," she smiled. "Is this your first visit?"

I nodded self-consciously. If she wondered at my lack of fashion, she gave no indication.

"We're glad to have you. Please sign our guest book, won't you?"

After signing, I found a seat near the back of the church. The singing actually brought tears to my eyes. *It's been too long, Lord.* I joined in the worship choruses.

The pastor was in his late fifties with sandy-colored hair and a full face, accentuated by large glasses. His smile was warm and seemed genuine. After reading the Scripture, he delivered a twenty-minute sermon, pacing back and forth across the wide platform, sometimes walking down to the pews and talking right to the congregation. I liked him. He reminded me of a grandpa.

Afterward I introduced myself to him and thanked him for the sermon. He was as pleasant in person as I had hoped. And just spending time in church made me feel clean inside. By midday I was free to drive home and make a couple of important phone calls.

Matt and Beth were elated and assured me of their continued support and prayers. Then I called Marie.

"This is your prodigal daughter returned to the fold!" I announced, relieved when her voice sounded stronger than the last time. "But how are you doing? Are you back to normal since your surgery?"

She laughed. "As normal as I'll ever be. Every day I'm gaining strength in my arm. But what's this about 'prodigal daughter returned to the fold'? You've got to say it plain for an old lady like me."

"O.K., Marie. I decided to give the Lord another chance."

"I'm delighted. He never let go of you, Darlene. The Bible says He's married to the backslider. I'm so grateful."

"I am too." For the next fifteen minutes I told her about my unconfessed crimes and some of the decisions ahead of me.

When I finished, Marie's tone was somber. "Darlene, you know it's not an easy road back. I'm convinced God has the answer for your wholeness, although I'm not sure you'll get away scot-free. But God will help you if you trust Him. Oh, honey, I'm uplifting you to the Father. I'll stand by you and do anything I can to help you. I love you, and He loves you infinitely more."

My throat ached. "Thanks, Marie, for not giving up on me." Silently I breathed another prayer of thanks to God for loving me through her and not giving up on me.

On Monday morning I decided to tell Joanne and Julie about my decision. They expressed concern, based on my past failures, that I could make a permanent change. But they assured me of prayer support.

Norma, too, seemed dubious about my change but offered the name of a Christian attorney as a starting place for making things right at the store. And she assured me of the availability of God's wisdom for the hard decisions of the next few weeks.

During my shift at Thriftway that night, I began to get an inkling of just how difficult these decisions would be. Brian stopped by the store.

"Am I glad you're here tonight, Mrs. Mainer!" he greeted me. "I'm out of cigarettes." He picked up a carton and slipped it under his coat.

I stared, strangely slow to respond. "Brian, tonight is the last night for freebies," I said at last.

"How come? Are you quitting?"

"No. Actually Brian, I've gone back to church. I'm living by a new set of rules."

"Don't tell me you got religion again! Well, whatever makes you happy. Just don't try to push it on me." He leaned over the counter and kissed me on the forehead. "I love you, Dar, but religion is definitely not my thing." He danced out the doorway with his cigarettes.

O God, can't I even be good? Why didn't I stop him? And if I'm still letting my friends steal, I'll probably be stealing myself before long. After all, I steal as easily as I breathe. I'll never change!

Discouragement gripped me. Then an inner voice spoke. *I know you can't change, Darlene. It's going to be My work in you. Trust Me.*

"But I've blown my resolve already," I argued. "How can I even claim to be a Christian?" When I started condemning myself, I knew I needed help, but how?

The answer came immediately: *Get an attorney and confess.*

Suddenly my fear of going to jail was overshadowed by a

growing conviction that God had spoken to my heart and would not abandon me. I knew I could not turn back; God had to be in full control; and this time, it would be His power in me providing the ability to follow through with my commitment. If I had to be in jail, which was a very real prospect, then God would keep me faithful to Himself. And for my part, I was determined never to turn back.

On my lunch hour the next day, I called the attorney.

"I can't help you," he said after listening to my story. "But I'll have a Christian defense attorney give you a call tomorrow. You know, I'm a prosecutor. I'll tell you honestly that there could be a minimum of one year for each count of grand theft. Since you're turning yourself in, there could be a two-and-a-half year prison term with about four years probation. With a bonding company involved, they usually prosecute."

I thanked him and hung up, while a pushy voice in my head started talking to me. *A little more time to be free and change your mind! You can still back out. All God wants is for you to be willing. You're forgiven, so forget it!*

How I wanted to listen to that voice! I didn't want to go to jail. But now I was committed to doing what God wanted. There was no backing out, even if it meant serving time.

The next morning I was startled out of a sound sleep by the phone ringing.

"Hello, Ms. Bogle? This is Bob Wilson from Beverly Hills. Mr. Kerny asked me to give you a call regarding a conscience theft case. Would you like to fill me in?"

I sat up in bed, propping the pillows behind me, and recounted the whole story, including my experience with the polygraphs.

Bob Wilson laughed. "They'll never believe you passed *two* tests while lying about everything." Then he got serious. "As a first-timer, Ms. Bogle, you'll get two to three years in prison and probably the same on probation. A bonding company will always push for prosecution. How are you fixed for money?"

I was still struggling with the idea of three years in prison. "If I go to jail, I won't *have* any money."

"Well, I'll need $1,500 to start the case. You'll also have to have money available to pay the store—I'd say about $7,000."

I was stunned. "I don't have that kind of money. I have good credit and could borrow, but if I'm going to jail, I can't pay it back. I don't think God would be glorified in that."

"I'll tell you what," he said kindly. "Pray about it and get back with me. You can reach me before eight just about any morning."

For a week I tried to sell my antiques, my furniture, and anything else I wouldn't need for three years with disappointing results. Discouraged and frustrated, I called Mr. Wilson with the news that the case would have to wait. It almost seemed that I was being forced to forget about the confession and simply go on with my life, even though I knew perfectly well what God had said.

My tension and depression grew. Some days I felt I was on the verge of an emotional breakdown. I dreaded the nights even more because of the inevitable encounter with cold sheets and the vacant space beside me. My innermost thoughts screamed into the darkness as I tossed from side to side. I was scared of going to jail, of living alone for the rest of my life, and especially of failing once again in my Christian commitment.

But when I read the Bible, I could feel invisible arms holding me. I began to read aloud from my King James each night and tape it. I listened to those cassettes every time I was in my truck when uncertainty kept me edgy.

Then Beth called. "Darlene, I have this friend in San Mateo. I'll give him a call and see if he can help. He's an attorney."

Three days later, I received a phone call at work. Larry Schneider, Beth's friend, instructed me to write out my confession, then he would contact the store. He also said not to worry about payment until the case was settled.

I had the letter of confession in the mail within the hour. I couldn't back out now even if I wanted to. And it only made sense to quit my job at the store.

I filled the next few weeks of waiting with prayer meetings, Bible studies, and frequent visits with Beth and Matt. I wrote a letter to Rebecca, who was still in Oregon, telling her of the change in my life and encouraging her to find a relationship with Jesus Christ. I also had several yard sales on Saturdays and began to unload all but a few personal items.

In the midst of one sale, Bubba returned home after seven weeks at the construction job in Tahoe. He walked into the almost empty house with a six-pack of beer and a bewildered expression. "Are we moving?"

"Not yet." I took a deep breath. "Bubba, I've decided to confess to stealing the money and intend to repay it. So I've retained a Christian attorney. I've also gone back to church."

He stared at me in disbelief. "They'll throw away the key!"

"Maybe so. But I've prayed about it and feel it's right. So I'm doing it—no matter what the cost."

"You're not playing with a full deck, Darlene," he retorted and stomped out of the house.

The next day Bubba was waiting for me when I got home from church. "I guess I'll have to go along with your decision," he said reluctantly. "I tried to have you declared mentally incompetent and committed. But they told me that unless you were doing harm to yourself or someone else, there's nothing I can do."

"You *really* did that?" I chuckled.

"Sure. Anyone who commits perfect crimes and then confesses to them isn't sane!" He puffed on a cigarette. "Why don't you just let God forgive you and forget about making waves? You'll ruin your life."

"Bubba, I've compromised all my life. If I'm ever going to make it and live totally for God, I've got to do it His way. I'm probably saner now than I've ever been."

Bubba stubbed out his cigarette and walked away muttering to himself.

Beth and Matt offered continuing support. "You know, Beth, it's really strange," I commented after one successful yard sale. "Every time I sell something, it's like a part of me is being ripped away. I have real pain connected with my memories."

"That must be rough," she sympathized. "You know, though, the Bible says that when we give up anything for Jesus's sake, He will restore it a hundredfold."

"Except I don't know if it's for Jesus's sake. I keep looking around at all that I've acquired, much of it illegally. If I go to jail for a few years, not much of it is worth coming back to. My standards have been out of line for years."

"Will you sell your truck?"

"If I'm convicted, yes. If not—well, it's the only brand-new vehicle I've ever owned. I'm pretty attached to it."

"We'll help you in any way we can, Darlene. Everything will work out."

"Maybe. But I'm still scared!"

Beth promised to check back at the end of the week. I had just hung up the phone, when I heard footsteps across the front porch. Recognizing Brian's outline through the sheer lace curtains, I opened the door smiling. "Hi, Brian. How's it going?"

His face was lined with tension. "Not too well. Do you have a few minutes?" He looked around the room nervously.

"We're alone," I assured him. "How about I get us some coffee?" I headed toward the kitchen.

"I guess so." He was right on my heels.

Suddenly I turned in the middle of the living room to stare at him. "Brian, what is your problem? You're acting as though someone's on your tail."

"Maybe they are. I'm getting our arrangement together. Just don't let anyone see you on Friday and don't leave the house. I'll bring your $1,000 Saturday morning, early."

I reached out and leaned against the couch. My knees were weak. How could I have forgotten about that?

I struggled to keep my voice calm. "Brian, I'm a Christian. I can't take part in a murder plot."

He stared. "Darlene, you promised! I'm counting on your alibi. You've got to."

Confidence surged from deep inside. "I don't have to do anything. And what's more, if you do it, I'll have to turn you in and testify against you."

"You can't, you're my wife!" His voice rose in desperation, and he began to pace like a caged animal.

My head was beginning to throb. "Brian, I've some news for you." I walked to my file drawer and pulled out the final decree papers addressed to Brian, still unopened after two years. "We are no longer married."

Brian took one look at the papers, threw them back at me, and stomped from the house, slamming the front door as he left.

Panic gripped me. Why had I waited to tell him about the divorce? Would he go ahead with his revenge plot anyway? What if he still held me to my offer of an alibi? How many more skeletons would rattle around in the closet of my past?

20.
Another
Miracle!

When I phoned Beth and told her of my confrontation with Brian, she brought up a point I had not considered. "Darlene, if he were going to kill someone for $5,000, what's to stop him from adding you to the list?"

At first the idea seemed preposterous. "Nothing, I guess, except that we used to be friends. But I don't think he'll be dropping back for a social visit in the near future."

"Why didn't you ever tell him about the divorce?"

"Pure selfishness. I figured if he ever inherited anything, and he thought we were married, he'd split it with me. I'll never inherit anything from my own family."

"Oh, Darlene. You're a joint heir with Jesus Christ!"

"I guess that's right," I replied thoughtfully. "But two years ago it didn't matter. Anyhow, I'm glad it's out in the open now and I can be straight with everyone."

"I don't think God is through with Brian yet. We need to pray that he leaves the area and is removed from your life. But I'll be praying that he'll find Christ too."

"I've been praying for him, and Rebecca, and *all* the people I know. It's really strange, Beth, I know God is in control, and deep inside I'm at peace. But I find I'm doing so many things just because it's right to do them, not because I feel like doing them. I argue with myself all the time about making things right with the store. God has been speaking to me about other things too. I'll need to buy more women's clothing and start looking more feminine. The one dress I have is getting worn out on Sundays."

I smiled at the thought of that outdated A-line.

"Don't you know anyone at church to go shopping with?"

"Not really. I don't have any close friends around here. Steven calls occasionally, but I don't want to spend much time with him. We end up talking about gay friends and that doesn't help my thought life. He just got promoted to area representative, so I don't see him around the plant very often." I paused. "You know, Beth, I still feel uncomfortable around most Christians. I guess I feel if they really knew me, they'd reject me. Besides, I don't know if I'll be here much longer. I could wind up in jail."

"Well, your former friends need to be replaced with new ones, Darlene. I know it's hard to leave friendships you've had for years, but God will replace them with very special people. Are you open to making new friends?"

"I guess so. The Lord has a full-time project just keeping me together emotionally. I don't want to go to jail. I don't feel that I can keep living here either. There are too many temptations."

"Maybe a move is the next step. But in the meantime, God is able to make you stronger than the temptation. I'm praying and so is Matt."

We hung up. Neither the temptation nor the waiting was easy. Another week passed with no word from Larry Schneider. Every time the phone rang, I jumped; every time a siren wailed, my stomach knotted. I finished recording the New Testament and began the Psalms.

Late one night the phone rang. "Dar, I have to move again. I have a proposition for you."

My face flushed when I heard her voice. "Rebecca, I can't have you move back here. My life is just getting straightened out." I fought my inclination to help.

"I don't want to move back," she said. "I've decided that the reason I'm having problems is that I wasn't cut out to be a mother. You're the only person I know with her life together enough to trust with my son. I want to give Randy to you."

"You *what*?"

"I know you love him, and he loves you. You'd give him a good home. I'll sign any papers you want, and you can be his mother."

"Rebecca, I can't make a decision like that on the spur of the moment. I'll have to pray about it. I'll call you back. What will you do with him if this doesn't work out?"

"Send him to my grandmother in Fresno. I just can't handle a kid right now."

"All right. I'll get back to you by tomorrow."

When I called Norma, she expressed concern that Randy would be Rebecca's rationale for staying involved in my life and keeping me involved with my past. Norma also reminded me that my future was uncertain, putting me in no position to make such a commitment.

I hung up and threw myself face down on the couch, choking back the sobs. An overwhelming sense of loss washed over me. Thanks to my cancer surgery, I would never be able to have a child of my own. I had denied the strong parental feelings that my special love for Randy had awakened, but these feelings were no less strong now.

"God, it's not fair! I can't have kids, and Rebecca doesn't want the one she's got." I pounded on the cushion. "And I really love Randy."

Then the voice I had learned to recognize as God's spoke to my heart.

Darlene, I understand. But Norma is right. Rebecca does want to keep a hold on you. Randy is her way. Release them to Me and trust Me to meet your needs and theirs.

"But God—"

Will you trust Me? Tell her no.

It was not a voice of condemnation or irritation but of compassion.

"Yes, Lord," I murmured, hardly daring to believe it could ever be all right. I reached for the phone. Less than twenty minutes had passed.

"I prayed," I told Rebecca, "and God said no."

"Did He send you a telegram?" she asked sarcastically.

"No, He just spoke to my heart. Besides, my own future is uncertain." And I explained about my confession to Thriftway.

"Darlene, you're crazy! Your religion is going to put you in the nut-house."

"I don't think so," I chuckled, remembering Bubba's efforts. "My future is in God's hands."

"Well, I'm sorry you're not going to take care of Randy's future!" The phone went dead.

I held the receiver for a few moments. What kind of future *would* he have? I had not done much good in his past! My heart filled with guilt and remorse over the influence our friends and sexual activities must have had on Randy's psyche. I replaced the receiver slowly.

It's just not fair, God. I could share Your love with him and maybe correct some of the damage I've done.

But God had said no, and I quieted myself, remembering when I had backslid attempting to mother my younger sister when I was not strong enough spiritually.

I continued to fill my days with Bible reading and church activities. The drive to church was peaceful because I chose the narrow streets of Monterey that took me near the ocean cliffs. Occasionally I stopped and listened to the pounding surf.

After one Sunday service I was heading for my truck when I recognized a man who worked at the plant. He saw me at the same moment and invited me to join a group of singles meeting at the wharf for lunch. I hesitated briefly, then accepted his invitation, realizing I did need to meet more people from church.

At the restaurant I sat next to Madeline. We were about the same age, had similar interests in reading, and had both been in Monterey about the same length of time. When she offered to pick me up for the next singles meeting on

Thursday—for which she said everyone "moderately dressed up"—I surprised myself and accepted.

But all week I fretted over what to wear. The gold print A-line dress was beginning to drive me crazy, although I kept avoiding a shopping expedition. Finally on Thursday night, I simply replaced my usual Western shirt with a man's blue pullover sweater and polished my black cowboy boots to a satin sheen.

When I heard the horn beep at seven, I clutched my King James Bible for security and hesitated at the door. I didn't feel like bringing the beige purse, and tonight my pocket seemed the wrong place to stuff my keys, so I stooped, lifted the pantleg of my jeans, and dropped them into my boot.

I was uneasy from the moment I got into the car. Madeline's shoulder-length, salt-and-pepper hair seemed color coordinated with her black lacy blouse and gray tweed, floor-length skirt. I cast sidelong glances at her, hoping everyone wasn't dressed as nicely. The pressure of my keys against my leg added to my discomfort.

We pulled up to an old Victorian house just off Monterey's Cannery Row. Suddenly I was glad I had ridden with Madeline instead of coming alone, as a fear of new people and places was making my stomach somersault. I couldn't even have a drink to relax! I swallowed hard and followed Madeline up the walk.

The group consisted mostly of people in their thirties and forties. After refreshments, group singing, and a short Bible lesson, we stood in a circle to share prayer requests.

"I'd like prayer for my cook," one man said. "She's an alcoholic and in jail with an uncertain future."

I'd like to tell you about my own uncertain future! I gritted my teeth in resolute silence, listening to the rest of the requests. I couldn't even begin to tell about my past.

The catalyst of the group seemed to be a genuine concern for one another. A gentle tugging in my heart convinced me to return.

Later Madeline dropped me off in front of my house. "I'll see you at church," she smiled.

"Would you care to come in for coffee?"

She glanced at her watch. "Sure, why not?" She parked the car, and we walked together to the house. But she looked around in surprise as we came through the front door. "Did you just move in?"

I had forgotten how bare the house looked. "Actually, I've been here quite a while. My roommate moved out. I've been selling a lot of things, trying to organize my life." *If we're going to be friends, she'll have to know the whole story.*

"I see. Have you ever been married?" She kicked off her shoes and curled up on the couch, tucking her long skirt around her feet.

I started the coffee percolating in the kitchen, then joined her in the living room. "I don't know if you're ready for the answer to that one." But I proceeded to fill her in on my lesbian relationships, my drag-queen husband, my return to Christ, and my confession of grand theft, all the while watching her face intently for any sign of rejection.

"Well, I can see why your house looks bare," she smiled when I had finished. "I haven't lived my life in a glass house either, Darlene. The players were different, but I can see we've shared similar emotions. You must be under a lot of pressure."

I was dumbfounded. I had been bracing myself for rejection, but she was accepting me. She said she understood. She wanted to be my friend.

"It is," I mumbled. "It's especially hard not having anyone to talk to."

"Why don't you talk with Pastor Edwards? I'm sure he would be supportive."

"I've been considering that. But now that I've told you my story, tell me about yourself."

By early morning our self-disclosure and prayer had brought us together as friends. Madeline smiled as she stood in the doorway. "Darlene, I feel God brought us together. I'll be praying about your situation, and whenever you need someone to listen, I'll be there."

I was grateful for her offer during the weeks that followed. It was gratifying to have a friend close at hand, not long-distance. Daily I struggled with my inner accusations taunting me that it was only a matter of time until I'd be locked behind bars. Nightly my dreams were haunted by scenes of women in prison attacking me. Voices in my head screamed. *You'll never be straight!* Suggestions of suicide offered an out that I had to reject continually. Sometimes a mysterious force seemed to turn my truck toward the cliffs or into the path of an oncoming car. *You're going to die! Give up and die!* Nothing would silence the voices.

I called Mr. Schneider's office every other day to see if there was any word from the store attorneys. The answer was always the same: "Be patient."

Meanwhile I continued to have my yard sales. One Saturday Steven and I combined yard sales to clear out his own garage. It was fun to share the day with someone, but many gay friends stopped. They wanted to talk, not purchase. I was careful to share with each one my commitment to Jesus Christ and my determination to break totally with a homosexual lifestyle. One comment pierced my heart: "I'll give you six months, Darlene. It you were really straight, you wouldn't be having a yard sale with Steven."

My inner conflicts were renewed. Couldn't I keep any gay friends?

Three weeks before Christmas 1977, I had almost $2,000 in savings. I decided to call Marlene and tell her the entire story. "The reason I'm telling you," I concluded, "is in case I'm in jail at Christmas, so you can cover for me with Mom. There's no need for her to know anything at this point. She's probably got enough to worry about."

"Personally, I think you were a fool to confess. I've never heard of anyone confessing when they passed two lie detector tests. By the way, do you have any furnishings left that I might be interested in?"

I went over my list and counted another fifty dollars toward my savings. "I'll keep you posted on any new developments." I promised Marlene. "Thanks for helping with my restitution project."

Every night I busied myself with constant activity, either finding somewhere to go or spending several hours reading Scripture.

One rainy night the week before Christmas, Madeline came over to pick me up for a singles party at Carmel Valley—casual, she had assured me—with the group from church.

"I'm glad I wore pants," I said, glancing at her long, dressy gown. "But I hope everyone's not as dressed up as you are!"

"Don't worry about it, Darlene. You look fine."

I felt out-of-place as soon as we walked through the door. The women were *all* wearing dresses. *They'll have to accept me as I am. But will I ever fit in and feel comfortable?*

The evening was low-key. We sang Christmas carols while Douglas played his guitar. At one point we went around the room sharing the earliest Christmas each of us could remember. I began to appreciate the people in the group as I listened to a wide variety of backgrounds: Many had come from broken homes; some from poverty; and a few from wealth. The discussion centered mostly around sharing and family descriptions of Christmas rather than gift-giving. What had brought us to the group was our singleness; what kept us there was a common bond in Jesus Christ. I felt less alone when I heard others sharing hurts and feelings of rejection. Maybe they would be able to understand my background and difficulties better than I thought.

Just before the gift exchange, Ingrid stood to sing a carol. A hush fell over the group as the beautiful and moving melody filled the room.

O holy night! The stars are brightly shining,
it is the night of the dear Savior's birth.
Long lay the world in sin and error pining;
Till He appeared and the soul felt its worth.
A thrill of hope the weary world rejoices,
For yonder breaks a new and glorious morn—Fall on
your knees! O hear the angel voices! O night divine!
O night when Christ was born—O night divine!

The song came alive in a way I had never known. My heart felt like a balloon cut free and soaring heavenward.

As Ingrid began the second verse, I sat motionless on the couch.

Truly He taught us to love one another;
His law is love and His gospel is peace.
Chains shall He break, for the slave is our brother,
and in His name all oppression shall cease.
Sweet hymns of joy in grateful chorus raise we,
Let all within us praise His holy name.
Christ is the Lord, then ever ever praise we,
*His pow'r and glory ever more proclaim.**

My eyes glassed over with sudden tears. The entire group was spellbound. *Chains shall He break. . . . Thanks, Lord, for a special promise of freedom hidden in these Christmas lyrics.*

Applause seemed almost sacrilegious. Afterward I walked over to Ingrid. "Would you write the words down for me when you have a moment? They really spoke to me."

"I'd be delighted." She hugged me. "Have a very special Christmas, Darlene."

I was embarrassed by the overt display of affection, but the warmth of Ingrid's acceptance helped to dull the pain of anticipating a Christmas alone.

---

*Adolphe Adam, "Cantique de Noel: Christmas Song (O Holy Night)," (New York: G. Schirmer, Inc., 1935).

Madeline and I shared stories of former Christmases as we drove back from Carmel Valley that evening.

At one point Madeline looked over at me with a smile. "Darlene, I want you to know that this year I'm counting you as my special gift from the Lord. I'm so glad that we're a part of one another's lives."

I nodded, misty-eyed again. "I am too, Madeline. God seems to know just how to meet our needs, doesn't He?"

Two days before Christmas when I came home at lunchtime to check my mail, I pulled a thick bundle of cards from the box. Glancing at the return addresses, my heart nearly stopped as I read Larry Schneider, Attorney-at-Law. The letter I had been waiting for!

I hurried into the house, walked to the couch, and sat on the edge, letting all but that one letter slip to the floor. "Father, I know my future is in Your hands. Please give me strength."

What if I'm going to jail before Christmas? I held my breath as I tore open the envelope.

Just then the phone rang. I grabbed the receiver.

"Hi, Darlene." It was Beth. "I just wondered if you heard from Larry yet."

"You won't believe it! I'm just opening the letter. Hold on." I pulled the letter from the envelope, scanned the first paragraph, and sighed deeply.

"Praise God," I said, an inner quietness filtering through my heart. "It says the store will accept full restitution with no prosecution if I will tell them in detail how I ripped them off. I continued reading. "They have conferred with their legal counsel, and everyone will go along with it since I confessed willingly. I have ten days to respond and pay the amount in full. I'm not going to jail!" Tears were freely falling down my cheeks.

Beth sounded exuberant. "Oh, Darlene, I'm so happy for you! You would have been so limited with felony charges and a police record. Do you have a way now to get the rest of the money?"

"Since I'm not going to jail I can take out a loan. My credit is good; I should be able to get $5,000 on signature only. That should take care of attorney fees, too."

"God is so neat. I knew He'd work it out, Darlene, and I believe He's working something special through it."

I thought once again of the words from "O Holy Night." "You know, Beth, I feel that one of my inner chains has been broken. I've been given another chance. It may take several years to pay off the loan, but every time I make a payment, I'll be thanking God for freedom!"

I started the paperwork for my loan the same day. I typed a two-page letter detailing how I had defrauded the store of both money and goods. I kept a carbon and sent the original to Larry with a personal check for the full amount of restitution, adding a postscript at the bottom: "Please submit your bill. Your sister in Christ."

Several days later I received a note from Larry:

"Dear sister: Merry Christmas. Please remit $75.00. Your brother in Christ, Larry."

21.
Old Familiar Demons

I was enormously grateful to be free and not to have heard anything from Brian. It astounded me that ever since my challenge to God two months earlier, I had not had a single cigarette.

But inside loneliness and fear of failure gnawed at my happiness. The store issue was settled, but many others hung in limbo. Would I really make it as a Christian? The inner condemning voice reminded me frequently of past failures. Nights and weekends were the worst when I fought aborting my commitment to do things God's way. I hated the empty time spaces of my life and sought activities to chase away the loneliness. I preferred to be anywhere rather than alone in my house.

The weekly meetings of the singles group provided emotional support and the opportunity to meet new people. On New Year's Day we met at Sandra's house just south of Big Sur. Small groups of people chatted with one another as children raced through the house. The men played football with the older boys, and everyone mingled as though we were at a family reunion.

I spent the day observing the activities and staying, for the most part, in the background. While Madeline chatted with Gloria, a petite woman with coal-black hair, I sipped a Pepsi and nodded at appropriate moments as they discussed a passage of Scripture.

This is sure different from any New Year's Party I've ever attended, I thought, remembering Rebecca and Randy. *Last year we were a family.* And I felt a growing emptiness in the midst of celebration.

God, You've done so much for me. You've worked miracles. You've freed me from a homosexual lifestyle. And yet I'm so lonely! I'm not ungrateful, but please take away the ache inside.

A few people included me in their conversations, but I longed for a physical embrace that would help hold me together inside.

I stayed for several hours and then drove home, still lonely. I knew I could not assume a Christian persona simply spouting platitudes and nodding at appropriate moments in other people's conversations. I needed a radical change inside and some way to satisfy the unmet emotional needs that had tugged at me for years—needs I had known how to meet up until now only in a physical way.

At work one thing was becoming evident: I could not take the pressure of seeing old friends. Although I had been promoted to the front office, I still saw several gay friends throughout the day, and the inner conflict was destroying me.

One Friday I confided to Julie. "I feel an obligation to go to lunch and share Christ with them," I told her, "but it stirs up so many memories."

"You need to make sure that the Lord wants you to share with them like that," she responded. "What has Steven said about your change?"

"He ignores it mostly. He feels it's possible to be a Christian and to be gay at the same time." I paused thoughtfully. "Plus he's concerned about our friendship. We've been close for a long time."

"How do you feel around him?"

"We disagree, and I know being gay is a sin, but we do have a special friendship. I'll always care about him. We haven't spent much time together since his promotion, but it's hard to stay home alone when I know he'd welcome a visit from me."

At that moment I noticed an acquaintance from the girls'

bar who was waiting by the door to talk with me. "There's a perfect example," I whispered to Julie. "My old friends still come to check on me."

I walked to the counter. "Hi, Marti. How are things?"

"Just great! I wanted to invite you to a pool tournament we're having tonight at the pizza place."

"I haven't been shooting much pool lately. You know I'm straight and have been going to church."

"Yeah, I know Darlene. But, hey, I'm a Christian too. You don't have to let it affect your whole life. You can come, have a soda, and just socialize. Don't tell me God is against your having fun."

"There's more to it than that. I'll think about it. I've got to get back to work. Talk to you later."

After Marti sauntered off, I returned to Julie's desk. "See what I mean? It's hard not to respond. I've been friends with some of these people for more than ten years."

"I can't tell you what to do, Darlene. But you do need to pray about whether to spend time with them."

"I will. And will you please pray too?"

I said nothing to anyone else about my inner conflict. But that night I went home and pulled out my pool stick. What could it hurt? And besides, it was Friday night.

I played in the tournament and drank Cokes all evening. I felt strange and even guilty about being there and argued with myself the entire time.

It's not a sin to be here. I can handle it. I'm straight. I'll ignore the girls.

But an inner taunting voice countered every positive thought. *You can't handle it. You're not straight at all. You still look at women. That's as bad as being with them. You'll never make it.*

I went home just before midnight, unaware that an emotional web was being spun which could trap me back into the gay scene.

The next morning the phone rang before eight. It was Beth.

"Hi," I said, propping the receiver next to my ear on the pillow. "Why are you calling so early?"

"I was concerned about you. I tried calling you all last evening."

"I went out for pizza."

"Oh, with the singles?"

I began to hedge. "Well, no. Actually, I had pizza and then I played a few games of pool."

There was a long silence. "Darlene, you didn't go to that gay pizza place?"

"Yeah. But there's nothing wrong with that, Beth. I just shot pool in a tournament. That's not a sin, is it?"

"Of course it's not, as long as you cleared it with Jesus. Did you do that first?"

"I didn't want Him to say no, Beth," I wailed. "And I wanted to be with old friends. I'm strong enough to stay out of trouble."

Beth's voice was kind. "I just don't want to see you caught in something you can't handle, Darlene. Satan isn't going to give up on you. I wish you'd call me the next time you feel lonely."

Satan? Is he involved in this? I didn't like to think about it.

"Don't worry, Beth. I'm not ever going back into gay life. I've come through too much in the last few months."

I got dressed and began to clean the house, resolved not to submit to temptation. I washed and waxed the truck, a weekly ritual. Then I remembered an errand that would take me downtown past the pizza place. It was broad daylight. I couldn't get into any trouble now.

But something invisible seemed to pull me toward the building. Beverly, one of the owners, was behind the counter.

"Hi, Darlene. It was good to see you last night."

"I enjoyed it too," I replied lamely, not even knowing what I was doing there.

Beverly opened a bottle of Coke and put it down in front

of me. "Say, I wanted to ask you something. How would you like to tend bar for me a couple nights a week? I want someone who doesn't drink."

"Oh, I don't think so, Beverly. It wouldn't be the best place for me."

"Well, think about it. I pay a good amount per shift plus tips." Suddenly she grinned. "What's the matter, Darlene? Don't think you could withstand the temptations?"

I took a slow sip of Coke before replying. "I'm sure I could. There's just no sense asking for trouble."

After I left, however, my mind was running on an exciting new track. Could I swing an extra bartending job? It would mean extra money toward my bills. I didn't even think to call Beth.

I was still in conflict the following morning when I arrived at church. To my surprise, the guest speaker was Reverend Stone, my old pastor from the Bay area.

I sat with his wife during the service while a new struggle emerged. Should I tell Reverend Stone the real reason I moved to Monterey almost eight years before? He had no reason to think I had *not* been serving God all these years. Then I remembered his hard, uncompromising attitude. He had all but told me he expected me to fail, so why should I bother to confirm his suspicions?

In the end, however, my need to restore relationships won out. I walked up to him after the service. "Reverend Stone, do you have a minute to talk?"

He smiled warmly. "Certainly, Darlene. My, but it's good to see you still serving Jesus."

"That's what I wanted to talk to you about." I cleared my throat, noting that he seemed different somehow, not so stern.

"When I left your church eight years ago, it wasn't for the reason I told you. I lied because I didn't want you to know I was going back to a gay lifestyle. I resented your assumption that a gay could not change, and I didn't want to be one more bad example. Well, I want to ask your forgiveness for those feelings."

He hugged me. "Of course I forgive you, Darlene. I'm concerned about where you are with Christ now."

I beamed at him. "I can reassure you on that score! I recommitted my life to the Lord several months ago after a long dry spell."

"That's what counts. Keep walking with Him, Darlene. He'll never fail you."

I walked out of church feeling ten feet tall. Reverend Stone *had* changed. I had never felt such warm acceptance from him before. *And Lord, I forgive him too.*

I had not been able to bring myself to tell him how hurt and angry I had felt that day. It seemed pointless now. And could I really blame him for thinking it was not possible to change? Sometimes I struggled with the same thought. But maybe I could prove his statistics wrong. *Lord, please help me make it this time because I love You.*

I resolved, after my conversation with Reverend Stone, to stop by and tell Beverly the answer was no. The lot behind the pizza parlor was nearly empty as I walked into the darkened building. Beverly was sitting at the end of the bar with a woman I didn't recognize.

"Where is everyone?" I asked.

"We don't open till three on Sunday," she replied. "I came in early to heat the oven. This is Roxie."

I nodded a greeting to the woman. "I can't stay," I went on, "but I wanted to tell you the answer is still no. This wouldn't be a good environment for me."

Beverly laughed. "I figured you'd turn me down. Too bad. I really want someone who doesn't drink." She turned toward Roxie. "Darlene got religion. Now she avoids us."

"I did more more than 'get religion'!"

Roxie grinned and held up a half-empty glass of wine. "I tried religion once, but it didn't work. There's too much to give up."

"Well, I get along fine on soda." I turned to leave. "I'll see you around."

"Want to shoot a game of pool?" Beverly asked. "That can't hurt you."

I hesitated. "Sure, why not?"

The afternoon passed quickly. Suddenly I realized it was only fifteen minutes till the evening service. Roxie walked me to the door. "Will you come back after church?"

"I don't know," I mumbled. "We'll see."

All through the service I struggled with feelings of guilt. Madeline wasn't there, and no one else knew me well enough to stop and talk. I suspected my clothes smelled like cigarette smoke, which made me glad I had talked with Reverend Stone that morning. Afterward, feeling at loose ends, I drove back to the pizza parlor.

There I sat in my truck for several minutes, gripping the wheel. At least here they knew my name! I hopped out of the truck, tucked my pool cue under my arm, and strode into the bar.

Roxie appeared out of nowhere, so drunk she could hardly stand. She threw her arms around my neck and planted a big kiss on my cheek before I could stop her. "Hey, take it easy," I said, leading her to a stool.

Beverly moved down the bar. "I'm glad you came back, Dar. Roxie's been talking about you all night." She grinned. "As a matter of fact, I wonder if you'd be willing to take her home. She's in no shape to drive, and she lives out past you in Carmel Valley."

I thought I was through with this scene. I pulled Roxie to her feet. "Get me her purse. She's in no shape to tell me her address."

As I helped her out the door, several voices called to me, "Have a good time, Darlene. Don't miss any opportunities."

I turned and said firmly, "I'll take her home, period."

One woman laughed. "We *know* you, Darlene."

Her words resounded in my ears on the trip to Roxie's. *No, you don't know me. None of you do!*

I dropped her off at her door and drove home, resolving never to let that situation come up again. Apparently I couldn't have any gay friends.

But ignoring the urge to join my old compatriots didn't make the desire go away. And that night's sleep was like many others—a nightmare of longings almost too strong to resist that threatened to throw me back into lesbian relationships. I woke up screaming. "I won't go back! I'll die first!"

The next Saturday I was awakened by a loud knock at the front door. I saw through the window that Roxie, Beverly, and Beverly's roommate all stood on the front porch.

The warning buzzers in my head were muffled by the inescapable sense of loneliness that clung to me, and I hesitated in the hallway. Many of my Christian friends were either married or lived somewhere else. Few, it seemed, were available for impromptu visits or walks on the beach, and my chaotic emotional needs demanded more than the structured singles fellowship could provide.

I had not shared my homosexual background with anyone except Madeline, and I did feel accepted by her. But I still felt emotionally isolated. How could anyone really understand who had not lived the homosexual life? Even a book Marie Fuller had recommended about emotional healing offered only ink-on-paper insights.

I opened the door and let them in.

We spent the day on the wharf and touring Cannery Row. *I hope I don't see any Christians.* I felt guilty and uncomfortable. When we returned to my house in late afternoon, Beverly and her girl friend took off, leaving Roxie standing on the front porch with me. At a loss to know how to get rid of her, I asked, "Do you have a car?"

"Over there." She pointed to a sports car. "Why?"

"Well, I'm going to wash and wax my truck and thought you might like to do yours."

I busied myself with my weekly project while Roxie stood

by and watched. *Help, Lord, I need to get out of this situation.*

Suddenly the phone rang. I raced to respond, Roxie right behind me.

"Darlene, this is Beth. I have a strong feeling something's wrong. Do you have a problem?"

I grinned sheepishly. "I sure do. Thanks for calling."

We talked in code for several minutes, finally deciding I should leave immediately for a trip to Los Gatos.

I hurried back outside and began to put things away. "Sorry, Roxie," I explained quickly. "I forgot about a dinner engagement. You'll have to leave."

"I was looking forward to knowing you better," she pouted. "Maybe some other time?"

"We'll have to see." I rushed up the front stairs. "So long!" I stepped inside, shut the door firmly, and sighed deeply. *Thanks, Lord! That was close.*

By the time I arrived in Los Gatos, I had a dozen excuses to justify my behavior. Beth met me at the front door.

"I won't tell you any of the lies I made up, Beth," I said. "I was lonely again and thought I could handle it at the pizza place. I have a couple of friends at church, but they don't fill the emptiness. At church I'm really just a face. If I told them about *me,* I know they'd back off. I need to touch people."

She put her arm around my shoulders as we walked slowly into the living room. "I know, Darlene. God has some real healing to accomplish in your life. It's going to take time. Have you considered more counseling?"

"I'm reading a Christian book about inner healing right now that Marie Fuller recommended. I'm not sure about actual counseling."

"I've read several books about the healing of memories. I think we need to pray that God will send someone into your life to help in that area."

I nodded thoughtfully. "I know I need to forget a lot of things. I hear accusing voices whenever I'm with old friends, telling me I'm going to fail again and that I'll never be totally free. I hear them at other times too. It seems like they're trying to drive me crazy. You know, I can't believe how I could do something so stupid as spending the day with lesbians. And I don't understand why I can't make wiser choices. I know I can't hang around homosexuals and expect to stay straight."

"I don't know how to help you, Darlene, but I'm sure God does. Let's just agree that He will send someone who knows how to minister in the area of inner healing."

Several hours later I was driving back to Monterey. "God, if You can forgive my sins," I prayed, "then You can take the pain away from my childhood memories."

Immediately the scene of my father's leave-taking so many years before came to mind. The oncoming headlights blurred through my tears as I became that child once again.

Daddy, why did you have to leave? Why couldn't you love me enough to stay? No one has ever loved me enough to stay.

I gripped the wheel with white knuckles, taking deep breaths to ease the knot in my throat. The emotional pain was too deep, too real for the instantaneous healing I yearned for. So I swallowed the tears and played a Scripture tape, terrified that healing would never come.

22.
"Chains Shall He Break …"

When I requested a transfer to the San Jose area to escape daily confrontations with gay friends, I was told there would be no openings for at least four months. All the same, I drove up one Saturday—about a hundred miles each way—to check out possible housing in the area around the plant. Then I remembered that a college friend had just moved to San Jose. So I found a phone and within fifteen minutes was knocking at Louise's door.

An older version of my college friend met me with a big smile. "Darlene, come in. It's been a long time."

Indeed it had. And it took us some time to catch up on the last fifteen years, with me hedging about my extracurricular activities.

"How are things between you and the Lord, Darlene?" Louise asked at last. "I remember back in college you were having quite a struggle."

"I'm still having quite a struggle, Louise," I replied with a wry smile. "But God seems to be resolving it. He's worked some real miracles in the last few months." And I shared with her about my life in the gay community, about breaking my connections with Brian and Rebecca, and about my confession and ongoing restitution.

"I've thought about you again and again since those shaky college years," Louise responded thoughtfully, "and wondered if God couldn't give you real stability in your life. Darlene, what do you think about inner healing and deliverance?"

My stomach lurched nervously. "I don't know a lot about

either one. I've been doing some reading about inner healing, but I think deliverance from evil spirits usually takes place in foreign countries, doesn't it? I certainly don't like to think of its happening here!" I shuddered. "And the thought of people possessed almost makes me ill. I believe in the devil, but I don't like to think about demonic activity."

"Well, you probably don't want to hear this, but my sister and her husband pastor a church near here, and she told me recently about her involvement in both ministries."

I remembered what Beth had said weeks before about Satan's not wanting to give up on me, and I thought about the incredible emotional pain that had always lurked within me. Maybe the ministries of deliverance and inner healing went hand-in-hand. If so, my "chance" encounter with Louise might be more than coincidental.

"I'd like to meet your sister," I said at last. "I've been looking for answers, and I suspect I need to be healed of some childhood pain. I just don't know where to begin."

"How about if I call her tomorrow and see if she'll meet with you? God must have planned your visit!"

I nodded, grateful for His timing and for Louise's gentle probing.

Louise called me the next day after church with her sister's number. She told me Mary would be waiting for my call after nine that evening. Oddly enough she added that Mary had been expecting Louise to call with a referral. Had God actually given her some kind of "advance warning"?

I hung up and began to pace, more nervous than before. What would I say? How would I start the healing process? What kind of things would I have to tell her? What if God told her things I had not? And what cost was I willing to pay for healing?

At nine o'clock sharp I called, Mary's voice was reassuring but businesslike. "Darlene, we pray about those people we believe God wants us to minister to. The program we've designed requires the approval of your own minister as well as a commitment to attend a weekly Bible study with us for about four months. If you're willing to abide by these stipulations, I'd like you to read a couple of books about deliverance from evil spirits before we meet with you."

"That's fine, Mary. I'm willing to do almost anything."

I agreed to call her back the following Friday, but my stomach tensed as I hung up the phone, and the inner voices ran wild.

Evil spirits—who are you kidding? Pastor Edwards will never agree to let you go somewhere else. He probably doesn't even believe in inner healing, not to mention deliverance. And if you tell him you were gay, he'll give you the cold shoulder.

Reason countered every argument. *No! I've promised to do this God's way. He doesn't want me to suffer. And if this is the right move, Pastor Edwards will agree.*

I stopped by the bookstore the next day and picked up the books Mary recommended. I also made an appointment to see Pastor Edwards. To my surprise, he not only expressed warm acceptance of me as a parishioner, my background notwithstanding, but he approved of my seeking help. When I called Mary on Friday with the news, she set up our first interview for Tuesday of the following week—just a week-and-a-half after my "chance" visit to San Jose.

That Tuesday as I drove to San Jose, having reread the material about inner healing and deliverance, a new fear unsettled my emotions: What if nothing happened? Of course, if nothing did happen, then I had no reason to be scared but I was all the same. I could think of a dozen reasons not to keep the appointment. But I wasn't about to back out now!

I located the church easily and walked up the steps to the large double-glass doors leading into the entry hall. Glancing at my reflection in the glass, I pulled my rose-colored Western shirt out over my belt. *There, I'll look more casual.* Then I slipped in and closed the door gently behind me.

Muffled voices floated from the second floor down a stone hallway. This was like a fortress. I tiptoed across the beige tiles, the taps on my cowboy boots nonetheless clicking the announcement of my arrival.

A woman in her midthirties with short, ash-blond hair stepped out of a room as I ascended the stairs. She was of medium height with delicate facial features. Her bright green sun dress was offset with a white drawstring purse bulging with Bible and notebook. Her voice was surprisingly soft. "Darlene?"

I smiled and nodded. "I guess you're Mary." *It's too late to change my mind now.*

She led the way to a room down the hall. It resembled a large family room with a couch, coffee table, easy chairs and a fireplace. She motioned toward the couch. "Have a seat, won't you?"

But I felt safer in a straight-backed metal chair against the wall and shoved my hands into my jacket pockets. "When do we start?"

"Another woman will be joining us in a few minutes. Her name is Carla. She's the one you'll be doing your Bible study with. Until she gets here, why don't you start telling me about your childhood?" She took the notebook from her purse and got out a pen.

I began self-consciously. In several minutes, a Mexican-American woman with wavy black hair came in and joined Mary on the couch. She seemed to be in her twenties and had sparkling brown eyes and a friendly smile. I studied her features while I continued to talk. Her tanned olive skin was not dark enough to blot out the freckles that covered her high cheeks and formed a racoon-mask pattern around her eyes.

Together they listened to the highlights of my life story. After several minutes I stopped. "I'm a little confused as to what exactly is going to happen here. How does this inner healing work?"

"We believe that healing and deliverance work as complementary ministries," replied Mary. "Deliverance is like surgery, after which comes the healing process. I believe that the homosexual bondage and struggles in your life are a result of the spiritual forces of Satan. They need to be broken and cast out before you can begin to be healed."

"You mean you think I've got demons?" I straightened up in my chair. "I've committed my life to Jesus. I can't have demons!"

Mary smiled understandingly. "Would you say you're living in freedom?"

"Well, no. I have some struggles. But I need healing, not this demon stuff." I folded my arms across my chest.

"Salvation includes deliverance as well as healing," Mary spoke patiently. "It's all part of Jesus Christ's work on Calvary and part of the ministry Jesus commissioned us to do. In Luke 10 He gave believers authority over all the power of the enemy. Besides, if you were free from Satan's bondage, you wouldn't be here."

"That's true. But people already look at me strangely when they find out I was gay. What are they going to do when they hear I have demons too?" I giggled nervously.

"The main thing is, Darlene, you can be free. It's your choice. Do you want to be free?"

"Of course I do. I'm just not convinced my problem is demons. I mean, how can you tell?" I shifted in my seat.

"Well, let me ask *you* a few questions. All those years in the gay community how much control did you have over your sexual appetites? And how has it been since then? Does it seem like an ordinary problem, or is it much stronger, much harder to gain the mastery over?"

I thought about my nightmares, about the desire that at times seemed almost to consume me. And I thought back to the years I lived with Rebecca, our pinups, and how we could not find enough aberrant sexual means to satisfy our lusts.

"It's strong," I responded. "I mean, it's very strong. And—

well, *now* it goes against my will, although it didn't before. I don't want to give in to temptation, but at times it threatens to overpower me."

"That's an indication, Darlene, that the problem is demonic and comes from enemy strongholds within, not simply an assault from without. You've had some rough childhood experiences, any one of which or all of them combined could have provided Satan an entry point. Have you had any involvement in the occult?"

"Yes—when I was younger and a little more seriously since then."

"Occult involvement only strengthens the devil's foothold. In deliverance, Darlene, the Holy Spirit reveals the names of specific evil spirits to us. Look at it this way. If your problem is not demons, then we've had a good prayer meeting. If it is demons, you can walk out a free woman. You can't lose!"

I settled back in my chair. "All right. What do you need to know?"

Mary took notes for the next hour as I responded to questions about childhood experiences of sexual abuse, feelings of abandonment, and the parade of substitute parents in my life. I shared my involvement with drugs and alcohol and highlighted my homosexual activity over the past seventeen years.

Finally Mary closed her notebook. "Let's spend a few minutes in prayer and call it a day. Then we'll get together on Saturday for the actual ministry."

I listened attentively while Mary prayed in a quiet but firm voice of authority. "Jesus, in your name we bind the power of Satan over Darlene's life. We take authority over all the workings of the enemy. Spirits of harassment, we bind you. I pray a hedge of protection around Darlene as she drives home and throughout the week until her deliverance is complete."

Suddenly I heard a noise like hornets buzzing in my head. Voices began to scream inside. *Stop! Stop her! Kill her!* It felt as though a spring were being tightened inside me, and I leaned forward in my chair grasping the seat in a vise grip.

Mary's voice was firm. "Darlene, tell me what's happening."

Pick up the table and kill her!

I lifted my head and looked at Mary. "You wouldn't believe me if I told you."

"Tell me, Darlene."

"I hear these voices telling me to stop you, to kill you. They said to pick up this table and throw it at you." Suddenly I giggled again.

"Spirits of violence and murder, I bind your working. Your time is short and you will not manifest yourself through Darlene."

I shook my head in confusion. "But I don't understand, Mary. I don't really want to hurt you."

"That was just a demonic ploy. I want you to pray now, Darlene."

I closed my eyes, and this time a surprising picture flashed across my mind, which I began to describe to Mary and Carla.

"I am sitting in the middle of a bare floor in a large room," I said slowly. "Jesus is at the door with His hand stretched out toward me. He's telling me to get up, take His hand, and walk out the door to wholeness. I'm just sitting there shaking my head. I'm telling Him that I can't move. I've been sick for so long that I'm comfortable with my sickness. I don't know what it's like to be healthy. I can't leave my room. But now He's saying that if I don't get up and take His hand, I'll never be well. So now I'm starting to push myself along the floor toward Him, reaching out. He's clasping my hand, pulling me to my feet. And now we're walking out the door." I opened my eyes and looked at Mary. "Say, this is neat!"

She smiled at me warmly. "This week is going to be a hard one for you, Darlene. Satan will try to keep you from returning on Saturday. You have the choice to listen to him or to walk into freedom. Go ahead and pray now, why don't you, notifying Satan of your intention."

Encouraged by that lovely mental picture, I spoke out boldly. "Satan, in the name of Jesus I choose to be free and never again to serve you willingly. I resist you in Jesus' name." As soon as I spoke those words, something inside me relaxed.

"One more thing, Darlene. When you come back on Saturday, plan on several hours of prayer. Carla and I will be fasting and praying all week, seeking God's wisdom. You will have to resist all Satanic suggestions this week about not needing to come back. And if you want to talk at any time, please give me a call."

"I will. And thanks, Mary. I feel better already."

"We'll be praying with you, Darlene, and the church here will be joining us. I believe you want total freedom, and I know this is God's time."

I nodded and waved good-by.

But from the moment I left the church, the inner voices started clamoring. *You don't need to go through this. You're a Christian. You can't have demons. You don't need other people to pray for you. Pray for yourself. If you go back, they'll make fun of you.*

I played a music tape in the truck and started to sing at the top of my voice to drown out the inner conflict. Then a quiet, reassuring voice spoke to my heart. *Darlene, it's time for you to let Me make some changes in your life. Don't be afraid. Trust these women. They will help you.*

Was it simply my own need for courage speaking?

And Darlene, it's time to start wearing women's clothes all the time.

I gasped aloud. "Lord, is that really You?"

All the time? Right away I thought of a dozen objections to giving up my jeans and boots. How could I go camping or ride a motorcycle? He couldn't mean wear women's clothes *all* the time!

"If this is really You, God," I said at last, "please have someone else tell me too. I can't give up my entire wardrobe just to please other people."

I smiled to myself. Now which of my friends would tell me to stop wearing jeans? *Not too many changes at once, Lord!*

By Friday night I was ready to call the whole thing off. I walked around the house arguing aloud. "God, I don't know how to function out there. What is well? What is healed? I know You said You'd be with me, but I'm scared."

Inside my head I heard a clear command: *Call Marie.* So I reached for the phone, eager to hear Mrs. Fuller's soothing voice.

"Hi, honey," she said. "How are things going?"

"Tonight, very frustrating. I'm an emotional wreck. I found someone who has a ministry in healing and deliverance, and I've made an appointment for tomorrow."

"Well, honey, that sounds like what we've been praying for all these years. So what's the problem?"

"They think demons are keeping me hooked on gay life. Marie, I'm scared. I don't know if I can go through what it takes to be healed."

"I understand how you must feel, dear. But it should come as no surprise to you that the source of sin is Satan. The Bible makes that clear. He doesn't want you to be free, and he's trying to keep you afraid so he won't be discovered. I think you definitely ought to go tomorrow and let God do what He wants to do."

"What if I hurt the people ministering to me? There are voices inside my head telling me to do all kinds of things."

"Remember, dear, the Bible says that fear comes from Satan, not Jesus. I have such a right feeling about this. Promise me you'll give God this chance."

"All right, Marie. But will you be praying too?"

"I will, dear. And will you call me back and let me know how things go? I love you, and Jesus loves you much more. He's committed to making you whole, Darlene. Let's just help Him all we can."

After our conversation I read my Bible late into the night.

The first rays of light were streaming through the window when I put on some clean white jeans and a new Western shirt, buffed my cowboy boots, and slipped on a leather vest. After all, none of my friends had confirmed that I should stop wearing men's clothes yet!

I arrived twenty minutes early and paced in front of the church, debating whether to go in. Then Mary opened one of the glass doors.

"Come in, Darlene," she called encouragingly. "We can get started sooner. I'll meet you upstairs in a minute."

I climbed the stairs, glancing around for a possible escape route, then entered the fellowship room and greeted Carla. Walking around her to the far side of the room, I again chose a chair against the wall and placed another straight-backed chair in front of it.

Carla smiled at me. "Hi, Darlene. How are you this morning?"

"Nervous."

Mary came through the doorway. "Why don't we move the chairs into a smaller circle? Darlene, would you move closer?"

I inched my chair forward and sat down, keeping distance between Mary and myself.

"We usually lock the door," Mary said. "Do you mind?"

"Is that to keep me in or someone else out?"

"It's to maintain privacy. You may leave anytime you like."

"All right. But one more thing. As much as I don't like being locked in—or out—I don't like people laying hands on me either. So don't touch me, all right?" Memories of Curt and Tony raced through my mind along with my childhood nightmares of being touched inappropriately and against my will. I knew my voice sounded hard, and my stomach knotted with tension.

"Calm yourself, Darlene. We don't need to touch you." Mary's tone was soothing. "Let's spend some time in prayer."

Mary began to pray aloud. I felt as though a huge spring

were being wound inside of me. I gripped the top of the metal chair beside me. *Shut up! Shut up!* I opened my mouth and took deep gasping breaths to relax. My chin was pressed against my chest and my eyes squeezed shut so tightly that the blackness seemed impenetrable.

Mary's voice came through nevertheless. "Satan, in the name of Jesus, we command you to reveal yourself and your nature in Darlene's life. Spirits of power and control, I take authority over you now and command you to come out of her. I send you to the depths of the ocean."

Carla was joining in verbal agreement. My breathing grew more painful; the spring inside my chest was tightening. I opened my mouth to talk, but my throat seemed paralyzed.

Her commands continued, until suddenly the spring broke and the pressure moved up my throat and out my mouth. I sank back against the chair and opened my eyes. Mary was looking at me. "How are you feeling? You need to tell me what's happening."

"I felt a pressure leave. My insides got unknotted."

The procedure was repeated a number of times as Mary called out spirits of homosexuality, fear, lust, anger, and a host of others. Each time the spring of tension knotted up my insides, then moved out of my mouth, allowing me to breathe normally again. Was this actually demons leaving?

Almost three hours had passed since we entered the room, Mary spoke directly to me. "Darlene, I believe the Lord told me that you need to renounce the spirit of occults before its power can be broken. Also you need to declare aloud that you receive the lordship of Jesus Christ. You have denied Him in times past, haven't you?"

"When I was heavily involved in the feminist movement, I said He'd never be Lord over me."

"Now you need to verbalize your acceptance of Him as Lord of your life and also speak directly to Satan and the spirit of occults to break their power."

I bowed my head. A force rose up from deep inside that

seemed to travel up my spine and across my shoulders. I could actually feel pressure moving inside my head, numbing as it went. When I tried to speak, I couldn't; only guttural sounds came out.

Mary's voice cut through. "Satan, in the name of Jesus we break your power right now. We bind your working and render you helpless."

I stared at her, shaking my head back and forth. "I—I can't talk."

"Yes, you can. Renounce the occult spirits by name and command them to leave." Her voice rang with authority.

"Spirit of occults . . . witchcraft . . . hexes, astrology, ouija board, mind control, hypnosis." I choked out the names. "I renounce your work in my life and tell you to leave now in the name of Jesus!" A pressure had grown into a ball between my shoulder blades. Now it traveled up through the nerves in the top of my head and down through my sinus passages. I expelled the pressure with a deep sigh, then leaned back in my chair.

Mary was watching me closely. "How do you feel, Darlene?"

"Lighter!" I flashed a smile.

"Let's just spend a few more minutes, shall we?"

I bowed my head, and my mind became a slide projector gone wild. My thoughts were jumping from scene to scene. I saw an old theatre with a flashing marquee. *Lust—Live Sex Acts.* Imps jumped up and down excitedly as they waited for the door to open. Suddenly Jesus came walking through the crowd and, taking a sign from under His arm, nailed it over the marquee. *Out of Business.* I smiled to see the creatures begin to keel over and dry up into wrinkled old beings, then die.

Jesus smiled at me, then spoke. *This is what they feed on. When you don't feed them, they die.*

I shared the mental pictures with Mary and Carla.

Suddenly another picture loomed across the screen in my

mind: a woman with a long, flowing dress, standing near a lamb. Looking closer, I saw that I was the woman and I appeared to be very feminine. "How out of character!" I exclaimed, eyes still closed, as I shared the scene.

Carla's voice reached me. "Darlene, I think the Lord wants me to tell you something."

I looked up at her, my heart beginning to sink.

"You may want to pray about this, but I think He wants me to tell you that it's time to get rid of your men's jeans and shirts."

I scowled. "I knew that was coming."

"You don't have to accept it just from me. The Lord will tell you if it's valid."

"He already has," I replied glumly. "I asked Him for a confirmation through someone else before I practically destroyed my entire wardrobe."

Mary nodded, smiling. "You know, I still don't feel we're through yet," she added. "Let's spend more time in prayer."

We bowed our heads again. Suddenly I was overcome with an intense longing to be held. I yearned to be hugged. *If only I could cry. I could really cry if Mary would just put her arms around me and hold me.*

I felt stripped of all my defenses. I felt too vulnerable even to ask.

After a silence both Mary and Carla prayed, asking the Holy Spirit to fill the empty places of my heart with His love. I mumbled a prayer of gratitude for releasing me to become His woman, then lifted my head. *Why can't I ask?*

Mary looked at me intently. "Darlene, what would you have done if I had reached over and put my arms around you?"

I barely breathed my response. "Cried."

Then I rose to my feet to signify that the session was over, still longing for a hug but too afraid of looking weak. We talked briefly, confirming the plans for our Bible study. Then I left.

My drive home was filled with praise as I sang every song I could remember. Inside I heard a new voice of proclamation. *I'm free, I'm free!*

My new liberation did not obliterate the realization that what had taken place in those five hours represented just the surgery. A lifetime of choices—difficult choices to walk in obedience to God's Spirit—lay ahead.

I had a new wardrobe to acquire though I had not the slightest idea what kind of clothes to buy or even where to get them. I was committed to meeting with Carla every week and spending much quiet time alone with God. And one final question arose as I pondered my deliverance: If this was the surgery, how would the inner healing work?

I wanted to tell everyone how wonderful it was not to have myself tied in knots and invisible forces locking me into relationships that would only leave me emptier than before. But even my songs of praise could not drown out the question *What next?*

23.
Walking
the Tightrope

Early the following Saturday, armed with my checkbook in one back pocket and a wallet full of credit cards in the other, I arrived at the shopping mall. I wandered first into the intimate apparel department of a major department store, searching for a feminine gown and robe.

How out-of-place I felt in my cowboy boots, jeans, and long-sleeved shirt! So I avoided eye contact with the sales clerks and hoped no one was paying attention. First I bought nylons and slips, using the height and weight chart for the nylons and guessing at the size of the slips.

Then I selected a long, silky green negligee trimmed in lace. It made me smile, remembering the mental picture of myself I had seen last week. Well, at least I would try to look pretty for the Lord. I only hoped I wouldn't look ridiculous.

Next I strolled into women's sportswear. Since it was still early, there were only a few customers. I appraised one long rack of casual slacks with my hands on my hips. How was I supposed to do this? I didn't even know what size I wore.

I looked longingly toward the men's department, then reached out and checked the price of a pair of slacks directly in front of me. They were more expensive than men's pants and not even made as well! I spun around in frustration, ready to do my shopping another day, when I nearly tripped over Gloria from the singles group. She looked as though she had just come from the beauty shop and her green tweed suit and black ruffled blouse accentuated her striking features.

"Oh, hi!" I said lamely.

She must have noticed my discomfort. "What are you doing, Darlene?"

"What does it look like I'm doing? I thought I'd try to buy some women's clothes to wear to work, but I'm lost in this maze. I can't figure out all this junk!" I ran my hand down the rack of slacks. "I don't know if I'm a six, a sixteen, or a thirty-six!" I sighed. "I'd be better off in the men's department where I know my way around."

She laughed. "Come on, Darlene. I'll help you."

I looked at this petite woman who appeared to have stepped out of the pages of a fashion magazine. "I don't think our taste in clothes runs in the same direction."

"You need slacks, right? How many?"

"At least four."

"Let's get some basic colors. Then you can find tops that match. That will expand your wardrobe." She pulled a pair from the rack and held it up, while I glanced around to make sure no one was listening to this shopping lesson.

"These should be the right length. See this tag? It says average. You are in the average range."

We took black, blue, brown and white slacks from the rack. "Now let's find some blouses to match?"

I smiled as we walked through the racks of bright colors and lace. "I take a 15 1/2 collar."

"Not anymore. It's time you learned how a woman dresses."

"Just joking." I pulled out a navy blouse with long sleeves and French cuffs.

"That's a little tailored, Darlene. Here, try this." She held up a red short-sleeved pullover with a scoop neck.

"You've got to be kidding!"

"Just take it and be quiet," she smiled and selected two or three other blouses trimmed with lace. "Let's go try them on."

I trudged to the dressing room, where each stall had a full-length mirror. Gloria stood outside the shutterlike door.

"Put on one complete outfit, then show me."

I pulled the pair of black slacks over my cowboy boots. "These pants don't fit right," I complained. "They're too loose. And besides, they don't have pockets."

Gloria's voice came through the shutters. "Quit mumbling and put on one of the blouses."

I slipped on the red pullover and stared in horror at the reflection in the mirror. "I can't wear this in public!" I shrieked.

The door opened and Gloria peered in. "What's wrong? It's nice."

"Nice?" I clutched the material tightly around my neck and crossed my arms to pull down the skimpy sleeves. "It's indecent! There's nothing to it."

"Now Darlene, stop it!" She straightened out the blouse to its normal position. "That's a nice blouse for summer, and you could wear it to work on hot days."

"I want a Western shirt," I grumped.

"Try on the others now. I want to see how they look." She closed the door firmly.

The second blouse was a multi-colored pink pastel with lace on the sleeves and around the V-neck collar. It had a string tie with little pink beads. I slipped it over my head and opened the door. "This at least is presentable."

She nodded approvingly. "It looks really pretty."

"Only problem is," I went on, "it's pink. I'd like it better in a darker color. And this neck is cut too low, and the lace is scratchy."

"Darlene, you've become so comfortable in long-sleeved, button-at-the-neck shirts that you haven't any idea how these things are supposed to feel. They look feminine and very pretty. Try on the other slacks, then we'll find a dress for church."

"I already have a dress." I knew very well it wouldn't do.

"I know. That's why we're going to find you another one."

The slacks fit fine and, with much grumbling, I took them to the cashier to keep until I found a dress. Gloria was beaming with delight.

"I'd like a dark tailored dress with long sleeves."

But Gloria picked out a brown-flowered, short-sleeved dress with a matching jacket. The dress was lightweight with a V-neck and an A-line skirt.

"It makes me look about twenty years older," I muttered on the way back to the dressing room.

"No, it looks casual and feminine." Then she laughed. "I know why the Lord sent me shopping today. You need a mother!"

Suddenly touched, I didn't know how to respond. "Very funny," I scoffed, disappearing into the dressing room to cover my embarrassment. But I suspected she was right.

The dress was midknee length. I laughed aloud as I saw myself in a short dress with high boots and bare legs.

"Just right," Gloria pronounced.

"But I can't wear my cowboy boots with this one, can I? All right, Gloria, I'll get it."

I mouthed silent words to my reflection. *God, please make me comfortable inside with the image You are creating on the outside.*

Gloria was tapping on a shutter. "Are you ready, Darlene? We need to pick out shoes, jewelry, and fingernail polish."

In a moment I emerged from the dressing room. "You know, Gloria, I'm glad I bumped into you. I feel like a foreign tourist with a language barrier."

"You'll learn, Darlene. It just takes time." She looked at me thoughtfully. "We need to get you a new hairdo. You'd look good in soft curls."

"Oh, please," I laughed. "I don't know how much of this I can take at one time."

She ignored me. "And you could use a more feminine watch. That wide leather band with metal knobs doesn't quite fit the image."

We shopped in several stores, acquiring everything I would need for a start. Despite my limited finances, I felt all my expenditures were right. I prayed again. *Lord, will I ever be comfortable in this feminine role?*

The next day after I wore my new dress, shoes, lingerie and carried a new purse to church, I sorted all my men's clothing. I saved two pairs of jeans and threw them into the camper (just in case I needed to move or go camping, I told myself) and one other pair of white pants on which I had sewn over a hundred patches, many given to me by friends. Everything else I boxed and gave to a young man who worked part-time at the plant and was preparing to leave for Bible school.

My shopping spree completed, I settled down to a weekly routine of activity, looking forward to a weekend trip to Los Angeles to visit Norma. The singles group increasingly filled the need in my life for Christian friends. And I looked forward to my weekly Bible study with Carla, although it was more than two hundred miles round trip. We were to spend three hours together in prayer, Bible lessons, and general sharing.

But before we began she reached out, took my hands in hers, and started to pray softly. Tears squeezed from behind my tightly closed eyelids, and a lump formed in my throat. I could sense her concern and love for me, which made me feel suddenly very vulnerable.

When Carla finished praying, I mumbled awkward thanks, then quickly retrieved my hands and my composure.

"How would you feel about using lotion on your hands to make them soft?" she asked unexpectedly as she opened her notebook. "They feel a little rough and calloused." She went on to introduce the study book we would be working through for the next four months.

What's wrong with my hands? I looked at the hardened skin and ground-in grease from servicing my truck, as if seeing it for the first time, and decided to follow her suggestion of hand lotion.

Driving home that night I realized something else, I had fingernails! I stared in amazement at how long they had grown in the last few weeks. It was the first time in my life I had not bitten them, and I had not even realized it. I supposed I would have to learn how to file them and use the subdued pink polish Gloria and I had selected together. How in the world did women keep from snagging their nylons with long nails?

I started watching the women in my singles group more closely, observing how they walked, dressed, and managed with long fingernails. Would I ever get the hang of everything? I had so much to learn about outer as well as inner beauty.

A telephone call awakened me one morning that week, stirring up some painful memories. "Darlene, this is Rebecca."

"Hi," I said in surprise. "Why are you calling so early?"

"You're the only one I know who cares enough to help me, Darlene. I've left Oregon and am moving back to California. I'm in Redding. My engine blew up, and I need a tow to Monterey."

"I have to work," I objected. "Redding is at least six hours away. Where's Randy?"

"I sent him to live with his grandmother. I'm alone. I don't have any money and I can't leave the car. It's full of my things."

I was out of bed and pacing the floor now. *I can share Christ with her. If she can see the changes He's made in me, maybe she'll accept Him too.* "All right, Rebecca. Tell me where you are. It'll be midafternoon when I get there. I'll have to rent a tow bar."

More than seven hours later with Rebecca's vehicle firmly secured to the back of my truck, we headed back to Monterey. After a long silence, Rebecca spoke. "Darlene, why did you *really* come get me?"

I glanced at her. "Someone had to. I wouldn't leave anyone stranded. Besides, maybe someday *I'll* need help."

Why didn't I just tell her about Jesus? How could I begin to share all the changes in me that had taken place?

"I doubt it," she said slowly. "You're too self-sufficient to ask."

"Well, if it were me, I'd probably junk the car and take a bus." I looked over at her again. "Besides, I wanted the opportunity to share what Jesus Christ is doing in my life."

"I didn't ask for any sermons!"

"You don't have much choice until we get back to Monterey," I laughed. "You're a captive audience."

"Do you ever miss me?"

I knew Rebecca was changing the subject because she rambled on without waiting for a reply. "And what are we going to do when we get back to Monterey?"

"The answer to your first question is yes. I do miss you. You were a part of my life for a long time. But Jesus Christ is filling the place that you once held. As for what we are going to do, I'm going home after I drop your car wherever you want it."

"You're still mad at me for leaving, aren't you?"

"No. In fact, Rebecca, if you hadn't left, I might not have renewed my faith in Jesus Christ. He's changed my life and set me free from the emptiness of gay life. He's my best friend."

She ignored this. "But I don't have a place to stay. . . ."

"I'm sure you'll manage once the ladies learn you're in town. I have learned one lesson well, Rebecca. Sometimes the best course of action is to run, meaning I'd be foolish to let you stay at my place. I'll never throw away my relationship with Jesus Christ. That's what I'd be doing if I let you back into my life."

"You make me sound evil."

"Evil?" I raised my eyebrows. "Rebecca, I am more convinced than ever that homosexuality is a demonic bondage."

"What are you saying—that I'm demon-possessed or something?"

It was the very question I had asked Mary before my deliverance, and I searched for the right words. "What I'm saying is that homosexuality is sin. When you keep committing the same sin, you allow that sin to take root in your heart. I've been set free from the sin of homosexuality and now I have the choice to remain free. It's not always easy, but that physical attraction isn't there any more."

"You're not even tempted to fool around?" Her smile was seductive.

"Temptation isn't the same as desire. Temptations come, but God is greater than any temptation and He gives me the power—and the desire—to say no."

"I don't believe you, Darlene. I lived with you, remember. I'll bet in six months you'll be involved again. Once gay, always gay."

"I won't bet with you, but I'll tell you one thing. The Bible says that the God who began a good work in me will finish it and keep me from falling. I trust God's Word."

"I'll keep checking on you, Darlene. I know you still have feelings for me or you wouldn't have come to get me."

"I came for one reason, Rebecca. I wanted to tell you face-to-face that you can be free—a whole, complete woman in Jesus Christ. I do have feelings for you. I love you because of Christ, and I'm praying that you find wholeness through His power."

She actually spat on the floor of my truck. "I think you're a traitor to the cause. I don't buy this religion stuff. You may think you're happy, but don't push it off on me. I still say you'll have a new girl friend in six months." She sank back against the seat.

"I've told you what I needed to say, Rebecca. Even if we're living in the same town, I want you to know that I will not have you at the house or spend any time with you. I have a new life and new friends who love Jesus, and I'll never go back."

"That's final?"

"That's final."

When we arrived in Monterey, I drove to the women's bar and unhooked the car. "If you ever get tired of this," I gestured toward the tavern, "just remember, there is a better way."

Then I drove home, my stomach in knots. Did I say the right things? Would it really make any difference? Did I do the right thing by going to rescue her? *God*, I prayed silently, *let my feelings for her be filled with Your love. It's really hard to stop caring.*

I tried to forget Rebecca and look forward to the trip south to visit Norma.

Early Saturday morning I headed for Los Angeles, listening to Bible tapes all the way and feeling much stronger by the time I arrived. Norma and I sat in her kitchen overlooking the garden patio and talked over tuna sandwiches and iced tea. There was much to share.

After I told her about everything new in my life including my recent contact with Rebecca, Norma responded with obvious concern.

"Darlene, I'm bothered about the contact you continue to have with Steven and Rebecca. I feel strongly that these relationships need to be severed."

"I have severed them for the most part, Norma. But I can't ignore old friends when they reach out to me."

"I just don't want to see you fall again. God has done so much in your life."

I nodded thoughtfully. "He'll have to let me know when I'm not supposed to respond. I know He's strong enough to complete the work in my life."

Norma stood and motioned for me to follow. "Let's spend some time in prayer. The kids will be home soon, and I don't want to be interrupted." I followed her down the hall to her office, which had been converted from a small pantry. She settled herself behind a wooden desk that filled one corner of the room. I plopped down in an overstuffed armchair.

"Darlene, there are so many areas in your life that still need healing. Maybe God will reveal to us how to help with the process." She bowed her head and began to pray silently.

When I closed my eyes, I felt like a little girl again, protected by the arms of the massive chair. I snuggled deeper. The little room was perfectly peaceful.

"Darlene, I sense that we are to pray for the healing of memories regarding your childhood. It's hard to reach out to others when you have so much pain of your own buried in the past."

I opened my eyes. Inner healing, according to Carla and Mary, was the other side of the deliverance coin. "How do we do that?"

"Tell me about your earliest childhood memory." Norma picked up a pencil to make notes.

"The most painful one is the day my father left," I began. I closed my eyes and allowed myself to picture the event again.

"I was about five years old. Dad told us he was leaving. Mom and Bubba and I just stood by the front door watching him go, and I burst into tears. I think I felt guilty, as though the reason he was leaving was that I had been bad." I gulped to swallow the lump in my throat as I shared the story in detail.

"What was the emotion you felt that day, Darlene?"

"Abandonment. I loved Daddy so much, and I was never really sure he loved me back. I tried so hard to please him and to be a big girl for him." I pressed my lips together so tightly that my teeth cut into them. *I won't cry!*

"Darlene, invite Jesus into that memory to come sit on the couch with you in the place of your father."

"You mean invite Him out loud?"

"Yes. He was there all the time, you know."

In my mental picture of our living room with Daddy already gone, I suddenly saw Jesus standing by the sofa, waiting for me to invite Him. "Please come sit with me, Jesus."

"I can see Him in my mind too," said Norma. "What's He saying to you?"

I listened. "He's saying, 'I'll never leave you, Darlene. I love you so much. You're my girl. I accept you!'" I smiled to myself, and in my heart the pain of that memory—miraculously, after all these years—was gone.

LONG ROAD TO LOVE

I sank back against the chair, once again comforted by its massive arms and high curved back. *I can trust Jesus,* I assured myself. *He won't abandon me.*

Norma's voice continued softly. "I feel we should ask the Lord to show us at least one of the events that caused you to fear men, Darlene. He can heal that too." She began to pray for the Holy Spirit to show me the cause of my fear.

I sat with eyes closed, shifting into a more relaxed position. Suddenly it looked as though someone had turned a movie projector into reverse at a fast rate. I sat bolt upright and gasped in disbelief at what I saw.

"I'm in a bedroom with my father," I managed. "Norma! He's molesting me. I'm not even a year old." I opened my eyes, trembling, shaking my head, trying to make the picture go away. "No! I won't believe it! It didn't happen! Tell me it's not really true!" I fought the rising panic, the tears that threatened to fall.

Then I felt an inkling of understanding. I collapsed against the chair stunned. My voice dropped to a whisper. "Norma, for the first time in my life everything begins to make sense."

The smothering feeling, the bells clanging, the red lights flashing every time I was with a man—these had not originated with the nightmare experience in the woods with Curt. That rape and the others had made me confused and angry, even fearful of men, but they had not *caused* the sensory experience; they had only triggered it.

"Darlene, you may never be able to substantiate that it really happened, but your memory believes the pain. Let's ask Jesus to heal that pain."

Norma prayed, but the painful picture of that scene in the bedroom with my father, as well as a hundred questions without answers, blocked total healing. On the trip home, my mind rode a roller coaster over thirty years of memories.

Much that happened in those early years I knew I would never be able to understand, even if I could remember. Had Mom known? Why hadn't she protected me? I thought about our struggles in years past, when another new revelation flashed into my mind: *Mom never knew love either. That's why she couldn't love me as I needed.*

In that moment God enabled me to forgive her. Another layer of my shell had been peeled back.

My feelings toward my father were harder to handle. I had no desire to forgive him. Anger raged in me as I remembered his own anger in the woods, ready to kill Curt for what he had done. He had done the same terrible kinds of things to his own infant daughter. *I'm glad you're dead! If you were still alive, I would hate you enough to kill you!* I shoved my feelings deeper, wanting to deny incest, to deny my rage, and to deny my pain.

As the weeks passed, I retreated more into my journal. *God, I am so alone, so empty. Everyone applauds the miracles You've worked, but no one hugs me or takes me home for dinner.*

Another day I wrote: *Would all these people really love me if they ever found out I'm not hard as nails, tough as steel? This new woman who is emerging is not full-grown. I'm a little girl, and I'm scared!*

The fear of vulnerability caused me to bend and stretch the truth sometimes to protect the strong image I still wanted to project. At church I wanted to reach out, love and be loved, but I sensed an invisible wall between others and me. Did they feel if they got too close, something would rub off? It became easier to pretend I didn't notice when heads turned away at my arrival or conversations ceased.

I panicked as I realized it was becoming harder to resist the compulsion to slip into former thought patterns. They fit my mind like a comfortable well-worn glove. I could share my fears only with my journal, which assured me of complete acceptance. Would I ever be totally healed?

24.
Complete
in Him

Almost eight months had passed since I recommitted my life to Christ. My weekly Bible studies with Carla were over, and without that accountability I felt lonely and vulnerable.

Uneasiness knotted my stomach. I knew I had gotten rid of the demons, so why was I feeling the urge once more to visit old friends? Emotions I had believed healed were surfacing again. I hated the guilt that tormented me when I lingered too long in conversation with Steven. He came to our plant only once a week now, and I knew God was helping me to break the ties of friendship. But I would ask Steven questions about old friends, then regret it as old memories flooded my mind.

The church was home, but I had found neither the warmth nor the level of friendship that I desired. Mary, Carla, and Norma, as supportive as they were, lived far away. *God, I can't fall again! I'll die first!*

Every evening for a week I read more of the Bible onto cassette tapes, while I struggled to overcome the depression that filled my mind. Something wasn't right. I could not shake a black cloud of fear.

When I confided my frustration to Pastor Edwards one evening on the telephone, he prayed with me and assured me of his continued availability. He said that the power of Satan was coming against me. And he recommended the ministry of two women in the church who might be able to help. Sunday morning after the service, Pastor Edwards introduced me to Paula and Laura.

"I've already spoken with them, Darlene," he said, "and

they're ready to set up an appointment to counsel with you, if you like."

Laura, a petite blonde, spoke. "The pastor told us about your background. It sounds as though you may have some open doors that need to be sealed shut. How about things in your home? Have you done a spiritual housecleaning?" Her words sounded almost clinical in contrast to her quiet, softspoken tone.

"I've gotten rid of a lot of things—occult books, for example. I don't know what else there might be."

"Can you meet with us Tuesday night at seven in the pastor's office?" asked Paula. "We'll talk about things in detail."

I readily agreed to meet with them.

Monday and Tuesday brought, much to my surprise, mental and spiritual warfare. Old familiar voices popped up with mocking harassment. *You'll never be free. Nothing's changed. Why bother to fight? It's not worth it.*

I turned to the Living Bible I had purchased recently and copied a verse onto a 3x5 card: *And I am sure that the God who began the good work within you will keep right on helping you to grow in His grace until His task within you is finally finished on that day when Jesus Christ returns* [Philippians 1:6, LB and hereafter]. I taped the card onto the doorpost of my bedroom. "God, please do what Your Word says!"

The light was on in the pastor's office Tuesday evening as I drove up to the church. I walked slowly down the hall and stood outside the door, listening. Muffled voices were engaged in conversation. I knocked lightly.

"Come in." Laura's voice was firm but friendly.

I opened the door and stepped into the room familiar to me from frequent visits with the pastor. Bookshelves lined the walls behind the large oak desk, and artifacts from trips around the world were interspersed between volumes of theology. Petite Laura looked out-of-place in Pastor Edward's black leather chair, and Paula smiled a greeting from the couch. I sat down next to her.

"I'd like you to answer some questions as a guideline for our counseling," said Laura, reaching over and handing me a sheet of more than thirty questions. She was obviously the leader.

I scanned the sheet.

Have you ever followed horoscopes or had your fortune told by use of card, tea leaves, or palm reading? Consulted a ouija board or crystal ball for fun, out of curiosity, or in earnest? Played with games of an occult nature such as ESP, Telepathy, the Pendulum; or practiced table lifting, levitation, astral projection (leaving your body), or automatic handwriting? Read or possessed occult or spiritualist literature or objects, books on astrology, interpretation of dreams for predicting the future, fortune-telling, magic—black or white—religious cults, ESP, clairvoyance, or psychic phenomena?

I finished reading the list, then looked up. "So far I answer yes to just about every question on the sheet. It says *ever*, so I guess I have to say yes. But I've been delivered of those demons, so I don't know that my positive responses are significant."

"Darlene, if you have left open doors spiritually speaking," responded Laura kindly, "they can all come back. It's that simple."

"Well then, let's get those doors closed." I handed the list back to Laura. "What now?"

"We're going to pray. I'll be speaking directly to any spirits inside of you, so don't be surprised if they answer from your mouth."

Laura bowed her head. "Father, in the name of Jesus, we plead the protection of the blood of Calvary over each one of us here, our homes, and our families. Satan, we bind you and your working right now and render you helpless in the name of Jesus." She paused. "Spirit of witchcraft, I command you to identify yourself now."

I closed my eyes tight as a shrill laugh erupted from somewhere deep inside me. It reminded me of an old witch stirring a pot of brew. I opened my mouth to speak but only piercing laughter came out.

"I command you to be quiet in the name of Jesus." Laura's voice was firm. "Spirit of witchcraft, what gives you the right to stay in this life?"

"I won't tell you!" The voice was sassy.

"I bind you to the Spirit of Truth and remind you to be subject to the authority of Jesus. Now, what gives you the right?"

A whimpering little voice responded. "Because she won't get rid of the pictures, or the books, or her pool cues."

I opened my eyes in amazement. Paula was taking notes.

But witchcraft was not the only spirit. To my dismay, every spirit I had thought was gone identified itself. This time I learned when they had entered, why, and how to break their power and keep them out.

During the ministry, I anguished over the many things I apparently needed to remove from my life. Many of the items were personal and connected to a multitude of hidden emotions. One spirit spoke the words I dreaded most: "I don't have to leave because she won't give up her friendship with Steven."

How can I give up Steven? He's my closest friend. We'd die for each other.

My response betrayed the bondage. As long as I was clinging to the past, I realized I could never live completely in the present.

"Darlene," Laura was saying, "I want you to renounce all involvement with each of these items. If you want to be free, you have to be obedient to rid your life of the things that will keep you in bondage."

My throat tightened; I coughed before I spoke. My body convulsed as I renounced each spirit and commanded it to leave. Finally I leaned back against the couch, exhausted. The ministry had taken several hours.

"I thought I had been through the hard part already," I said. "I hope I never have to go through this again."

Paula handed me the list. "Shut these doors, and you won't."

I glanced at the paper. How could so many things still have been a part of my life?

I want to be clean, Lord, I prayed on the way back to my car. *I don't want anything to be more important to me than You! I'll get rid of everything I own if that's what it takes.*

Then I thought about Steven. My surge of new determination conflicted with the loyalty I felt toward my old friend. *Yes, even his friendship, Lord,* I thought at last. *If I have to stand completely alone, I will.*

The next evening after work I stood in my living room with the list. I decided to start at the top and work down.

I pulled my pool stick from the front closet. As I held it in my hand, my mind flooded with a hundred memories of games won and lost. *No! I'll do it!* I strode outside and broke the stick in two, symbolizing the death of a former way of life. But pain cut through my emotions.

One by one I was able to draw a line through the items on my list. Valuable pictures and books by noted homosexuals seemed to plead for life as I shredded them in preparation for a bonfire that would finalize their hold on my life. I knew the time had come for the white patched pants to go too.

Feminist and occult jewelry of silver and gold stopped me short. Maybe I could sell some of it and accumulate money toward my debt. *Or maybe,* I thought, sensing a wrongness about profiting from my spiritual housecleaning, *I could give this jewelry away.*

Lord, these things are me! There won't be anything left. Tears sprang to my eyes. Then, remembering my session with Laura and Paula, I scooped everything into a sack to be burned.

Next on my list was drugs. I didn't have any drugs! But in

the medicine cabinet I noticed several bottles of outdated Valium and other tranquilizers that Brian had brought home from the hospital when we lived together. I hadn't remembered these prescription drugs were here.

At that moment I heard a familiar, loving voice inside my head. *Satan is trying to kill you, Darlene. You would have remembered when you were depressed.*

I leaned against the wall, realizing it would take several more hours to clear my list. *Lord, can we wait until tomorrow?*

I was startled by the answer: *This is a lifelong project.*

Later that week I stood in the backyard watching a bonfire destroy three thirty-gallon sacks of memories and empty love. I wept as a verse of Scripture flashed through my mind: "Don't store up treasures here on earth where they can erode away or may be stolen" (Matthew 6:19). Knowing I was doing right did not lessen the pain.

It provided the perfect setting, nevertheless, for Marie Fuller to visit for the weekend. The days she spent with me included a whirlwind of introductions as I took her to meet my singles group, and especially Madeline. We went for coffee with Paula and Laura, and I shared with her my recent experiences of learning to walk in deliverance.

On Sunday afternoon I drove her to San Francisco, where she would spend several days with Elaine and visit Beth and Matt. Standing next to my truck, I gave her one long hug before heading back to Monterey.

She held me close for that extra special moment of prayer that I had come to expect. "Thank You, Jesus," she prayed, "for the work of grace You're doing in Darlene's life. Keep moving her toward wholeness. Have Your way in both our lives. Amen."

I squeezed her hand. "Thanks for your love and prayers all these years, Marie." I turned, then glanced back quickly. "He's really doing it, you know. After all those years of frustration, I'm finally learning what it means to be on the road to wholeness and the right kind of love."

She nodded. "Darlene, I wish I could tell you the road gets easier or that someday you arrive. I'm still finding areas in my life that need conforming to His image." She waved and blew me a kiss. "Honey, God wants your obedience above any sacrifice. He wants you free, and you're going to know freedom only as you hear His voice and do it. I don't know any place in the Bible that says you'll always feel good about obeying. It just says do it. You still have some hard choices ahead, but given the alternative of being in bondage again, there's really no choice at all. Trust Him. I do!"

"I will, Marie. But it's sure easy to compromise and justify doing things my own way."

I sat in the truck for a moment before pulling away. *Lord, if she's still finding things to change, I guess I can stand the process too. But I wish it were easier.*

In the weeks that followed Marie's visit, I felt committed to write letters to people I had wronged. Topping the list were Brian's parents, to whom I confessed my part in the deception. And I sealed every letter with a prayer.

I also wrote to friends I had not seen for years to share my recommitment to Christ. Joy and Sharon had both gone overseas on mission assignments, yet both responded within a few weeks with delight and encouragement. Separately they told me that for ten years they had prayed for me. Emotion choked me as I thought how their love, along with that of many others, had followed me through the years.

In addition to writing letters, I paid back money I had stolen from individuals and asked several people for forgiveness. It was not easy, of course, but daily I felt the inner shell of hardness melting away. I was gratified one evening to get a phone call from Mom Mainer, thanking me for my honesty, saying they still loved me, and promising to stay in touch.

One last major project required attention. I took several volumes from my bookshelf of poetry: poems I had written to lovers, to loneliness, to God for release from the desire that burned in my soul, and to the demon thoughts that sought to destroy me all those years. I read every poem, the memories far from dead.

Lord, this isn't me anymore. I prayed at last. *I want my writing to glorify You.*

It took me two hours to shred them, tearing each page in an effort to separate myself from the pain of my former life. Scalding tears dripped onto the growing pile of paper. Would destroying the words erase the memories? I was too familiar with my past and frightened of the future with its unknown changes.

The very next morning at work while I was reading through papers on my desk, I heard a familiar inner voice. *Darlene, it's time to sell your truck.*

I shook my head to make sure I had heard right. *Lord?*

I want you to sell your truck, today. It's a final connection to your old image.

I went out to my supervisor's desk. "May I take a few hours off this morning? I'm buying a car."

Given his approval, I waved and hurried out the door, my purse over my shoulder. *Where to, Lord?*

I remembered a small used car lot across town with a good reputation. Within minutes I had slipped behind the wheel of a small white station wagon.

"I've never driven a standard transmission," I said to the salesman. "Do you have an automatic?"

"The gas mileage is better on this one," he told me. "Don't worry. I'll show you how to drive it."

Less than an hour later I returned to work, holding the paperwork on a new little Datsun. The dealership had offered such a good trade-in on the truck that I could purchase new furniture for my house and fulfill my commitment for the remaining months of the house lease.

It was going to be a trip learning to use a stick shift, but I was tickled at the thought of driving a vehicle that projected the image of the woman I was becoming!

And so the months passed. Christmas came and went. It

was nearly two years since I recommitted my life to Jesus Christ. Loneliness still had the power to open old wounds, especially during holiday celebrations, and tears often filled my eyes as I saw husbands and wives walking arm in arm or cuddling their children. But increasingly I found the acceptance and love I had long sought through relationships with people in the church, and especially in the singles group, despite recent growth and a large turnover.

Then came another turning point. Just after Christmas my supervisor at work informed me that our plant in San Jose, the one to which I had requested a transfer the year before, would have an opening the first of February. Was I interested in a promotion to office supervisor?

I was stunned. I had forgotten all about my plan, since I had made it after all in Monterey. Now at long last, the job was being offered, and I no longer wanted it. The Bay Area was where I had started out many years before, joining Dad and Bubba in Oakland after dropping out of college and being discharged from the military. I knew too many people, too many gay bars up there.

God's reassuring voice inside stilled my panic. *Darlene, knowing where the bars are isn't a problem. I'll keep you anywhere.*

That afternoon during my break at work, I called a couple of friends for prayer support including Madeline.

"I've just been offered a job transfer," I told her. "It will mean moving back to the Bay Area. Will you pray about it?"

"Sure I will." She paused. "I don't want you to move, Darlene. If this were a year ago, I'd say no right now. But in the past year you've really grown spiritually. I know you can make it no matter where God sends you. I'll support whatever decision you feel He wants you to make."

"I'm really scared at the prospect of moving where I don't have a tight support system of accountability. I'd have to really be sure."

"And you'd have to find a *new* support system. Why don't

we get together tonight for dinner? We can pray together then."

"Thanks, Madeline. I'll see you about seven."

After I hung up, I remembered a Bible verse from that very morning: "The Lord will work out his plan for my life, for your lovingkindness, Lord, continues forever. Don't abandon me, for you made me" (Psalm 138:8).

Tears trickled down my face. Everything in me wanted to stay, but suddenly I knew I was supposed to go.

When Madeline and I met at the restaurant, I shared my inner conviction with her.

"I feel it must be time to move out into other areas," I told her. "Besides, I know I can't stay protected all my life."

"You might be right, Darlene. But you've been the sister I never had. I'll miss you." She leaned over the table to give me a hug. "I'll never forget our first talk two years ago. It seems like a hundred years since you were facing those grand theft charges!"

"God has worked a lot of miracles since then." I grinned. "The best is knowing that I can have women for friends and not be tormented with sexual thoughts. I can give and receive because I've learned about real love and because I don't have to hold on to someone out of jealousy. But it's going to be hard to tell the singles group good-by. I'll make the announcement this Thursday." Suddenly I panicked. "Madeline, there are only three weeks till I'll be gone!"

"I know," she responded softly. "But you'll come back to visit us."

I nodded. She was right, of course.

As I walked into the meeting Thursday, I was surprised to see so many old-timers, long-time members who had married or dropped out. We had our coffee hour and formed a large circle for singing. Then Gloria walked to the center of the group, pulling her chair behind her. "Darlene, come here please."

My face flushed. "Are you serious?"

"Yes. Take this seat here, if you don't mind."

I sat down in the empty chair.

"Earlier this week," Gloria said to the group, "Darlene had to decide whether to move to San Jose and accept a job promotion. After prayer and discussion with friends, she feels it's God's will to go. So tonight a few of us wanted to surprise her with a toast night. I know that she has meant something special to many people in this room. If you'd like to share in a sentence or two, this is the time to do it. I'd like to start.

"You newer people missed Darlene's spiritual beginnings. She's come a long way since her days of jeans, cowboy boots, and looking like she just left a Mack truck parked in the street! Now she wears blouses with lace, dresses, and three-inch heels! Anyway, I love her and appreciate her more all the time."

My face burned with embarrassment.

Madeline stood up. "It seems a lifetime, though it hasn't been, since Darlene and I first got to know one another. She has been God's gift of friendship to me. I'm going to miss her terribly, just as I know *all* of us are going to miss her." She gave me a special smile.

Rose was already on her feet, a social worker with Child Protective Services with whom I had recently become friends. "I only got to know Darlene two months ago, when she and I went out after singles group and talked until 3 A.M.! Not only has her sharing been a help in my profession, but getting to know her has been an experience I'll never forget."

Other people shared special moments from the group meetings over the last two years. I did not even try to stop the tears streaming down my face.

Finally I stood. "For those of you who are new, I'm the woman who, just two years ago, could scarcely cry. You can see that's changed! This group has meant more to me than I can express. It's made up of people who care, who pray, and who take time to be friends. I know God has good things in store for me in San Jose. But I'll sure miss you all."

I started back to my seat when Gloria grasped my hand. "Not yet!"

Two women stepped out of the kitchen with a huge sheet cake. I could read the blue lettering across the room: *Goodby, Darlene. You are loved by Jesus—and us!*

Epilogue

It has been six years since that night at singles. Some of my rough edges have been smoothed, since my relationship with Jesus Christ is a constant process of growth. Every day provides opportunities to choose God's way instead of my own. True to His Word, Jesus has never abandoned me or withdrawn His presence. I have learned new steps of obedience and found a loving body of believers who keep me accountable.

The good things that have happened since my move far outweigh the times of struggle or loneliness. Many doors have opened for ministry to others seeking a way out of homosexuality. I speak at churches and many women's groups, always sharing the miracle of transformation God has worked in my life.

Some in the gay community have responded and found that God is able to work the same transformation in their lives. Others have expressed anger when presented with a viable alternative to their chosen lifestyle. I have participated in debates and been challenged by gay leaders, all the while presenting the case that homosexuality is not biological or genetic but volitional.

Some blame environment, genetics, or emotional influences, but none of these is the *cause*. Homosexuality is a choice, characterized by God as sin. And regardless of the influences in a person's life, God's love can put that person back together and give him or her the power to live a moral life. What makes the difference is the personal assumption of responsibility and the decision to change.

In love, I have held others to the choice of God's best for their lives and witnessed the process of their restoration. I can assure them with deepening conviction: Jesus Christ will never leave them to make it on their own. He is committed to staying with them and working toward their wholeness.

I have also experienced healing as I have faced the

fractured beginnings of my life and have forgiven those who made me a victim of sexual abuse, although I still struggle sometimes with memories of my father. My anger and hatred have diminished as I have spent time in therapy and confronted my feelings. My self-image has improved with the realization that I am not to blame for Dad's actions or those of the men who violated me. God has turned me from an abandoned daughter into a daughter secure in His love.

Together, God and I have worked to restore relationships within my family, especially with my mother. Through a unique experience not long ago, I gained new understanding and appreciation for her. One afternoon she was rushed unexpectedly to the hospital and given a slim chance of recovery. I flew home. After a brief, anxious visit in the Intensive Care Unit, I drove to her empty house. My mind was flooded with old memories—and new fears.

Then I caught a glimpse of her journal beside the bed. For the next three hours I was captivated by her remembrances, which enabled me to see my mother in a new and tender way. I hesitated, then made an entry from a daughter's viewpoint. I wrote of my fear of losing her, closed the journal, and prayed she would recover to read the entry.

She did, and the journal helped us begin to develop a friendship based on honesty and caring. Building such a relationship is not unlike the process of healing, a process I always want to speed up both for myself and for others.

In fact, I would prefer to eliminate all emotional pain and find instant healing. But sometimes *reliving* the pain is the only way to relieve it. I have counseled and wept with others as they despaired of the process and given thanks for the dozens of people God placed in my life to comfort me when I lost hope of ever making a complete change. I find now that I am less impatient with my own journey toward wholeness. Knowing what to do and then choosing to do it, unfortunately, is just the beginning.

My message whether to one person or to hundreds, is

hope for anyone trapped by the bondage of homosexuality. I am living proof that there is a way out. No one is beyond the ability of Jesus Christ to redeem and restore to wholeness. When I am tempted to become discouraged, I remember the prophet Isaiah's declaration that we are carved in the palm of God's hand. He is able to keep us safe, even from our fractured images of the past.

Marie Fuller used to say, "Darlene, we may be products of our environment, but we do not have to continue to be victimized by our past."

My heart is moved with compassion as I meet with hundreds of people victimized by the lie of homosexuality. I can see the part Satan has played, holding them in bondage by ingraining habits so deep that many of them feel they were born that way. I am committed to bringing these people the message that they can turn from Satan's lie to the freedom of God's truth: "When someone becomes a Christian he becomes a brand-new person inside. He is not the same anymore. A new life has begun!" (II Corinthians 5:17).

Deliverance from a homosexual lifestyle is more difficult than simply breaking demonic bondage, although that represents the initial surgery. The path is filled with hard choices every day. But deliverance sets a person free to make the *right* choices. When the spirit of homosexuality left me, so did my desire for lesbian involvement.

I am completely heterosexual in my orientation—too much so, sometimes! If it is God's will, someday I will marry. At this point I am primarily concerned with becoming the woman God wants me to be, that's a full-time project. So I leave the future with Him and live one day at a time.

It seems like a lifetime since that first Sunday when my toes were still pointed from my cowboy boots, until today when I am more comfortable in lace and high heels. People still say the funniest things. Recently, a woman approached me after a speaking engagement and said with a puzzled expression, "You don't look like a typical lesbian."

I smiled and replied, "I sure hope not!" Then I remembered the prayer I prayed while standing in front of a mirror eight years ago on my landmark shopping expedition, and I breathed a new prayer of gratitude. *Thanks, Lord, for making me comfortable inside with the woman You're creating outside.*

I pray that my story will rekindle hope for anyone caught in the sin of homosexuality and remind them that God is no respecter of persons. He will totally change any life committed to Him. All who come to Him can claim His promise:

> "There was a time when some of you were just like that, but now your sins are washed away, and you are set apart for God, and he has accepted you because of what the Lord Jesus Christ and the Spirit of our God has done for you" (I Corinthians 6:11).

Glossary

HOMOSEXUAL *A male or female attracted to the same sex. Does not have to engage in such activity to be a homosexual.*

HETEROSEXUAL *A male or female attracted to the opposite sex. Does not have to engage in such activity to be heterosexual.*

LESBIAN *A female homosexual. (Also called dyke, butch, or femme.)*

QUEEN *An effeminate male homosexual. (Also called fairy or faggot.)*

STRAIGHT *Any heterosexual.*

GAY *The acceptable terminology to describe both a member and the life of the homosexual community.*

BISEXUAL *A male or female person who enjoys sexual activity with the same or opposite sex equally.*

GAY BARS *Hangouts for the gay community. Men have their bars, and women have their bars, but in most cases homosexual members of the opposite sex are allowed.*

TRICK *Refers to the person and act of picking up a person for a sexual encounter. Mostly a queen's terminology.*

CHICKEN HAWK *An older homosexual who seeks young boys for sexual encounters.*

CHICKEN *A young male.*

DRAG *Wearing the attire of the opposite sex.*

DRAG QUEEN *A male homosexual who impersonates a female by wearing women's clothing, makeup, and a wig. As a female impersonator, he would dress to present a show for entertainment.*